REPRESENTATIVE GOVERNMENT IN IRELAND

REPRESENTATIVE GOVERNMENT IN IRELAND

A Study of Dáil Éireann 1919–48

BY

J. L. McCRACKEN

PROFESSOR OF HISTORY IN
MAGEE UNIVERSITY COLLEGE, LONDONDERRY

LONDON
OXFORD UNIVERSITY PRESS
NEW YORK   TORONTO
1958

Oxford University Press, Amen House, London E.C.4

GLASGOW NEW YORK TORONTO MELBOURNE WELLINGTON
BOMBAY CALCUTTA MADRAS KARACHI KUALA LUMPUR
CAPE TOWN IBADAN NAIROBI ACCRA

© *Oxford University Press 1958*

PRINTED IN GREAT BRITAIN

TO MY WIFE

PREFACE

THIS book is an attempt to contribute to the understanding of representative government by making a detailed study of a single institution. A legislative assembly entitled Dáil Éireann—the assembly of Ireland—was created in 1919 by the extreme nationalist groups which were striving to effect a complete separation of Ireland from England. When they failed in their purpose and were obliged to accept dominion status for twenty-six of the thirty-two counties of Ireland the name was retained and continuity was claimed for the elective house of the Irish Free State parliament. From a series of constitutional amendments culminating in 1937 in a new constitution the dáil emerged with authority unimpaired. Throughout the thirty years under review the dáil was not only the constant element in the constitution but also what the head of the government once called it 'the most important institution of the state'. So it is that an examination of the dáil sheds light on the general working of representative government in Ireland.

Certain features of Irish constitutional development have more than local significance. Born in revolution, the state emerged as a dominion with a written constitution in which provision was made for such constitutional devices as voting by proportional representation, the appointment of non-political ministers, the use of the referendum, and the initiation of legislation by the people. New political parties were fashioned; two successive senates were created in an attempt to find an acceptable second chamber of the oireachtas or parliament; and a parliamentary tradition was built up in spite of persistent extra-parliamentary movements. Above all the reluctant dominion was in the forefront of the movement for loosening the Commonwealth ties and itself contributed notably to a new conception of Commonwealth relations.

This book was prepared during my tenure of the Sir Robert Woods Research Lectureship in Trinity College, Dublin. I wish to express my sincere thanks to the Board of Trinity College and to the Committee of the Trinity College Educational Endowment Fund (now the Trinity College Trust) for having made it possible for me to undertake the work, and to the Trustees of Magee University College, Londonderry, for a generous grant in aid of publication.

To the many people who gave me assistance I owe a deep debt of gratitude. I should like to record my appreciation of the unfailing courtesy and helpfulness of the staff in the Library of Trinity College, Dublin, the National Library of Ireland, the Library of the Oireachtas, and the Library of Magee University College, Londonderry. I am greatly indebted to three party officials, Miss M. Davidson of the labour party, Miss A. J. Martin of Fine Gael, and Mr. T. Mullins of Fianna Fáil, whose willingness to help far exceeded anything I had the right to expect. The manuscript was read in whole or in part by Dr. Basil Chubb, Professor R. Dudley Edwards, and Mr. F. C. King. I am grateful to them for their many helpful suggestions. Others to whom I wish to express my thanks are Mr. J. J. Killeen for much indispensable information, Miss M. Comerford for assistance in elucidating obscure points, Mr. M. Heffernan for information on the first farmers' party, Mr. P. O'Keeffe for his kindness in lending me a valuable collection of documents, Mr. R. A. Harrison for generous assistance with the chapter on legislation, Professor H. O. Meredith for undertaking the laborious task of preparing the index, and Professor T. Finnegan for most welcome encouragement and advice. Mr. J. C. Beckett and Professor T. W. Moody were ready at all times, as they have been for a quarter of a century, to help me in every way they could. A special word of thanks is due to Dr. Donal O'Sullivan who read and re-read the manuscript, correcting errors and making innumerable suggestions, and never wavering in his conviction, which at times I did not share, that the work would be brought to a successful conclusion. Finally, I wish to thank my wife who contributed in many ways to the making of this book.

It only remains to state that much as I owe to others the conclusions reached are my own. For them and for all faults and errors I accept responsibility.

Londonderry
June 1958

CONTENTS

PREFACE vii

I. THE RISE OF SINN FÉIN 1

II. THE ORIGIN AND NATURE OF THE REPUBLICAN DÁIL 19

III. THE WORK OF THE REPUBLICAN DÁIL 35

IV. THE ORIGIN OF THE CONSTITUTIONAL DÁIL 45

V. THE COMPETENCE OF THE DÁIL 57

VI. PARLIAMENTARY ELECTIONS 67

VII. THE COMPOSITION OF THE DÁIL 86

VIII. THE POLITICAL PARTIES 102

IX. THE MECHANISM OF THE DÁIL 119

X. THE DÁIL AND THE SECOND CHAMBER 137

XI. THE DÁIL AND THE EXECUTIVE 153
  (i) The nominal executive
  (ii) The real executive

XII. THE DÁIL AND THE EXECUTIVE: LEGISLATION 170

XIII. THE DÁIL AND THE EXECUTIVE: EXTERNAL AFFAIRS 183

APPENDIX: Maps showing geographical distribution of parties 205

BIBLIOGRAPHY 217

INDEX 225

I

THE RISE OF SINN FÉIN

DÁIL ÉIREANN in its original form was the creation of the reconstituted Sinn Féin party which came into being through the combination of various separatist groups in the autumn of 1917. The origins of the party must be sought in the early years of the century when Irish nationalism was experiencing something of a rejuvenation.

Throughout the nineteenth century political interest and endeavour in Ireland were directed towards two objectives: the reform of social and economic conditions and the winning of some measure of national independence. By the end of the century much had been achieved in the first sphere. But neither constitutional agitation nor revolutionary action had succeeded in undermining the Union. The limited form of self-government which would have satisfied moderate nationalists had proved as unobtainable as the independent republican status to which the extremists aspired. The one achievement of note had been the conversion of Gladstone to home rule. With the liberal party's victory in the general election of 1906 the home rule movement entered upon its last phase. The Irish parliamentary or nationalist party, under the leadership of John Redmond, was strong in the support of the great majority of nationalists throughout Ireland. The liberals were sympathetically disposed to home rule. The hostility of the House of Lords remained as the one great obstacle. The introduction of the Home Rule Bill in 1912 following on the removal of the Lords' veto in 1911 was a triumph for the nationalist party and raised its influence and prestige to the highest pitch. But already forces were at work which were to destroy it absolutely within a few years.

A series of events about the turn of the century gave a fresh orientation to Irish nationalism. Like the nationalist movements in nineteenth-century Europe, the new nationalism in Ireland was prefaced by a literary revival. In 1893 Dr. Douglas Hyde founded the Gaelic League with the object of preserving the Irish language and promoting interest in Irish art, literature, and music. Although the league was non-political in the sense that it held itself aloof from all political parties it tended to produce a state of mind favourable to the advanced nationalist movements. Patrick Pearse, one of the leading figures in the 1916 insurrection, declared: 'The Gaelic League will be recognized in history as the most revolutionary influence that ever came to Ireland.'[1] Those who fell under its influence and the influence of the literary renaissance that centred round it were inspired with a spiritual enthusiasm, an ardour and vitality which were alien to the parliamentary party. The new spirit found an outlet in literary societies and in several small periodicals devoted to Irish literature and politics. The release of the Fenian Thomas Clarke in 1898 after fifteen years imprisonment and the celebrations to mark the centenary of the 1798 rebellion stirred emotions which were fostered in newly-established patriotic clubs. The Anglo-Boer war and the participation of an Irish brigade on the Boer side further stimulated anti-British feeling.[2] In 1899 Arthur Griffith became editor of a newly-founded paper called the *United Irishman* in which he expounded the political creed of self-reliance and independence. One of his articles early in the following year suggested the formation of a central authority to bring into touch with one another the various groups which were working 'to uplift the mind and heart and soul of the country'.[3] The proposal resulted in the founding of a friendly and cultural society called Cumann na nGaedheal. Another central body, the national council, was formed in 1903 to agitate against demonstrations of loyalty on the occasion of a royal visit to Ireland. Meantime, at the third annual convention of Cumann na nGaedheal in October 1902 Griffith had outlined what came to be known as the 'Hungarian policy', a policy the essence of which was expressed in a resolution adopted by the convention: 'That we call upon our countrymen abroad to withhold all assistance from the promoters of a useless, degrading, and demoralizing policy until such times as the members of the Irish parliamentary party substitute for it the policy of the Hungarian deputies of 1861 and, refusing to attend the British parliament or to recognize its right to legislate for Ireland, remain at home to help in promoting Ireland's interests and to aid in guarding its national rights.' Griffith elaborated his policy in a series of articles in the *United Irishman* which were reprinted in book form in 1904 under the title *The Resurrection of Hungary*, and in a further series entitled, 'The Working of the Policy'.[4]

[1] R. M. Henry, *The Evolution of Sinn Féin*, pp. 48–49.
[2] D. Macardle, *The Irish Republic* (1951), p. 62.
[3] *United Irishman*, 15 Mar. 1900. [4] Henry, op. cit., pp. 68–69.

The articles created a demand among the small band of separatists for the formation of a political party or at least the formulation of a political programme. At the annual convention of the national council on 28 November 1905 what was by this time known as the policy of Sinn Féin (Ourselves) was promulgated.[1]

Early in 1906 the *United Irishman* was replaced by *Sinn Féin* as the organ of the party. In it, as in its predecessor, Griffith expounded the 'Hungarian' policy. He saw in a dual monarchy the solution to the Irish problem. Since the Renunciation Act of 1783 had asserted Ireland's right 'to be bound only by laws enacted by his majesty and the parliament of that kingdom', he contended that the country was entitled to the constitutional status it had secured in 1782. To make this claim a reality he proposed a policy of self-reliance and non-cooperation designed to render England's position in Ireland untenable. The nucleus of a civil service would be formed by inducing the county councils to throw open the offices in their gift to competitive examination. Arbitration courts would be established to supersede the ordinary courts. Consular agents would be appointed to promote Irish commerce. Pressure would be exerted on the banks and the stock exchange to make them more sympathetic to Irish commercial undertakings. The Irish waterways would be developed and an Irish mercantile marine founded. Special stress was laid on the need to develop native industry and manufactures. Following the doctrine of Friedrich List, Griffith advocated a system of protection. To coordinate this policy in the absence of a national parliament Griffith proposed to constitute in Dublin a 'council of three hundred' composed of the Irish members of parliament, the general council of county councils, and representatives of the urban councils and poor law boards. The council would issue decrees which the local government bodies would enforce so far as they had the legal power.[2]

For the first two years after its formation Sinn Féin was successful in a modest way. Its propaganda was carried on in its weekly paper and in clubs and branches in various parts of the country; pamphlets and a handbook were published, debates were organized, and lectures were delivered; and some successes were won in local government elections. In 1908 the party had its first opportunity of contesting a parliamentary election. C. J. Dolan, the nationalist member for North

---

[1] *The Republic of Ireland*, 7 Feb. 1922; *Freeman's Journal*, 29 Nov. 1905; P. S. O'Hegarty, *History of Ireland under the Union*, pp. 650–3.

[2] A. Griffith, *The Resurrection of Hungary*, pp. 93–96; *Sinn Féin Tracts, no. 1: Sinn Féin in tabloid form* (1917).

Leitrim, joined Sinn Féin, resigned his seat, and offered himself for re-election as a Sinn Féin candidate. He was decisively beaten. The lesson drawn by the Sinn Féin organizers was that their publicity was not widespread enough, but their efforts to remedy the situation by transforming their paper into a daily and increasing its size from four pages to eight resulted only in the failure of the daily paper.[1] For the next few years the movement made little headway and no candidates were nominated for the 1910 general election. The fact is that as the prospects of home rule brightened the appeal of the constitution of 1782 weakened. Sinn Féin itself recognized this when in April 1910 it announced its intention of doing nothing to embarrass Redmond in his struggle for a Home Rule Bill. Yet it continued to assert Ireland's claim to complete independence: 'no legislature created in Ireland which is not supreme and absolute will offer a basis for concluding a final settlement with the foreigners who usurp the government of this country'.[2]

Two other separatist groups were at work in these pre-war years. In 1896 James Connolly founded the Irish socialist republican party and two years later a paper called *The Workers' Republic*. The party was primarily designed to serve the interests of the workers in the industrial sphere, but it was republican and nationalist in sympathy and it was ultimately responsible for bringing the urban workers into the left wing nationalist movement. While it participated in such activities as the centenary celebrations of the 1798 rebellion and the organization of the Irish brigade during the Anglo-Boer war it did not for years constitute a separate political party. After the general elections of 1910 it began to consider political action. A proposal to form a combined industrial and political organization was defeated by three votes at the party's annual congress in Galway in 1911, but in the following year the congress in Clonmel reversed this decision and founded the Irish trades union congress and labour party. The other group was composed of a number of republicans who drew their inspiration from the Irish Republican Brotherhood, the secret, oath-bound, Irish-American sponsored society which had been in existence since Fenian days.[3] The I.R.B. thus formed the link between the separatist movements of the nineteenth century and those of the twentieth. Its aim was the establishment of an independent republic

[1] *Sinn Féin* appeared as a daily paper from August 1909 to January 1910.
[2] Henry, op. cit., pp. 71–87.
[3] I.O. (C. J. C. Street), *The Administration of Ireland*, pp. 163–70.

by force. This policy found expression in *Irish Freedom*, a small periodical founded in 1910 and controlled by the I.R.B. acting under the pseudonym of the 'Central publication committee of the Wolfe Tone clubs'. The motto of the paper was a quotation from Wolfe Tone: 'To subvert the tyranny of our execrable government, to break the connection with England, the never-failing source of all our political evils, and to assert the independence of my country—these were my objects.'[1]

The separatist groups were all essentially minority movements drawing their support mainly from urban areas and especially Dublin. They were at one in their desire to break the connexion with Great Britain and in their distrust of the parliamentary party, but otherwise there was little community of outlook among them. Sinn Féin was a middle-class movement, capitalist in its economic policy and indifferent or hostile to the workers as in the strikes of 1911. It was accused by labour of having attempted to attract foreign capitalists to Ireland by the inducement of cheap Irish labour. The republicans were more sympathetic to labour movements. *Irish Freedom* published articles on working conditions, praised the co-operative movement, and supported the strikers of 1911. Yet the republicans earned the rebuke of the labour party for opposing the acceptance of British trade union aid for Irish strikers. While the republicans held that the Irish nation must be built on Sinn Féin principles they joined with the labour party in rejecting the dual monarchy scheme and in scorning Griffith's aversion to physical force. It was only in reaction to the events following on the introduction of the Home Rule Bill in 1912 that the groups began to draw together.

From the beginning of the home rule movement opposition to self-government had been vehement amongst the great majority in the protestant counties of Ulster. As early as 1877 the possibility of the protestant counties seceding from a self-governing Ireland had been mentioned. William Johnston, a prominent Orangeman, declared in the House of Commons that if an Irish parliament were set up, Ulster would not be satisfied with anything less than a parliament of its own.[2] Organization against a renewed attempt to pass a home rule measure began in 1905 with the institution of the Ulster Unionist Council to take 'consistent and continuous' political action against

---

[1] Henry, op. cit., pp. 88–93; *Irish Freedom*, 15 Nov. 1910.
[2] M. MacDonagh, *The Home Rule Movement*, Dublin, 1920, p. 107; 233 *Parl eb.*, 3s., 1173.

home rule. By the time the Home Rule Bill was introduced in 1912 a vigorous campaign was in full swing. Ulster unionists and English conservatives vied with one another in the violence of their denunciations. A scheme was prepared for the creation of a provisional government and of an army to serve it. On 28 September 1912 and the following days 218,000 men in Ulster signed a covenant pledging themselves to resist the setting up of a home rule parliament by every means in their power and to refuse to recognize its authority if it was forced upon them.[1] When it became clear that the Home Rule Bill was going to pass in spite of unionist opposition Sir Edward Carson, the Ulster leader, moved an amendment for the exclusion of the whole of Ulster from the home rule area. This amendment was rejected in January 1913,[2] and the unionists and their supporters pushed on with their plans for resistance. The Ulster Volunteer Force was organized; elaborate military preparations were made culminating in the Larne gun-running of 24 April 1914;[3] and the campaign of the English conservatives bore fruit in the Curragh incident which revealed the unreliability of the army for coercive measures against Ulster. In face of this storm the government weakened to the extent of introducing an Amending Bill under which individual Ulster counties would have the option of contracting out of the Home Rule Bill for a period of six years. The compromise was reluctantly accepted by the nationalists, but rejected by the unionists who demanded the permanent exclusion first of the whole of Ulster and then of the present six-county area. No progress towards a settlement had been made when the Great War broke out. On the day war was declared Redmond wrote to Asquith asking him to have the Home Rule Bill passed immediately, even if its operation had to be suspended for a time.[4] In spite of unremitting unionist opposition the government accepted Redmond's suggestion. The Amending Bill was dropped. The Home Rule Bill was passed in September, but a Suspensory Act postponed the coming into force of home rule until after the conclusion of the war. Moreover, Asquith gave an undertaking in the House of Commons that force would not be used against Ulster and that parliament would be given an opportunity of amending the Act in such a way as to secure general consent both in England and Ireland.

[1] R. McNeill, *Ulster's Stand for Union*, London, 1922, pp. 117–26.
[2] Ibid., pp. 132–3.
[3] Ibid., pp. 160–6, 190–226.
[4] D. Gwynn, *Life of Redmond*, p. 362.

In the existing state of feeling in Ireland it was almost inevitable that the organization of the Ulster Volunteers would inspire a similar movement on the other side. Redmond was urged by at least one member of his party in the summer of 1913 to follow the example of Ulster, but he refused to depart from parliamentary action.[1] The physical force party was eager to see a nationalist volunteer movement launched. The I.R.B. decided in July 1913 to organize a force but to wait until an opportunity arose of using individuals and bodies less suspect than themselves so that the government would not be disposed to suppress the movement immediately. Meantime, Pearse and others prepared the way with a journalistic campaign. In October 1913 the I.R.B. found what they considered a suitable opening in an article published in the Gaelic League journal by Éoin MacNeill, professor of Early Irish History in University College, Dublin, and vice-president of the Gaelic League. The O'Rahilly was deputed to approach MacNeill, without disclosing the I.R.B.'s interest, and to encourage him to action. The outcome was the formation of a provisional committee of twelve members of whom only three were members of Sinn Féin, the most prominent members of that group and of the I.R.B. being deliberately kept in the background. The inaugural meeting of the Irish Volunteers was held at the Rotunda in Dublin on 23 November 1913. Four thousand men were enrolled at this meeting. Plans for the organization and training of the force were rapidly completed; an auxiliary force of women called Cumann na mBan was formed; and the Fianna Éireann, a youth movement organized by Constance Markievicz in 1909, became a preliminary training ground.[2] Redmond was profoundly disturbed by these developments.[3] The Volunteers were controlled by men who had little use for home rule; they had declared their intention of putting the force at the disposal of an Irish parliament, but the Irish parliament envisaged by the Home Rule Bill was to have no power to control an army; and the official organ of the movement, *The Irish Volunteer*, often contained statements which were disturbing to the parliamentary party. To attempt to have the movement suppressed seemed to Redmond a dangerous course, but to gain control of it was relatively easy. He threatened to call out of the Volunteers all his supporters unless he was permitted to nominate twenty-five of his followers to

---

[1] S. Gwynn, *John Redmond's Last Years*, p. 92.
[2] Macardle, op. cit., pp. 95–100; O'Hegarty, op. cit., pp. 668–72.
[3] D. Gwynn, op. cit., p. 245.

the provisional committee. Though the republican element on the original committee disliked the proposal they realized that to refuse would lead to a split, to the probable suppression of the republican section, and to enhanced difficulties in securing arms. On 16 June 1914 a majority of the committee decided to accept Redmond's ultimatum, and the minority which dissented appealed to those who felt as they did 'to subordinate their personal feelings and persist in their efforts to make the Volunteers an effective, armed, national defence force'.[1] Nine days after the formation of the Irish Volunteers the government issued a proclamation prohibiting the importation of arms into Ireland. The Irish Volunteers were no more deterred by this proclamation from organizing a gun-running than their Ulster counterparts. A consignment of rifles and ammunition was landed at Howth, co. Dublin, on 26 July 1914 and at Kilcoole, co. Wicklow, on 1 August. Dissension between the two sections of the Irish Volunteers had occurred over the distribution of these arms and over the use of the money subscribed for the purchase of arms before the outbreak of the Great War precipitated a split. When the decision to go to war was announced in the House of Commons Redmond pledged the Volunteers to defend Ireland without consulting, or even informing, the committee. His action was criticized but endorsed by the committee. When, however, in a speech at Woodenbridge, co. Wicklow, on 20 September 1914 he called upon Irishmen to fight 'wherever the fighting line extends' the members of the original committee broke off their association with the Redmondites and promised to call a convention to reaffirm the original aims of the force. The total number of Volunteers was estimated at 180,000. Of these the great majority followed Redmond, took the name National Volunteers, and were committed to full support of the war, in which, indeed, many of them took an active part. The minority, some eleven or twelve thousand, continued to be called the Irish Volunteers and to profess the original policy, but they had been driven into the company of the more radical nationalist groups whose instrument they became increasingly until they were committed to rebellion.

In their response to these developments the separatists displayed a unanimity which had been conspicuously absent hitherto. The Home Rule Bill was scornfully received. Sinn Féin dismissed it as 'the rottenest bargain ever made by a victorious people with a mean,

[1] D. Gwynn, op. cit., pp. 310–20; Henry, op. cit., pp. 153–5; O'Hegarty, op. cit., pp. 677–9.

pettifogging, despised government', and the republicans summed up their attitude in the sentence, 'Damn your concessions; we want our country!'.[1] To the proposed partition of the country the separatists were completely opposed. Sinn Féin's declaration, 'England may continue to oppress this country, but she shall not dismember it', was re-echoed by the republicans: 'We shall never let them go, never'; and by labour: 'To it labour should give the bitterest opposition.'[2] More divergence of view appeared in the attitude of the separatists to the Irish Volunteers. Sinn Féin, as befitted a party which was opposed to force, bestowed only a qualified blessing on the movement. By the time the Volunteers came into existence labour had a volunteer force of its own. Labour disputes in Dublin in 1913 resulted in the formation of the Citizen Army from among the strikers. Despite the similarity of organization and aim the Citizen Army held itself distrustfully aloof from the Irish Volunteers. Many of the members of the Volunteer committee were suspect in labour eyes. The organizers of the Citizen Army resented the loss of recruits to the Volunteers, resented the indifference with which the Volunteers treated them, and resented the Volunteer policy of leaving controversial issues in abeyance. To the republicans, however, the formation of the Irish Volunteers, even as a defensive force, was a welcome development. Republicans served on the original committee, and *Irish Freedom* declared that in this departure from endless talk reality was touched at last. The action of Redmond in asserting his authority over the Volunteers brought the separatists together again in protest. *Sinn Féin* advised those members of the Volunteers who were in earnest to form their own committee independent of Redmond; *The Irish Worker* accused the committee of having handed the Volunteers over to a 'gang of place-hunters and political thugs'; and *Irish Freedom* published a leader on the arrangement entitled, 'The kiss of Judas'.[3] The attitude adopted by Redmond on the outbreak of war drew forth violent protests from the separatist organizations. Sinn Féin, the republicans, the Irish Volunteers, and the Citizen Army all declared for neutrality in opposition to the unionist and nationalist parties which were committed to the war. A common outlook and a common misfortune—for the papers of all these groups were suppressed within four months—tended to draw them together. There were still differences in plenty among them but the public habit,

---

[1] Henry, op. cit., p. 103.   [2] Ibid., p. 149.
[3] Ibid., pp. 141–5, 154–5.

dating from this period, of styling them all Sinn Féiners was not without its element of justification.[1]

Between the outbreak of the war and the 1916 rising a vigorous propaganda campaign was sustained in the separatist press—which under one name or another survived all government suppressions—and in a stream of pamphlets. In the autumn of 1914 a paper called *Éire* appeared as a weekly, but after its second number it became a daily. It is indicative of the changed relations among the separatist groups that although it was launched 'in order to report the proceedings of the Irish Volunteer convention'[2] *Éire* was edited by Griffith the founder of Sinn Féin. In this paper the recruiting campaign was denounced and the war news was analysed day by day in a way unfavourable to the allies. After about six weeks the paper was suppressed. Griffith's next venture was a bi-weekly called *Scissors and Paste* which consisted merely of extracts from other newspapers. Though the paper contained no original comment the selection and juxtaposition of the extracts made it as seditious in the eyes of the government as its predecessor had been and it was suppressed after just over two months. In May 1915 *The Workers' Republic*, edited by Connolly, took the place of *The Irish Worker*, which had shared the fate of *Sinn Féin* and *Irish Freedom* in December 1914. After an interval Griffith founded a new weekly called *Nationality* in June 1915. It continued to appear till the 1916 rising. The trend of separatist thought can be illustrated by one extract from this journal which represented a movement that had not originally been in favour of physical force: 'The things that count in Ireland against English conscription are national determination, serviceable weapons and the knowledge of how to use them.' The propaganda of these journals was supplemented by a considerable pamphlet literature. Early in 1915 the Irish publicity league launched a series entitled, 'Tracts for the Times', the first of which was, significantly, *What Emmet means in 1915*. The Sinn Féin case was argued in a pamphlet called *When the government publishes sedition*, an examination of the census returns to show that the population of Ireland had shrunk by half since the Union; in *Daniel O'Connell and Sinn Féin* which contended that O'Connell was really a Sinn Féiner; and in *How Ireland is plundered*, an account of the financial relations between England and Ireland. Cumann na mBan was responsible for a 'National Series'; the death of the old Fenian leader O'Donovan Rossa in August 1915 provided

[1] Henry, op. cit., pp. 164–8.   [2] *Éire*, 26 Oct. 1914.

inspiration for pamphlets on his life and work; and the Defence of the Realm Acts provided others. This pamphlet campaign reached an eloquent climax in the last four 'Tracts for the Times' which were written by Pearse between the end of 1915 and March 1916, a fortnight before the rising.

The war not merely accelerated the progress of amalgamation among the separatist groups, it also brought them all under the influence of the I.R.B. The supreme council of the I.R.B. resolved immediately to seize the opportunity of Britain's preoccupation in the war to organize an insurrection. By way of preparation they summoned a secret meeting of men prominent in the various branches of the left wing nationalist movement, including representatives of Sinn Féin and labour. At this meeting it was decided to resort to arms in one of three eventualities: if the Germans invaded Ireland; if Britain applied conscription to Ireland; or if the war was drawing to a close without a rising having taken place, so that the insurgents might declare war on Britain and claim representation at the peace conference. In September 1914 the supreme council created a military committee, charged with the task of securing control of the Irish Volunteers and of planning the insurrection.[1] The nominal leaders of the Volunteers still adhered to their original policy of maintaining the Volunteers as a defensive force, trained and ready to resist conscription or any attempt at suppression, but not designed to take the offensive. From the time of the split with the Redmondites, however, their authority was consistently undermined by the I.R.B., some of whose leading members held key positions in the force. Contact was made with Germany, the co-operation of Connolly and of the Citizen Army was secured, and plans were completed for a rising at Easter 1916 without their knowledge. It was not until a few days before the rising that MacNeill discovered what was afoot. When he did he used every means in his power to prevent the outbreak short of denouncing the leaders to the government.

The rising was thus the work of a minority group within a minority movement. It took even the officials at Dublin Castle by surprise and it was naturally an even greater surprise to the general public. Outside of their own circle next to nothing was known about the leaders or their aims. The rising was almost universally condemned.[2] Thousands of Irishmen were serving in the British army; in the eyes

[1] Macardle, op. cit., pp. 123–9.
[2] P. S. O'Hegarty, *Victory of Sinn Féin*, p. 3.

of their relatives and friends the rising was nothing less than a stab in the back. Yet there were those who realized how easily this abhorrence might be transformed into ardent admiration. James Stephens, writing in London a few days after the outbreak, foresaw the reaction: 'She is not with the rebellion, but she will be, and her heart, which was withering, will be warmed by the knowledge that men thought her worth dying for.'[1] John Dillon, Redmond's principal lieutenant in the parliamentary party, was in Dublin throughout the fighting. As soon as he was able he wrote advising Redmond to be extremely cautious about making any public statement and to urge most emphatically on the government the folly of numerous executions. Dillon was convinced that harsh repressive measures would swing public opinion round in favour of the insurgents.[2] Redmond had already expressed his 'feeling of detestation and horror' before Dillon's letter reached him; in spite of it he reaffirmed his condemnation in a statement to the press. He did, however, agree with Dillon on the question of wholesale executions and advised Asquith to follow the example of Botha in South Africa.[3]

It is not surprising that Redmond's advice was ignored. A policy of repression had been the panacea for Irish ills too often in the past to be abandoned at a time of national danger. Pearse surrendered on 29 April. On 3 May executions after secret trial by courts martial began. In all, ninety persons were sentenced to death and fifteen were actually executed, the executions being spread out, a few a day, from 3 May to 12 May. Some 3,000 people were arrested throughout Ireland; of these a large number were transported to England and many were sentenced to penal servitude for long periods or for life. These events set in motion a revulsion of feeling in Ireland and stimulated anti-British sentiments among the Irish-Americans. In England, too, protests were raised, the *Manchester Guardian*, for example, declaring that the executions 'were becoming an atrocity'.[4] P. S. O'Hegarty, a member of the supreme council of the I.R.B., writes:

Had the English but the wit to see it, the insurrection played right into their hands ... But the completeness of their victory, their crushing of the insurrection with the approval of the Irish parliamentary party and the mass of Irish public opinion, took away their political sanity. The army and the *Irish Times* demanded blood, and blood they got. But when Sir John

[1] W. K. Hancock, *Survey of British Commonwealth Affairs*, i. 99.
[2] D. Gwynn, op. cit., pp. 474–5.
[3] Ibid., pp. 474, 482.
[4] Macardle, op. cit. pp. 183–9.

Maxwell shot to pieces the government of the Irish republic he put an end to the English domination of Ireland.[1]

The downfall of the Irish parliamentary party is equally traceable to the rising and its aftermath. As sympathy for the insurgents grew Redmond's immediate condemnation of the rising was remembered against him. By respecting the prime minister's appeal to avoid raising the Irish question in the House of Commons while the government sought a solution he dealt a further blow to the prestige of his party. The offices of the *Freeman's Journal* were destroyed in the fighting so that the party lost the services of its newspaper at a critical period. Redmond's appeals to Asquith behind the scenes to stop the executions were unknown to the Irish public. When on top of all this the government failed to secure agreement on the Home Rule Act the fate of the party was sealed. As the star of the parliamentary party waned that of Sinn Féin climbed steadily towards its zenith.

The first post-rising attempt at a settlement on the basis of the Home Rule Act resulted only in bitterness and recrimination; both unionists and nationalists were convinced that they had been misled by Lloyd George. The re-establishment of the old machinery of government, with a unionist chief secretary and a unionist attorney-general, served to discredit the parliamentary party further. The only immediate step taken by the new cabinet under the premiership of Lloyd George was the release of many of the interned prisoners in December 1916. At the beginning of 1917 Sinn Féin was presented with the opportunity of testing the state of feeling in the country. A by-election was pending in North Roscommon, a constituency which had been represented by a nationalist for nearly forty years. The candidate selected to contest the election in the interests of Sinn Féin was Count Plunkett, the father of Joseph Mary Plunkett, one of the executed 1916 leaders. He was elected by a large majority. Three months later a vacancy occurred in South Longford and Sinn Féin nominated Joseph McGuinness, at the time a convict in Lewes prison. The election was hotly contested for the nationalists realized that their future hung upon it. Dillon wrote to Redmond: 'If we are beaten I do not see how we can hope to hold the party in existence. If we win there will be a fresh chance for the party.'[2] The result was a narrow victory for Sinn Féin; McGuinness was elected with a majority of thirty-seven votes.[3]

---

[1] O'Hegarty, op. cit., pp. 3–4. [2] D. Gwynn, op. cit., p. 546.
[3] Macardle, op. cit., pp. 208–9, 214–15.

These successes were achieved to the accompaniment of constantly mounting excitement in the country. Demonstrations of all kinds, clashes with the police, and widespread arrests became increasingly frequent. To some the remedy for the situation seemed to lie in the application of conscription to Ireland. Lloyd George preferred instead to offer home rule to that part of Ireland which clearly demanded it, but Redmond rejected his appeal to enter into further negotiations and led his followers out of the House of Commons in protest against the renewed proposal to partition the country. The second Sinn Féin victory in a parliamentary election was followed quickly by another effort on Lloyd George's part to resolve the deadlock. He put forward two suggestions: either that a home rule parliament should be established immediately in the twenty-six counties, together with a council of Ireland composed of representatives of the two parts of the country, or that a convention of Irishmen should be set up to devise a form of government within the Empire which would be acceptable to all parties. His second proposal was accepted, but the possibility of the convention achieving anything was rendered remote by the intransigence of the Ulster unionists and by the refusal of Sinn Féin to participate. The Sinn Féin attitude was all the more damaging in view of further evidence of its growing strength. When John Redmond's brother, Major William Redmond, M.P. for East Clare, was killed in action his seat was contested by Éamon de Valera who was elected by an overwhelming majority. A month later Sinn Féin secured another victory in Kilkenny where William T. Cosgrave was returned with nearly twice as many votes as his opponent.

While the separatists were steadily winning adherents at the expense of the parliamentary party they were still far from unanimous about the goal towards which they were striving. At a convention summoned by Plunkett in April 1917 divergent views ranging from the old Sinn Féin of Griffith to extreme republicanism were expressed and the only conclusion reached was to form a national council. This body denied the right of any foreign parliament to legislate for Ireland, demanded representation for Ireland at the peace conference, and pledged itself to use every means in its power to win complete freedom for the country.[1] Later in the year the national council appointed a committee to prepare a draft constitution for a new organization which was to be formed at the tenth annual convention

[1] Macardle, op. cit., pp. 213–14.

or árd-fheis of Sinn Féin in October. By this time a division had appeared among the republicans, some of whom adhered to the I.R.B. while others were opposed to its secret control.[1] The conflicting policies were so hotly championed in the committee that no progress was made until de Valera devised a formula which proved generally acceptable. The Sinn Féin convention which met on 25 October 1917 in the Mansion House, Dublin, was attended by some 1,700 delegates. Although the newspapers had for some time been applying the name Sinn Féin to the whole movement it was still technically the name of Griffith's organization only and some of the republicans resented its application to them. Now, at this convention the name was officially adopted by the unified separatist movement. The new constitution embodied the compromise which had been worked out by the preliminary committee. The aim of Sinn Féin was declared to be the securing of international recognition for Ireland as an independent republic. Once that status had been achieved the people of Ireland might by referendum choose their own form of government. The rest of the constitution was largely devoted to a restatement of the old Sinn Féin programme. In accordance with the resolution adopted in the Sinn Féin convention of 1905 a national assembly would be convoked in Dublin to give effect to the following programme: the introduction of a protective system for Irish industries and commerce by the combined action of local government bodies; the establishment of an Irish consular service and an Irish mercantile marine; the institution of a national stock exchange; the carrying out of an industrial survey of Ireland and the development of mineral resources, communications, and fisheries; the reform of the educational system and the creation of a national civil service embracing all employees of local government bodies who would be recruited by public examination; the establishment of arbitration courts for the settlement of disputes; and the abolition of the poor law system. Having adopted a constitution the convention proceeded to the election of a president. Griffith, the founder of the old Sinn Féin, was unacceptable to the republicans; Plunkett was a possible choice; but both of these men stood down in favour of de Valera who was elected unanimously. The Irish Volunteer organization remained distinct from the new Sinn Féin party, but at its annual convention held on 27 October 1917 de Valera was elected president. While the civil and military wings of the separatist movement were thus united under the

[1] Macardle, op. cit., p. 231.

same leadership the effective control of the Volunteers was in the hands of the I.R.B.

Meantime the Irish convention instituted by Lloyd George was pursuing its deliberations without any sign of success. Redmond was working hard for compromise in the knowledge that a breakdown in the convention would be fatal to his party. In November 1917 he warned Lloyd George that the convention was the last hope of a peaceful settlement. If it failed Sinn Féin would be supreme, and Ireland would have to be ruled by the bayonet.[1] While it remained in existence the parliamentary party retained sufficient support to enable it to win a number of by-elections. The nationalist candidate was elected in South Armagh in February 1918; in March the party had a further success when, on the death of Redmond, his seat in Waterford was won by his son Captain William A. Redmond; and in April it was successful at a by-election in East Tyrone. But these electoral victories did not presage a revival of the party.[2]

The reconstructed Sinn Féin party at once embarked on a vigorous campaign. Not only were new Sinn Féin clubs organized and meetings and reviews held but the first attempts were made to implement the policy of undermining and superseding the British administration in Ireland. In the west, grazing land belonging to large estates was cleared of cattle, divided into allotments for tillage, and given out at fixed rents which were collected by the local Sinn Féin clubs and paid to the owners of the land. The Sinn Féin food control committee organized a census of supplies and a scheme of distribution: in Ennis and elsewhere, for example, a market for potatoes with a rationing scheme of sale was instituted; and in Dublin a consignment of pigs on the way to the docks was seized and sold to local curers for home consumption.[3]

The government replied to these activities and to the sporadic outbursts of violence with an intensified police and military drive. An order was issued prohibiting the carrying of arms by unauthorized persons and the possession of arms in Tipperary, Galway, and Clare; a few days later Clare was proclaimed a military area; a strict censorship was established; meetings were broken up; and widespread arrests were made. These measures had so little effect that strong pressure was brought on the government to extend conscription to Ireland. The urgent need for more men disposed the government to

[1] D. Gwynn, op. cit., p. 570.   [2] Macardle, op. cit., pp. 244, 247.
[3] Ibid., pp. 240–2; Henry, op. cit., pp. 248–9.

listen. At a cabinet meeting on 28 March 1918 the decision was taken to apply conscription to Ireland as soon as the Irish convention had presented its report. The report was eventually completed on 5 April, after fifty-one meetings, but it was signed by only forty-four of the ninety members and in the circumstances it made no contribution towards finding a solution of the Irish problem. Four days later, when the House of Commons reassembled, Lloyd George announced the terms of a new Manpower Bill under which conscription could be applied to Ireland at any time by order in council. This renewed threat of conscription drove the parliamentary party to action which was tantamount to a vindication of the Sinn Féin contention that agitation at Westminster was futile. In protest against the bill the nationalist members withdrew from the house and returned to Ireland to help organize resistance. A conference summoned by the lord mayor of Dublin, which met in the Mansion House on 18 April, was attended by representatives of the parliamentary party, Sinn Féin, the labour movement, and other nationalist groups. An anti-conscription pledge was drafted at this meeting; and an appeal made to the catholic bishops who were assembled at Maynooth. On Sunday 21 April the pledge was signed at the church doors. Two days later the trades union congress staged a general strike. A further demonstration of solidarity was given in the Kingscounty by-election when the parliamentary party withdrew its candidate in favour of Sinn Féin.

To meet this situation the government acted with promptitude and vigour. Lord Wimborne was replaced as lord lieutenant by Field Marshal Lord French, and other members of the Irish executive were changed, including the chief secretary. On 12 April 1918 the police captured a certain Joseph Dowling, formerly a member of Casement's Irish brigade, who had landed from a German submarine with instructions to make contact with the Sinn Féin leaders. This German plot, as it was called, led to the arrest of most of the Sinn Féin and Volunteer leaders on the night of 17 May and the following day. Seventy-three persons were deported to England at once and others followed. These arrests were not intended as a preliminary to the application of conscription and in the proclamation announcing the discovery of the German plot it was stated that steps would be taken to encourage voluntary enlistment. Nor did they serve the purpose of crippling Sinn Féin; just over a month later Griffith, himself one of the arrested men, was returned at a by-election in East Cavan in spite of the strenuous efforts of the parliamentary party to hold the seat.[1] All this time the amount of violence was increasing and the government's repressive measures were becoming more severe. Large areas of the country were declared 'proclaimed districts' or 'special military areas'. In July 1918 Sinn Féin, the Volunteers, Cumann na mBan, and the Gaelic League were proclaimed dangerous and illegal organizations, and all public meetings and processions were prohibited. Cathal Brugha, Michael Collins, and other leaders of the Volunteers, for their part, were increasingly authorizing or condoning acts of violence and preparing plans for a ruthless opposition to conscription. Such was the state of Ireland when the Armistice was signed.

[1] Macardle, op. cit., pp. 249–57.

II

THE ORIGIN AND NATURE OF THE REPUBLICAN DÁIL

LLOYD GEORGE'S decision to hold an immediate post-war general election provided Sinn Féin with the opportunity of gauging its strength throughout the country. Nomination day was 4 December 1918. Long before that Sinn Féin was publishing lists of candidates.[1] An election manifesto was prepared restating the aims of the movement. Its purpose was to establish a republic. This was to be done by withdrawing the Irish representatives from the House of Commons; by using every means to make it impossible for Britain to hold Ireland by military force or otherwise; by establishing a constituent assembly of members chosen by the Irish constituencies to act as the supreme national authority and to develop Ireland's social, political, and industrial life; and by appealing to the peace conference for the recognition of Ireland as an independent state. Sinn Féin, the manifesto declared, stood less for a political party than for the nation; it represented the old tradition of nationhood handed on from the dead generations. The right of a nation to sovereign independence was stated to rest upon immutable natural law and to be incapable of forming the subject of compromise. As for the parliamentary party, its presence at Westminster was an obstacle on the path which led to the peace conference.[2]

The parliamentary party, realizing that its very existence was at stake, made strenuous efforts to recover the ground it had lost.[3] But in eight marginal constituencies in Ulster an attempt was made to avoid three-cornered contests by an agreed division between the two anti-unionist parties. After Dillon had rejected a Sinn Féin proposal that a plebiscite of non-unionist voters in the constituencies should be held to decide whether parliamentary party or Sinn Féin candidates should be nominated, and after a conference between Dillon and MacNeill had broken down Cardinal Logue succeeded in persuading them to agree to an equal division of the seats. But there was

---

[1] *Nationality*, 12 Oct. 1918.   [2] Ibid., 19 Oct. 1918.
[3] Macardle, *The Irish Republic*, p. 262; P. Béaslaí, *Michael Collins and the making of a New Ireland*, i. 245.

much confusion and recrimination. The delay in reaching agreement led to Sinn Féin nominating candidates and forfeiting deposits in the four constituencies allotted to the parliamentary party. Moreover, Dillon was accused of breaking faith by failing to direct his followers to vote for Sinn Féin in the constituencies where no parliamentary party candidate had been nominated.[1] Sinn Féin was on better terms with the labour movement. So many members and potential supporters of the labour party were enrolled in one or other of the left wing nationalist organizations that the labour leaders decided not to contest the election, although they were critical of Sinn Féin's social and economic policy.[2] Apart from the four constituencies surrendered to the parliamentary party and the constituencies of Dublin University and North Down, Sinn Féin contested every constituency in Ireland. In unionist strongholds the policy adopted was to nominate some prominent member of the party who was standing in another constituency as well.

The election campaign was conducted by Sinn Féin under great difficulties. When parliament was dissolved on 25 November 1918 extra troops were sent to Ireland. Already the government had arrested and imprisoned 1,319 of the lesser leaders of the republican movement and had deported without trial 115 of the most prominent figures. The Sinn Féin election manifesto was severely cut by the censor.[3] The £150 deposits of Sinn Féin candidates were confiscated. Most of the candidates were in prison; only 26 were able to appear in their constituencies. Republican literature was suppressed and those circulating it were arrested; meetings were broken up; and one after another the Sinn Féin directors of elections were arrested and their offices raided.[4] The result was all the more striking. On nomination day 26 Sinn Féin candidates were returned unopposed for constituencies scattered widely over the country.[5] When the election count was completed it was found that Sinn Féin had captured 47 of the 79 contested seats. The unionists had won 26 and the parliamentary party 6, 4 of them the Ulster seats allotted to the party by the agreement with Sinn Féin. Sinn Féin had thus secured a total of 73 seats which were held by 69 members, one of them a woman, the first woman to be elected to the House of Commons. In 24 of the 32 counties of Ireland only Sinn Féin candidates had been elected. It

[1] *New Ireland*, 14 Dec. 1918.   [2] Ibid., 9 Nov. 1918.
[3] Macardle, op. cit., pp. 921–2.
[4] *Irish Bulletin*, 1 July 1920; *Nationality*, 30 Nov. 1918.
[5] Ibid., 14 Dec. 1918; *Irish Times*, 5 Dec. 1918.

should be noted, however, that 31 per cent. of the electorate did not vote; that only 47 per cent. of the votes were cast for Sinn Féin; and that in all probability, as a contemporary commentator pointed out, many of those who supported Sinn Féin were motivated less by sympathy for the full republican programme than by resentment against the conscription threat, Dublin Castle rule, and the subservient policy of the parliamentary party.[1] De Valera himself interpreted the election result very much in this way. He declared in the dáil that he regarded the vote for Sinn Féin not 'for a form of government so much, because we are not republican doctrinaires, but it was for Irish freedom and Irish independence, and it was obvious to everyone who considered the question that Irish independence could not be realized at the present time in any other way so suitably as through a republic'.[2]

The copy of *Nationality* which announced the full election results bore the heading 'Ireland's declaration of independence'.[3] Another Sinn Féin paper declared: 'It is no longer a question of parties in Ireland today. . . . Sinn Féin becomes, as it were, the governing power of Ireland . . . the great representative organization of the Irish people in Ireland and throughout the world.'[4] The same paper hailed the election results as a 'great act of repudiation of English rule', and claimed 'Ireland is thrown entirely upon her own resources so far as England is concerned'. Sinn Féin's intentions had been made abundantly clear. Soon after the election, on 7 January 1919, a meeting was held which is usually described as the first Irish republican congress but which was evidently regarded at the time as a meeting of the dáil. Among the Gavan Duffy papers in the National Library of Ireland is a printed letter, dated 2 January 1919 and signed by H. Boland and T. Kelly,[5] which reads: 'We have the honour to call you to the first meeting of the Dáil Éireann which will hold a private session in the Mansion House, Dublin on Tuesday next January 7 at 10 a.m.' A printed card in Irish, bearing the member's name, was enclosed. The function of the meeting, which was attended by twenty-six representatives, was wholly preparatory. Count Plunkett, the senior Sinn Féin member, was elected chairman for the day and a temporary secretary and staff were appointed. A protest was issued for publication drawing attention to the fact that thirty-seven of the elected Sinn Féin members were imprisoned or exiled. The rest of the

---
[1] *Round Table*, ix. 581.
[2] *Dáil Official Report, 1921–2*, p. 9.
[3] *Nationality*, 4 Jan. 1919.
[4] *New Ireland*, 28 Dec. 1918.
[5] Honorary secretaries of Sinn Féin.

proceedings was concerned with the intended public meeting of the dáil. A select committee was appointed to consider draft standing orders and a draft constitution for the dáil; ceremonial and terminology were discussed; the decision was taken to summon the representatives of all Irish constituencies, regardless of party; the question of substitute members for representatives in jail was considered; and the date, place, and programme for the first public meeting were decided upon.

Meantime the government was in two minds about the attitude it should adopt to the abstentionist M.P.s and to the assembly which they were preparing to bring into being. Rumours were prevalent that a general round-up was intended, but it was decided in the end to take no immediate action.[1]

The public inaugural meeting of Dáil Éireann was held in the Mansion House on 21 January 1919. Only 27 of the 69 Sinn Féin members attended: 2 were absent through illness; 5 were on special missions abroad; 1 was deported; and the remaining 34 were in prison. Michael Collins and Harry Boland were in England arranging the escape of de Valera from Lincoln jail, but in order to mislead the government they were officially recorded as present.[2] A large crowd of spectators and press representatives attended the meeting. The organizers had decided to dispense with any ceremonial.[3] A prayer was read in Irish by Rev. Michael O'Flanagan and all the formal pronouncements were in Irish, with French and English translations. The first business was the appointment of Seán T. O'Kelly as speaker; in his absence Cathal Brugha was selected to preside for the day. Four temporary clerks were also appointed. A roll call followed, with the names of all the representatives of Irish constituencies included. A short constitution was then adopted. The rest of the proceedings was primarily propagandist. A formal declaration of independence, in the spirit of continental nationalism, was read in the three languages. Three delegates were chosen to attend the peace conference, a message to the free nations was issued, and a statement of social aims was promulgated.[4] At a private session on the following day a temporary ministry was appointed, with Cathal Brugha as prime minister, Eóin MacNeill as minister for finance, Michael Collins as

---

[1] *New Ireland*, 25 Jan. 1919.
[2] *Irish Press*, 21 Jan. 1944; Béaslaí, op. cit. i. 256.
[3] *New Ireland*, 25 Jan. 1919.
[4] *Proceedings First Dáil*, pp. 9–24.

minister for home affairs, Count Plunkett as minister for foreign affairs, and Richard Mulcahy as minister for defence.[1]

The English press adopted a scornful attitude to these developments in Dublin. 'Nobody here in England is bothered about the tomfoolery of the Sinn Féin parliament in Dublin', declared one.[2] *The Times*, while admitting that everything was done decently and in order and that not a word was uttered which could provoke discord or ill-feeling,[3] branded the ceremony as 'the stage play at the Mansion House', spoke of the 'futility of the whole performance', but in view of the 'darker forces which are profiting by its gospel of lawlessness' concluded 'that there was never a moment in Irish history when the government could less afford to be tender with disorder and with wholesale defiance of constituted authority'.[4] The Dublin daily press mingled apprehension with its scorn. The *Irish Times* held that the event was in one sense futile and unreal but that in another it conveyed a grave warning to the Irish people. 'The press gallery witnessed a solemn act of defiance of the British Empire by a body of young men who have not the slightest notion of that Empire's power and resources and not a particle of experience in the conduct of public affairs.'[5] The *Freeman's Journal* believed that if the proceedings were seriously meant Ireland was on the eve of one of the most tragic chapters in its history.[6] Sections of the American press also were sceptical of the dáil's potentialities. The *World* wrote: 'If the Sinn Féin parliament were taken seriously it might be viewed as a momentous event', and the *Tribune* referred to 'this most ideal and least real of all revolutions'.[7]

There followed a long interval in the dáil's activities. It was not until 1 April 1919 that it met again to welcome its members who had escaped or been released from prison. Five meetings were held during this second session in April, two of them in public. One more meeting was held in public, on 9 May 1919, but from that time on the efforts of the government to suppress the republican movement drove the dáil underground. In all, the first dáil held six sessions in 1919, three in 1920, and three in 1921, making a total of twenty-one meetings. The majority—fourteen—were held in 1919; in 1920 the dáil met on only three occasions—in June, August, and September; and in 1921 on four—twice in January, once in March, and once in May. Attendance varied from a maximum of fifty-two at the meeting of

[1] Ibid., pp. 26–27.
[2] Quoted in *Nationality*, 1 Feb. 1919.
[3] *The Times*, 22 Jan. 1919.
[4] Ibid., 23 Jan. 1919.
[5] *Irish Times*, 22 Jan. 1919.
[6] *Freeman's Journal*, 22 Jan. 1919.
[7] Quoted in *The Times*, 23 Jan. 1919.

1 April 1919 through a figure of over forty at the three 1920 meetings to just over twenty at the 1921 meetings.

On 10 September 1919 the government suppressed the dáil as a dangerous association. Thereafter it met in secret: at the home of Walter L. Cole, 3 Mountjoy Square; in Flemings Hotel, 75 Gardiner Place; or in the basement of the Mansion House.[1] The proclamation was received with anger and defiance by the Sinn Féin leaders. In the last issue before its suppression *Nationality* declared, '. . . this is the first time in the history of the English in Ireland that they have risen to the heights of proclaiming the elected representatives of Ireland a dangerous association'.[2] The *Irish Bulletin*, the official organ of the dáil, regarded the proclamation as tantamount to a declaration of war on the Irish nation. Griffith asserted that the government had proclaimed the whole Irish nation an illegal assembly. Even individuals and organs remote from Sinn Féin condemned the government's action. Sir Horace Plunkett, chairman of the abortive Irish convention, said that the dáil had at least as much moral sanction as the English government and ten times its moral influence,[3] and the *Daily Mail* admitted that the proclamation had the effect of throwing water on lime.[4] On 11 November 1919 military and police raided 76 Harcourt Street, Dublin, the headquarters of the dáil, seized all its papers, and arrested the clerical staff. The members were also by now liable to arrest[5] so that it had become necessary to forbid the attendance of certain key men in the movement at meetings of the dáil. A formal notice of a meeting in October 1919 addressed to P. O'Keeffe was accompanied by a letter which stated, 'Enclosed is a summons to the next meeting of Dáil Éireann. As it is possible that this meeting will be suppressed and as some of the deputies must still be available to carry on the work the ministry will be glad if you will abstain from attending.'[6] The *Irish Bulletin* of 13 August 1920 set out the prison records of the deputies. Of the members elected in 1918 12 had been sentenced to death; 21 had been sentenced to terms of penal servitude ranging from life to three years; 27 had been imprisoned or deported without trial; 65 had been imprisoned, many of them more than

---

[1] *Who's Who in the Seanad Election* (1925), note on W. L. Cole; and information supplied by Mr. P. O'Keeffe.
[2] *Nationality*, 20 Sept. 1919.
[3] *Irish Bulletin*, 26 Nov. 1919. [4] Ibid., 10 Dec. 1919.
[5] Frank Lawless, member for co. Dublin North, was arrested in the raid on the dáil headquarters.
[6] Letter dated 21 Oct. 1919 among papers lent to the author by Mr. P. O'Keeffe.

twice and some of them five times; only 2 had neither been arrested nor wanted by the police. At least 10 had been or were on hunger strike, one of them, Terence MacSwiney, representative for Mid Cork, died on 24 October 1920 after a fast lasting for seventy-four days. When the number of members at liberty had shrunk dangerously low the dáil considered the advisability of appointing substitutes for the arrested members. Since this would have destroyed the representative character of the assembly it was decided instead that the dáil should resolve itself into a provisional government when the membership had been reduced to five.[1] The way in which the suppression of the dáil and the proscribing of its members affected the dáil's activities will appear later.

A brief, simple, provisional constitution drafted by Seán T. O'Kelly, George Gavan Duffy, and Piaras Béaslaí[2] was adopted at the inaugural meeting. Dáil Éireann was declared to possess full powers to legislate and was to be composed of delegates chosen by the people from the existing constituencies. Executive power was to be vested in a ministry composed of a prime minister chosen by the dáil and four other ministers nominated by the prime minister and approved by the dáil. These ministers, for finance, home affairs, foreign affairs, and defence, were to be members of the dáil and at all times answerable to it. The dáil was to have power by vote to dismiss the ministry or any of the ministers if a written order in the form of a unanimous resolution was presented for that purpose seven days previously. Every meeting of the dáil was to be presided over by a chairman or vice-chairman chosen by the dáil for the year, or in their absence by a substitute or provisional chairman. Whatever money the ministry needed was to be granted by vote of the dáil to which the ministry was to be answerable for the expenditure of that money. The accounts were to be audited twice a year, in November and May, by auditors selected by the dáil but not members of it. Amendments might be made to the provisional constitution if a written unanimous order embodying them was made by the dáil seven days previously. A set of standing orders to regulate the conduct of business was also adopted. The language of business was stated to be Irish or English but all official pronouncements were to be made in Irish. The dáil was to be convened by the chairman who was to be responsible for the maintenance of order and the regulation of business. Each deputy was required to sign the roll. Rules were laid down concerning the

[1] *Proceedings First Dáil*, p. 280.   [2] *Irish Press*, 21 Jan. 1944.

orders of the day, questions, the conduct of debates, the closure, divisions, the quorum, the admission of visitors, and the voting of supplies. In fact, these standing orders read like an abbreviated and simplified version of the standing orders in operation today.

The original ministry selected under the leadership of Cathal Brugha was intended merely as a stopgap. It was with the escape of de Valera and the release of the other republican prisoners that the dáil executive was fully constituted. At the meeting on 1 April 1919 de Valera was elected príomh-aire or prime minister and he nominated ministers to the seven portfolios of home affairs, foreign affairs, finance, defence, labour, industry, and local government. In addition, directors were appointed to departments of agriculture and propaganda.[1] Two days later the dáil appointed a director of trade and commerce who was included in the ministry in June.[2] The election of Seán T. O'Kelly as ceann cómhairle or speaker was confirmed and J. J. O'Kelly was selected as deputy chairman.[3] The appointment of clerks was left to the speaker and their remuneration fixed at two guineas a day, while the house was in session. At the meeting on 1 April it was announced that four clerks had been appointed for the session.[4] By June the dáil was employing seven full-time officials: a clerk of the dáil, an official translator, a private secretary, an accountant, an assistant, a typist, and a messenger.[5] When the question of remuneration for members of the dáil was raised by Brugha it was decided to allow them third-class railway fare from their constituencies to Dublin and a maximum of 15s. a day lodging expenses.[6] Later a proposal was made that they should receive an allowance of £250 a year but on the suggestion of Collins, the minister for finance, it was resolved instead to establish a deputies' expense fund out of which any deputy might claim each month a sum not exceeding one-twelfth of £250.[7] The salaries of ministers who devoted their full time to political work were fixed at £600 for the president and £350 for the other ministers.[8] Subsequently the ministerial salaries were increased to £500 a year and those of the directors of departments to £400.[9] With the completion of these arrangements the dáil was organized for the implementing of the policy its leaders had outlined.

The term 'president' first appears in the dáil proceedings on 17 June 1919 when de Valera was in America working for the recognition of

[1] *Proceedings First Dáil*, pp. 34, 36.
[2] Ibid., p. 112.
[3] Ibid., p. 30.
[4] Ibid., p. 26.
[5] Ibid., p. 124.
[6] Ibid., p. 31.
[7] Ibid., p. 234.
[8] Ibid., p. 41.
[9] Ibid., p. 209.

The Origin and Nature of the Republican Dáil 27

the republic.[1] While there he became convinced that his position would be strengthened if he held the title of president. The difficulty was that the dáil constitution had not provided specifically for a president of the republic though de Valera contended that the position was implied in the office he held. After his return it was decided that as 'an act declaratory of the true situation' he should be formally proposed to the dáil as president of the republic, and this was done when the dáil ministry was re-elected on 26 August 1921.[2]

One other development calls for mention. Originally deputies had been required merely to sign the roll of membership. But on 30 August 1919 Griffith, who was acting as president in the absence of de Valera in America, supported a motion by Brugha setting out a form of oath to be taken by deputies, Volunteers, clerks of the dáil, and others whom the dáil might decide upon. 'They should realize', Griffith said, 'that they were the government of the country. This oath would regularize the situation. . . . If they were not a regular government then they were shams and imposters.' The oath, which was accepted by thirty to three, pledged the taker to 'support and defend the Irish republic and the government of the Irish republic which is Dáil Éireann against all enemies, foreign and domestic', and to 'bear true faith and allegiance to the same'.[3]

The republican government established in January 1919 was enabled to test its influence in the country on two occasions: in 1920 when the local government elections took place, and in 1921 when a parliamentary election was held as a result of the Government of Ireland Act, 1920. In preparation for the triennial municipal elections which were fixed for January 1920 the government introduced proportional representation into Ireland in the hope that it would militate against Sinn Féin by enabling minorities to secure representation.[4] The result was a victory for Sinn Féin. It secured a majority in 72 of the 127 municipal corporations and councils in the country and, with nationalist members, in 26 others. This success was followed up in June when in the elections for county and rural district councils Sinn Féin candidates captured 28 of the 33 county councils, 172 of the 206 rural councils, and 138 of the 154 poor law boards. As a result of these elections every county council, every rural district council, and every board of guardians in Leinster, Munster, and Connaught was controlled by Sinn Féin. The Government of Ireland Act came into

---
[1] Ibid., p. 112.   [2] *Dáil Debates*, xli. 1096; *Dáil Official Report, 1921–2*, p. 77.
[3] *Proceedings First Dáil*, pp. 151–3.   [4] *Irish Bulletin*, 14 Jan. 1920.

force in May 1921. The general elections for the two parliaments established under its terms were fixed for 24 May. While declining to recognize the act the dáil decided to participate in the general elections for the lower houses and to regard them as an election for the second Dáil Éireann.[1] With the election for the Southern senate contemplated by the act the dáil refused to have anything to do on the ground that it was a partly nominated body.[2] De Valera issued a proclamation reaffirming the aims of Sinn Féin.

> The policy of Sinn Féin remains unchanged [he declared]. It stands for the right of the people of this nation to determine freely for themselves how they shall be governed and for the right of every citizen to an equal voice in the determination; it stands for civil and religious equality and for the full proportional representation and all possible safeguarding of minorities. In world politics it stands for an association of nations based upon self-determination and equality of right amongst the constituent members, favouring mutual guarantees against aggression and the settlement of international disputes on the basis of right and justice instead of force. It stands for Ireland undivided and a unit with regard to other nations and states but in home affairs for such devolution of administration and authority as would make for the satisfaction and contentment of all sections of the people and would not be inconsistent with efficiency and economy. . . . You who vote for Sinn Féin candidates will cast your votes for nothing less than for the legitimacy of the republic, for Ireland against England, for freedom against slavery, for right and justice against force and wrong, here and everywhere.[3]

The parliamentary party decided not to contest the Southern election. An agreement on the division of seats in Ulster was signed by Joseph Devlin and de Valera on 6 April,[4] and Dillon announced his decision for the rest of Ireland in a letter to the press on 9 May in which he declared: 'The policy and proceedings of the British government for the past three years make it practically impossible for a nationalist Irishman to fight Sinn Féin at this election.'[5] In a letter to J. P. McCabe, vice-chairman of Blackrock urban district council, who had announced his intention of contesting co. Dublin as a nationalist, he wrote: 'In my judgment the wisest and most patriotic course for members of the nationalist party is to take no part in the coming elections for the Dublin parliament. . . . Any attempt on the part of the nationalists to secure a share of the representation at the

---

[1] *Proceedings First Dáil*, pp. 291–2.   [2] *Irish Bulletin*, 2 May 1921.
[3] Ibid., 4 May 1921.
[4] *Proceedings First Dáil*, p. 266; *Freeman's Journal*, 8 Apr. 1921.
[5] Ibid., 9 May 1921.

coming elections in the south would be treated as a hostile act by the republicans.'[1] The Irish labour party also resolved not to accept the Government of Ireland Act or to nominate candidates but called upon its members to vote for candidates who stood for the ownership and government of Ireland by the people of Ireland.[2] As for the unionists in the area, they did not desire or did not venture to put forward candidates. The result was that Sinn Féin was returned to power without the necessity of an election, the 124 candidates being returned unopposed. The only opposition and the only candidates prepared to recognize the parliament of Southern Ireland envisaged in the act were the four members for Dublin University, who were also returned unopposed. Sinn Féin contested the Northern elections too and secured six seats, but all except one of the Sinn Féin candidates elected for Ulster constituencies represented constituencies in the twenty-six counties as well, so that their successes in the north brought only one additional member to Dáil Éireann. The membership of the dáil thus stood at 125, for although a letter was addressed to each unionist member elected in the north informing him that he was eligible for membership of the dáil on taking the republican oath none of them, naturally, availed themselves of the invitation.[3] The *Irish Times* summed up the situation created by this second Sinn Féin electoral victory by saying: 'The Southern elections have put Sinn Féin in a position of indisputable strength as the spokesman of a large majority of the people. They have created a popular assembly which, though it refuses to become a parliament, must be the country's brain and voice for all purposes of political negotiations.'[4]

What was the composition of this revolutionary assembly? The first dáil consisted of the 69 Sinn Féiners who were successful in the general election of 1918; the second dáil of the 124 candidates who were returned unopposed on the nomination day of candidates for election to the parliament of Southern Ireland, plus the one Sinn Féiner[5] elected in the Northern Ireland general election who did not sit as well for a constituency in Southern Ireland. Sixty-three members of the first dáil sat also in the second.

P. S. O'Hegarty in his *Victory of Sinn Féin* alleges that mediocrities were deliberately selected as candidates by the Sinn Féin organization in 1918, that loyalty to the party rather than ability was the

[1] *Irish Times*, 11 May 1921. [2] Ibid., 2 May 1921.
[3] *Supplement to Irish Bulletin*, 20 June 1921.
[4] *Irish Times*, 14 May 1921.
[5] Seán O'Mahony, member for Fermanagh and Tyrone.

criterion.[1] Part of this statement is undoubtedly true; in the circumstances uniformity of outlook and solidarity counted for more than individual brilliance. But on the whole the revolutionary dáil compared favourably in its composition with its more normally selected successors. Certainly there was no ground for the *Morning Post*'s diatribe against it. The issue of 5 September 1921 contained a paragraph headed, 'The Irish junta: what it really stands for. Gunmen government.' It ran:

Dáil Éireann is closed for repairs and the hundred and twenty members for murder who have made the Mansion House melodious for the last two weeks have gone home to tell the Dum-Dum Friends' League what it feels like to be really great. Dublin looks quite dull without them. Drovers' leggings and dirty necks—the official uniform of the Sinn Féin commandant— have disappeared and this morning a dilapidated young proletarian with a football fringe and no collar, spitting flamboyantly into the Liffey, was pointed out to me as the clerk of the house.

Two general comments may be made about the members of the revolutionary dáil. The first applies mainly to the first dáil and in some measure bears out part of O'Hegarty's criticism. Forty-six per cent. of the successful Sinn Féin candidates in the 1918 election were not normally resident in the constituency for which they were elected though many of them had been born in it or had some family connexion with it. In other words they were men who had come to Dublin and fallen under the influence of one or other of the advanced nationalist organizations, men who were leaders in these movements or were well known to the leaders. To this extent O'Hegarty is probably right in asserting that there was some management in the selection of candidates. In the second dáil the percentage of nonresident members fell to twenty-five but even this is considerably higher than the average since 1922. The other general comment is that the revolutionary dáil contained a high proportion of young men. Observers at the inaugural meeting remarked on this fact[2] and it is borne out by statistics. The following table shows the ages of members on election as far as it has been possible to ascertain them.

In the first dáil 33 per cent. of the members were under thirty-five and 73 per cent. were under forty-five. In the second dáil the percentages for these age-groups were 38 and 75 respectively.

---

[1] O'Hegarty, *Victory of Sinn Féin*, pp. 75–76.
[2] *Irish Times*, 22 Jan. 1919; *Nationality*, 25 Jan. 1919.

Age on Election

5-year age range	Number of members 1918	Number of members 1921	Percentage of total ages ascertained 1918	Percentage of total ages ascertained 1921
20–24	2	3	3	3
25–29	11	13	18	14
30–34	7	20	12	21
35–39	15	19	25	20
40–44	9	16	15	17
45–49	6	4	10	4
50–54	6	12	10	13
55–59	2	2	3	2
60–64	0	4	0	4
65–69	2	1	3	1
70 and over	0	1	0	1
Total of ages ascertained	60	95	100	100

The percentages are given to the nearest 1 per cent. and therefore do not necessarily total 100.

The dáil was preponderantly Roman catholic in religion; only two members of the first dáil—Barton and Blythe—were protestants. A third protestant—Childers—became a member of the second dáil. Information on the education of members is not complete but at least 60 per cent. of the members of the first dáil and 56 per cent. of the members of the second had a secondary education. Twenty-eight per cent. of the members of the first dáil and 26 per cent. of the members of the second had received university education or professional training. One notable difference between the revolutionary dáil and its successors was the small number of members who had taken a part in local government before their election—only 10 per cent. of the members of the first dáil and 24 per cent. of the members of the second. No doubt the explanation lies in the youth of the members and in the fact that up to 1917 at any rate Sinn Féin was a minority movement in the country. The members served their apprenticeship not in local government but in such movements as the Irish Volunteers, the Gaelic League, the Gaelic Athletic Association, or Sinn Féin. Two members, however, one of whom sat in both the first dáil and the second and the other in the first only, were former members of the Irish parliamentary party and of the House of Commons. Two members of the first dáil and seven members of the second were near relatives of executed 1916 leaders or of other prominent members of the party who had given their lives for the cause. Four of the six women members of the second dáil belonged to this category.

Finally, an analysis of the members by occupation reveals the urban and esoteric nature of the movement to which they belonged. Before such an analysis is attempted a word of warning is called for. Many members of the revolutionary dáil were not following their normal peace-time occupations. Since 1916 they had been subjected to periods of imprisonment or internment. In these circumstances the extent to which they continued to derive a livelihood from their occupations depended on the nature of those occupations. Obviously a farmer or merchant whose affairs could be looked after by relatives was more favourably placed than a doctor or teacher. Some had been dismissed from their posts as a result of their participation in the 1916 rising. Thus 10 per cent. of the members of the first dáil and 7 per cent. of the members of the second were former employees of the post office. Some had been barely launched upon their careers when they were caught up in the revolutionary tide. Some had abandoned their original occupations for full-time service in the political or military wings of the republican movement. A number of these were destined never to return to their original occupations. To some extent, then, the following analysis is misleading but at least it has the merit of indicating the social groups to which the members belonged.

In the following table the bulk of the members of the revolutionary dáil are classified under three of the occupational groups employed in the Irish *Census of Population* of 1926 and 1936.

Occupational Analysis of Members
A. *Professional Occupations*

	First dáil	Second dáil
Barristers	3+2*	3+3*
Solicitors	2	6
Medical doctors	5	9
Teachers	7	15
Journalists	9	10
Engineers	2	4
Veterinary surgeon	1	1
Accountants	1	2
Total number	30	50
Percentage of total membership	43	40

* Qualify for classification under this heading but principally occupied in another profession.

B. Commercial, Finance, and Insurance Occupations

Shopkeepers	9+1*	18
Company director	1	1
Insurance officials	3	1
Chemist	1	1
Commercial traveller	1	1
Auctioneer	..	1+1
Total number	15	23
Percentage of total membership	22	18

* Qualify for classification under this heading but principally occupied in another profession.

C. Agricultural Occupations

Farmers	7	12+6
Percentage of total membership	10	10

D. Miscellaneous Occupations

Foundry manager	1	1
Local government employees	2	1
Solicitors' clerks	2	2
Clerks	..	4
Trade union official	..	1
Publicans	2	2
Hotel proprietor	1	1
Cinema proprietor	..	1
Tailor	..	1
Printer	..	1
Blacksmith	..	1
Carpenter	..	1
Building contractor	..	1
Full-time employees of nationalist organizations	5	7
No occupation	4	15
Total number	17	40
Percentage of total membership	25	32

From the foregoing data certain conclusions may be drawn. The revolutionary dáil was clearly an urban middle-class body which could make no claims to being a cross-section of the whole community. The professional and commercial classes were heavily over-represented. Sixty-five per cent. of the members of the first dáil and 58 per cent. of the members of the second were included in these two groups; yet in the *Census of Population,* 1926 only 6 per cent. of the total population were classified under the two headings. Equally significant is the fact that agriculture was poorly represented. In both the first dáil and the second 10 per cent. of the members were farmers, but the 1926 *Census* shows 31 per cent. of the population engaged in agricultural occupations. Other occupational groups, and especially skilled and unskilled manual workers, were sparsely represented among the members. A more detailed examination of the occupational groups throws further light on the composition of the dáil. In group A the lower professional social group predominated. Journalists and teachers together made up respectively 23 and 20 per cent. of the total membership of the first and second dáil. In group B the preponderant place was taken by shopkeepers; in each dáil there was only a single representative of larger commercial undertakings. In group D the majority belonged to the non-manual wage-earning social group. The conclusion would seem to be justified, then, that the core of the republican movement, or at least the indispensable element which was prepared to avow its republicanism openly, was constituted from among the lower social groups within the middle class.

III

THE WORK OF THE REPUBLICAN DÁIL

IN theory Dáil Éireann was the supreme authority in Ireland, endowed with full legislative power and exercising executive functions through a ministry responsible to it. But in fact the dáil as an assembly exerted little influence on the course of events. It was a proclaimed body, meeting secretly for short sessions at irregular intervals. There was little opportunity for normal parliamentary activity. The legislative output of the dáil was negligible; for the most part the dáil contented itself with receiving reports from ministers and registering its approval of propositions laid before it. Its principal function was to act as the focus of republican propaganda. Both Gavan Duffy and Béaslaí complained that there was too much of the atmosphere of mutual congratulation in the dáil. Other deputies were dissatisfied with the role assigned to them. When one criticized the appointment of a secretary of the dáil at a salary of £500 a year without the dáil's consent Griffith defended the ministry's action by contending that if it was to be precluded from making necessary appointments while the dáil was not in session it would be powerless.[1] When it was suggested that the existing ministry should be replaced by a number of committees composed of dáil members Griffith agreed, as a compromise, to form consultative committees to assist the ministers.[2] The matter was raised again at a later session by J. J. Walsh who spoke of the 'practically entire exclusion of three-quarters of the people's representatives from effective work on the nation's behalf'.[3] In supporting him Seán MacEntee asserted that there could be no real opposition to the ministry. Meetings of the dáil were got through so hurriedly that there was very little discussion on many important subjects. The ministry's reply was that few deputies had accepted the invitation to serve on the consultative committees, that it would be difficult and dangerous to retain a majority of the deputies constantly in Dublin, and that the dáil exercised ultimate control in that it could remove any minister with whom it was dissatisfied.[4] However true

[1] *Proceedings First Dáil*, p. 123.　　[2] Ibid., p. 131.
[3] Ibid., p. 213.
[4] Ibid., p. 214.

this last contention may be, the dáil ministry was the agent through which republican plans were put into execution.

The work of the republican dáil may conveniently be considered under four heads: propagandist activity; preliminaries to constructive work; constructive achievements; and the prosecution of the war against Britain.

At the inaugural meeting of the dáil a number of declarations were promulgated which served the twofold purpose of putting Ireland's case before the world and of strengthening republican consciousness at home. The declaration of independence professed to be a ratification of the republican proclamation of Easter 1916. It asserted the exclusive right of the elected representatives of the Irish people to make laws binding the country; it demanded the evacuation of the English garrison; and it claimed for Irish independence the recognition and support of every other nation.[1] This appeal was reinforced by a message to the free nations of the world, calling upon them to support the Irish republic by recognizing Ireland's national status and her right to its vindication at the peace conference.[2] As a further gesture three delegates to the peace conference were selected. A third declaration took the form of a democratic programme which derived its inspiration from the 1916 proclamation. It asserted that all rights to private property should be subordinated to the public right and welfare, that the country should be ruled in accordance with the principles of liberty, equality, and justice for all, and that every citizen should receive an adequate share of the produce of the nation's labour.[3] This flood of rhetoric was swollen at subsequent meetings by such pronouncements as the message to the Irish abroad, issued at one of the April meetings,[4] and the statement on depopulation and over-taxation, made in the presence of Irish-American sympathizers.[5]

Throughout its career the republican dáil maintained its propaganda drive through its publicity department. This department had its beginnings in the Sinn Féin organization. In April 1918 a department of propaganda was established at Sinn Féin headquarters under Robert Brennan. Its functions at first were to supply the Sinn Féin leaders with data upon which to base public statements, to provide material suitable for foreign press correspondents visiting Ireland, and to prepare statistics and statements for presentation to the

---

[1] *Proceedings First Dáil*, pp. 14–16. [2] Ibid., pp. 18–20.
[3] Ibid., pp. 21–23. [4] Ibid., pp. 54–55.
[5] Ibid., pp. 88–95.

The Work of the Republican Dáil

peace conference. Later, a service was instituted of weekly notes written from the Sinn Féin point of view and sent out to the provincial press. Upwards of forty newspapers received these notes. As the general election approached the department devoted itself almost exclusively to the issue of election literature. After the election and before the first session of the dáil the foreign relations committee of Sinn Féin decided to prepare a series of pamphlets on the various aspects of the Irish question. Some of these were already published and others were in the press when the dáil met and the position of the department was changed. The Sinn Féin propaganda department continued in being but propaganda outside Ireland was entrusted to a new department under the republican government. The two departments co-operated in the bulk of the publicity matter issued. The first director of publicity under the dáil was Laurence Ginnell who remained in charge of the department until his arrest in May 1919 when his duties were taken over by Desmond Fitzgerald. He in turn was arrested in February 1921 and replaced by Erskine Childers.[1] One of the most important functions of the dáil department was the issue of the *Irish Bulletin*, the daily organ of the republican government. It was first published in November 1919 in the form of cyclostyled sheets, a form which it retained to the end. At first it merely gave a summary of British military acts, but at the suggestion of the director of publicity for Sinn Féin it was expanded into an organ for the presentation of the Irish case and the recording of the civil and military activities of the republican government.[2] It was circulated mainly outside Ireland; according to the report of the department to the dáil it was being regularly received by 900 newspapers in 1921. In spite of the difficulties it was able to maintain uninterrupted publication. When its offices in Molesworth Street, Dublin, were accidentally discovered by auxiliary police on 26 March 1921 publication was maintained, without a break, from a private house. Bundles and packages were smuggled out in laundry and grocery baskets, in a pram, or by cyclist messengers who dispatched them from various city post offices. Some of the larger packages contained stamped addressed bundles which were in turn posted by the recipients.[3] A list of addresses to which the *Bulletin* was sent had been seized in the raid. Shortly afterwards spurious issues began to reach these addresses; the

[1] 'History and Progress of Department of Publicity.' Typewritten sheet dated Aug. 1921 among Gavan Duffy Papers in the National Library of Ireland.
[2] Frank Gallagher, 'Literature of the Conflict', in *Irish Book Lover*, xviii. 69–71.
[3] James Carty, *Bibliography of Irish History*, 1912–21, p. xxv.

Castle authorities apparently were not aware that the *Bulletin* was still being published. From this time on genuine copies were stamped with the words 'Official copy' in green ink.

The republican leaders can hardly have expected success in their efforts to secure a hearing at the peace conference. They were aware that the colonial secretary had turned down the demand of the South African nationalists for representation on the ground that 'under the South African constitution the parliament and government of the Union can alone be regarded as authorized to speak on behalf of the people of South Africa'.[1] They must have realized that the British government would exert the strongest influence to exclude an Irish delegation. But the appointment of delegates to the conference, the dispatch of a letter by Seán T. O'Kelly, the republican representative in Paris, to M. Clemenceau and all the peace conference delegates claiming admission for Ireland to the League of Nations, and the publication in booklet form of the Irish case under the title *The Irish Republic and the Peace Conference*, all this was an essential part of the forceful propaganda campaign. Indeed the whole ministry of foreign affairs was very much an instrument of propaganda. The activities of the ambassadors and consuls whom it appointed were not diplomatic in the proper sense of the word. They received no recognition from foreign governments. If they served any purpose other than to stress the claim to independence by their very existence they were significant only as agents for the dissemination of propaganda.

It was the aim of the republican leaders to set up 'a polity within a polity', but it was inevitable in the circumstances that a considerable part of the republican programme could not be implemented immediately. Thus de Valera admitted in reply to a deputy's question about the ministry's social policy that the democratic programme contemplated a situation somewhat different to that in which they actually found themselves.[2] Many of the republican government departments were little more than shadow departments whose work, at most, was preparatory. The ministry of education, for example, could do no more than secure promises of support for the revival of the Irish language from the catholic bishops, institute inter-family competitions in Irish, and attempt to improve the status of Irish in the universities. The ministry of fisheries sought to encourage the formation of co-operative societies, helped the people of Gorumma, co.

[1] *Nationality*, 18 Jan. 1919; 22 Feb. 1919.
[2] *Proceedings First Dáil*, p. 78.

Galway, to purchase a motor-boat, and bought a steam trawler for the transport of fish to the Welsh coast. The departments of trade and industry sponsored a boycott of British and Ulster goods which succeeded only in outraging unionist opinion.[1] A commission of inquiry into the resources and industries of Ireland was instituted,[2] but its elaborate report had no immediate significance.

So far there has been nothing to suggest that the dáil was succeeding in its declared aim of supplanting the British administration in Ireland. But in the sphere of local government and finance, of agriculture and justice it went far, for a time at any rate, towards making its claim a reality. The local government elections of 1920 brought Sinn Féin to power in the local government bodies throughout the greater part of Ireland. These bodies proceeded to declare their allegiance to Dáil Éireann and to pledge themselves to carry out its decrees in so far as they affected them. On 29 June 1920 Collins, the minister for finance in the dáil cabinet, proposed that the councils should break off all connexion with the central controlling body, the local government board. A commission on the question reported in favour of a break on 17 September. This involved the loss of the grants-in-aid paid by the board to the local bodies, amounting to one-eighth of the income of these bodies. To make good the loss the commission recommended the withholding of the principal and interest on British debts and the drastic curtailment of expenditure on hospitals, child welfare, and health services for tuberculosis and venereal disease. A saving of £370,000 could be effected in this way, leaving a deficit of £270,000 which, the commission suggested, might be met by diverting land annuities and income tax to the dáil. Not all of these recommendations were accepted, but the break was effected and from October 1920 practically all the local government bodies functioned under the supervision of the dáil department of local government which had its staff of engineering, medical, and accountancy officials operating throughout the country.[3] Naturally this change was not brought about without violence. The British government announced that local rates would be held liable for war damage; the republican government replied that it would resist and punish any attempt to collect them. The British government also regarded the payment of rates to any other than authorized rate collectors as invalid and

---

[1] W. K. Hancock, *Survey of British Commonwealth Affairs*, i. 112–13.
[2] Ibid., p. 123.
[3] *Proceedings First Dáil*, pp. 218–22.

arrested republican rate collectors. The crowning blow of the republicans was the burning of the Dublin Customs House in which the local government board was housed.

Another field in which the dáil succeeded was in finance, though here it was not a case of supplanting the British machinery. For the upkeep of its civil and military establishments the dáil relied on money raised by loan. On 4 April 1919 the dáil decided on the issue of republican bonds to the value of £250,000 in sums of £1 to £1,000.[1] The press announcement of the loan declared:

The proceeds of the loan will be used for propagating the Irish case all over the world; for establishing in foreign countries consular services to promote Irish trade and commerce; for developing and encouraging Irish sea fisheries; for developing and encouraging the re-afforestation of the country; for developing and encouraging Irish industrial effort; for establishing a national civil service; for establishing arbitration courts; for the establishment of a land mortgage bank, with a view to the re-occupancy of untenanted lands; and generally for national purposes.

In June Most Rev. Dr. Fogarty, de Valera, and James O'Mara were appointed trustees of the loan, and the prospectus of the loan for home subscribers was approved. It was to bear interest at 5 per cent., payable six months after the Irish republic received international recognition.[2] An external loan of the same amount was launched in America, and in June de Valera went to America to float it and to work for the recognition of the Irish republican government.[3]

A second sphere in which the dáil was able, for a time, to supplant the British machinery was in the administration of justice. The republican courts owed their origin to a decree of the dáil in June 1919 which aimed at establishing national arbitration courts but which left each constituency to act on its own.[4] The lead in implementing this decision was taken by West Clare, where within a fortnight the local deputy summoned a conference which decided to set up at once a district arbitration court and parish arbitration courts. This became the model for a general scheme adopted by the dáil in March 1920. By May these arbitration courts were established throughout the part of the country controlled by the republicans. At first they received little publicity or attention, but an agrarian crisis which developed in the west in the spring of 1920 brought them to the fore. Land hunger in the west was nothing new, and the cessation

[1] *Proceedings First Dáil*, p. 41.
[2] Ibid., pp. 132–4.
[3] Ibid., pp. 114, 251.
[4] Ibid., p. 122.

of emigration during the war had greatly aggravated the problem of uneconomic holdings. To the landless men of the west revolution meant a social revolution, and the weakening of the British machinery of government provided the opportunity for action. A great wave of cattle-driving, fence-levelling, and invasion of the large grazing ranches broke out. But the Irish revolutionary leaders were essentially bourgeois in outlook. Their attitude is summed up in a sentence from the *Irish Bulletin* of 5 August 1921: 'The mind of the people was being diverted from the struggle for freedom into a class war and there was even a possibility that the I.R.A. itself, largely composed of farmers' sons, might be affected.' To deal with the situation Art O'Connor was sent to the west with wide powers to act. On 17 May he held at Ballinrobe the 'first public sitting of any court directly under the dáil'. This was the beginning of a vigorous drive to stem the rising social revolutionary tide and to replace the British by republican courts. As a means of settling the agrarian problem land courts were established under the department of agriculture to deal with a multitude of claims to land. So numerous were these claims that the dáil was obliged on 29 June 1920 to issue a decree making it necessary to obtain a licence from the ministry of home affairs before a claim could be made in court.[1] At the same time the department of agriculture launched a land acquisition scheme in an attempt to remove the cause of the agitation. In September 1920 the dáil established a national land commission to carry on both the judicial and administrative sides of the land policy.[2] The second aim was also manifest in the decree of 29 June, for it established courts of justice and equity and empowered the ministry of home affairs to set up courts of criminal jurisdiction.[3] The ministry availed itself of these powers. By September 1920 there existed (*a*) parish courts, composed of three members, meeting once a week and dealing with petty civil and criminal cases; (*b*) district courts, composed of five members, meeting once a month and dealing with more important civil and criminal cases or cases which came by appeal from the parish courts. In addition, at three sessions during the year a circuit judge presided over the district court which then became a circuit court with unlimited civil and criminal jurisdiction. There were four circuit judges and four circuit

---

[1] *Proceedings First Dáil*, pp. 178–80.
[2] *The constructive work of Dáil Éireann, No. 2;* i. *The department of agriculture and the land settlement commission;* ii. *The commission of inquiry into the resources and industries of Ireland;* iii. *The department of trade and commerce.* Dublin, 1921; *Proceedings First Dáil*, pp. 199–202. [3] Ibid., p. 178.

districts. (c) At the apex there was a supreme court in Dublin, composed of not less than three members appointed for three years, functioning both as a court of first instance and a court of appeal. The legal code administered by these courts was the law as it existed on 21 January 1919 with any amendments subsequently made by the dáil. Citations were also to be allowed from the early Irish law codes or any commentary upon them in so far as they were applicable to modern conditions.

From this time until the British offensive drove them underground again the republican courts virtually supplanted the British courts in the greater part of the country. Even unionist landlords were glad to seek their protection against the dark forces of social disorder. With few exceptions the members of the legal profession were ready to appear before them. The Incorporated Law Society considered a resolution aimed at preventing solicitors from attending parish and district courts, but it was dropped. The Council of the Bar of Ireland passed a resolution declaring it unprofessional for counsel to attend the republican courts, but a general meeting of the bar decided to take no action against counsel who ignored the resolution. Since the imprisonment of offenders was not feasible the penalties imposed by the courts generally took the form of fines or deportations. Republican police were also active in performing the functions formerly discharged by the Royal Irish Constabulary. The British government declared the republican courts illegal on the ground that they functioned under the authority of the dáil. On 6 July 1920 the inspector-general of the Royal Irish Constabulary issued an order forbidding unauthorized persons to arrogate to themselves the duties of the police.[1]

It remains to consider the military activity of the republicans. The military wing of the revolutionary movement was in existence long before the dáil was constituted. The Irish Volunteers, or rather a section of the Volunteers, had been responsible for the 1916 insurrection. After its suppression the Volunteer movement had been inactive until it received a new lease of life with the emergence of the reconstituted Sinn Féin. In August 1918 the first copy of its new official paper—*An t-Óglách*—appeared. Here the Volunteers were told that they were the army of the Irish republic, the agents of the national will. It was their duty to obey the leaders whom they had chosen at their annual

[1] *The constructive work of Dáil Éireann, No. 1; The national police and courts of justice.* Dublin, 1921.

convention. These leaders should conform the policy of the Volunteers to the national will by co-operating with the bodies and institutions which in other departments of the national life were striving to make the Irish republic a tangible reality.[1] When the dáil was established in January 1919 the leaders of the Volunteers contended that the republic had become a tangible reality. Henceforth it was the duty of the Volunteers to surrender their autonomy and accept the authority of the minister for defence responsible to the dáil.[2] After 30 August 1919 every member of the organization took the oath of allegiance to the republic, and the old name of the Irish Volunteers was replaced by more comprehensive titles like 'the Army of Ireland', 'the Army of the Republic', or 'the Irish Republican Army'. There existed, too, the personal link between the military and the civil branches of the republican movement in that de Valera had been elected president of the Volunteers just after his election as president of Sinn Féin.

The fact remains, however, that the I.R.A. was an independent body. De Valera's statement at the public session of the dáil on 10 April 1919 was a recognition of this state of affairs. He said: 'The minister of national defence is, of course, in close association with the voluntary military forces which are the foundation of the national army.'[3] Already by this time the policy of attacking the agents of the government had been adopted by local squads of the I.R.A. acting on their own initiative. A group in co. Tipperary had decided on action in January 1919, and it was only by chance that they did not strike until 21 January, the day on which the dáil was formally instituted.[4] Such independent action continued. With the resources at their disposal a guerilla campaign was the only type of war that the republicans were in a position to wage and guerilla fighting calls for much individual initiative and the utilization of local knowledge. Although the dáil ministry contained a minister for defence the dáil seems to have exercised little control over the course of the fighting. Miss Dorothy Macardle says: 'Cathal Brugha's policy was militarily in advance of that which the dáil as a whole would have initiated at this time [spring 1919] and Michael Collins favoured action which even Cathal Brugha did not always approve. . . . The dáil refrained from interference, entrusting the military policy of the republic to its

[1] *An t-Óglách*, 15 Aug. 1918.   [2] Ibid., 31 Jan. 1919.
[3] *Proceedings First Dáil*, p. 47.
[4] Dan Breen, *My Fight for Irish Freedom*, chap. vi; Macardle, *The Irish Republic*, p. 290.

very able minister for defence.'[1] It is significant that as the direction of the campaign fell more and more into the hands of Collins a bitter personal enmity grew up between him and Brugha, the minister for defence. The latter did, however, accept full responsibility for the actions of the I.R.A. and submitted reports to the dáil. The dáil voted money for the army; for instance on 29 June 1920 it allotted a million dollars for defence out of the American loan.[2] It also endorsed the military policy; the only dissentient at any time was Roger Sweetman, the member for Wexford North, who resigned his seat in protest against the policy of violence.[3] Still, the looseness of the connexion between the dáil and the I.R.A. enabled the British to claim that the guerilla warfare was the work of irresponsible murder gangs. It was in answer to this charge that de Valera, after his return from America, asked the dáil to acknowledge formally the existence of a state of war. He felt, he said, that the dáil was hardly acting fairly by the army in not publicly taking full responsibility for all its acts.[4] In a statement to some foreign press correspondents after this debate he re-asserted the responsibility of the dáil for the military campaign:

... one of our first governmental acts [he said] was to take over the control of the voluntary armed forces of the nation. From the Irish Volunteers we fashioned the I.R.A. to be the military arm of the government. This army is therefore a regular state army, under the civil control of the elected representatives, ... and under officers who held their commissions under warrant from these representatives. The government is therefore responsible for the actions of this army.[5]

The grim story of the struggle is outside the scope of this work. It is enough to say that it falls roughly into three phases. In the first, which lasted till the summer of 1920, the republicans were on the offensive, attacking police barracks, ambushing police and troops, and shooting key men in the British administration. The appointment of Sir Hamar Greenwood as chief secretary and Sir Neville Macready as commander-in-chief in March 1920 was the preliminary to a strong counter-offensive which was conducted by the 'Black and Tans' and the 'Auxiliaries'. The third phase began towards the end of 1920. It was a period in which the British government oscillated between vigorous military action and a search for peace. The fighting became more violent and the policy of systematic reprisals was adopted. On the other hand a series of peace feelers were put out which eventually led to a truce.

[1] Macardle, op. cit., p. 291.   [2] *Proceedings First Dáil*, pp. 172–3.
[3] Ibid., p. 243.   [4] Ibid., pp. 278–9.   [5] Macardle, op. cit., p. 437.

IV

THE ORIGIN OF THE CONSTITUTIONAL DÁIL

FROM mid-1920 onwards the struggle in Ireland was conducted with ever-increasing violence and yet the constant clamour of certain of the British military authorities for more drastic powers is evidence of the fact that the British might have conducted the war with greater ruthlessness. Their restraint may be attributed to three factors: sensitiveness to world public opinion, especially public opinion in America and the dominions; the division of opinion within Great Britain itself; and the ingenious plans of the British prime minister.

America remained in this period the great reservoir of moral and material support for the republicans. Even though the agents of the Irish republican government failed to win recognition from the American government they succeeded in arousing an interest and stirring up an agitation to which American politicians could not be completely insensitive. Through the activities of individuals and organizations in America events in Ireland were given a publicity which the British government could well have done without. Thus at the time of the peace conference three delegates were sent to Paris by one of the Irish-American organizations to agitate for the admission of the Irish republican delegates to the conference. Lloyd George allowed them to visit Ireland in the hope that their impressions would do something to allay the growing anti-British feeling in America. But the envoys, who were welcomed at a special session of the dáil, strongly condemned British rule in Ireland and presented a lurid report on British atrocities. They concluded by urging the peace conference to consider the Irish case. A resolution to the same effect was passed by the American senate. Later, an unofficial commission of inquiry into conditions in Ireland was instituted in Washington and an Irish relief scheme was organized.[1]

In Great Britain the government's handling of the Irish situation evoked loud protests. Newspapers like the *Daily News*, the *Manchester Guardian*, and the *Westminster Gazette* consistently opposed Lloyd George's Irish policy. Hugh Martin wrote a series of articles

[1] Macardle, *The Irish Republic*, pp. 294–7, 407–9.

in the *Daily News*, the spirit of which is epitomized in the sentence, 'We shall have to give up either the hypocrisy of pretending to concern about freedom in Czecho-Slovakia or the infamy of stamping on freedom in Ireland'. Even *The Times* and the *Daily Mail* were having qualms. The Society of Friends collected money for relief in Ireland. The labour party demanded an inquiry into the actions of the crown forces in Ireland, and when this was refused it set up a commission of its own, under the chairmanship of Arthur Henderson, which presented a report highly unfavourable to the government. Prominent public men in England denounced the government's Irish policy in no uncertain terms. Sir John Simon said that it was 'turning Mr. Lloyd George's heroics about the rights of small nations into nauseating cant'; Asquith protested against the 'hellish policy of reprisals';[1] Philip Snowden asserted that Ireland was being ruled like a conquered province,[2] and the archbishop of Canterbury declared in the House of Lords: 'Not by calling in the aid of the devil will you cast out devils.'[3] Pamphlets condemning the government's policy were produced by G. K. Chesterton, A. Clutton Brock, J. L. Hammond, Brigadier-General Sir Henry Lawson, and others. A 'Peace with Ireland Council', under the chairmanship of Lord Henry Bentinck, included among its members such well-known persons as Professor Gilbert Murray, Sidney Webb, Ramsay MacDonald, Basil Williams, Oswald Mosley, General Sir Hubert Gough, H. W. Nevinson, R. H. Tawney, F. D. Acland, and Sir Maurice and Lady Bonham-Carter. Its objects were to acquire accurate information on the state of Ireland, to protest against the 'lawless policy of reprisals', to demand the withdrawal of the Black and Tans, and to secure official permission for an immediate meeting of the elected Sinn Féin representatives.[4] This volume of protest was not without its effect on those responsible for the campaign in Ireland. Even Sir Henry Wilson and Sir Neville Macready, the champions of more ruthless military action, were obliged to admit that they could do little without the support of English public opinion.[5]

Lloyd George reacted to this clamour from at home and abroad with characteristic subtlety. It convinced him that the good name of Britain was endangered and it strengthened his belief that force alone

---

[1] Macardle, op. cit., p. 444.   [2] *Irish Bulletin*, 6 Apr. 1920.
[3] Hancock, *Survey of British Commonwealth Affairs*, i. 126–7.
[4] *The Peace with Ireland Council* (London, 1920).
[5] Neville Macready, *Annals of an Active Life*, ii. 564; C. E. Callwell, *Field-Marshal Sir Henry Wilson: His Life and Diaries*, ii. 253–4.

could not solve the Irish problem. Yet while using it to restrain his more hot-headed confederates he sustained the pressure on the republicans long enough to enable him to dispose of the Ulster problem and vehemently enough to shake their intransigent attitude and bring them to the conference table. By this time home rule had ceased to have any relevance to the situation, and Lloyd George decided to replace the act of 1914 by fresh legislation. The Government of Ireland Act which became law in December 1920 provided for the creation of two states in Ireland—Northern Ireland, consisting of six Ulster counties, and Southern Ireland, consisting of the remaining twenty-six counties—each with its own parliament and government. With a view to the eventual establishment of a parliament for the whole country and to facilitate co-operation a council of Ireland was to be established, consisting of representatives from each of the parliaments and a president nominated by the lord lieutenant. The two parliaments were given powers to replace this council by a parliament for the whole of Ireland. The legislative authority of the proposed parliaments was restricted and Ireland was to retain forty-six representatives at Westminster.

The British government knew perfectly well that there was not the slightest chance of this act being acceptable to the republicans. In fact it contained a provision for the establishment of crown colony government in Southern Ireland if a majority of elected members failed to take the oath of allegiance to the king. The Ulster unionists were also hostile to the act, maintaining that they wanted to have nothing to do with home rule in any shape or form, but they accepted it as the only safeguard against being placed under Dublin rule. By doing so they strengthened the position of Lloyd George in any subsequent negotiations with the republicans, for he could henceforth point to the partition of the country as a *fait accompli*. The act came into operation in May 1921. A catholic nobleman, Lord Fitzalan, was appointed lord lieutenant and he issued a proclamation summoning the two parliaments. The republican leaders decided to regard the election for the House of Commons of Southern Ireland as an election for a second dáil, but to boycott the senate election.[1] The result was that only the fifteen nominated senators and the four representatives of Dublin University attended the formal opening of the Southern parliament on 28 June 1921.[2] The newly elected dáil

---
[1] *Irish Bulletin*, 2 May 1921.
[2] *Supplement to Irish Bulletin*, 6 July 1921; *Irish Times*, 29 June 1921.

held its first session on 16 August 1921 and at once turned its attention to a consideration of the British peace proposals.[1]

These peace proposals may be said to have had their beginnings in a letter written to *The Times* by Brigadier-General G. K. Cockerill, M.P., suggesting a truce and a conference 'analogous to that of an international conference' between representatives of the British government and Dáil Éireann.[2] In the autumn unofficial conversations were held between a representative of the foreign office and a certain Patrick Moylett at which the possibility of an armistice and amnesty followed by a conference was discussed.[3] Nothing came of either of these moves. An advance was made in December when unofficial conversations began through the medium of Dr. Clune, catholic archbishop of Perth, Australia. After an interview with Lloyd George the archbishop came to Ireland and made contact with Griffith and the other republican leaders. But the advice of the military authorities, backed by what he considered evidence of a weakening within the ranks of Sinn Féin,[4] induced Lloyd George to break off the negotiations. The fighting continued with greater violence than ever, but the peace feelers were still being put out. A. W. Cope, assistant undersecretary for Ireland, was next empowered to investigate unofficially the possibilities of negotiations. He had conversations with Father O'Flanagan and Lord Justice O'Connor, with Cardinal Logue and Most Rev. Dr. Fogarty, and probably also with Michael Collins. Moreover, people unofficially in touch with British ministers were continually inviting prominent republicans to explain their views. On 21 April 1921 Lord Derby came to Ireland under an assumed name to interview de Valera. He made it known that the British government was ready to offer something more generous than the status accorded in the 1920 act, something more nearly approaching dominion home rule. De Valera replied that the only satisfactory basis for a settlement would be the recognition of Ireland's full rights. This raised a question which was to prove a formidable stumbling block to the opening of negotiations. Having reported back to London Lord Derby wrote to inquire if de Valera insisted on the prin-

[1] *Irish Bulletin*, 17 Aug. 1921.   [2] *The Times*, 6 Oct. 1920.
[3] Macardle, op. cit., pp. 412–13.
[4] Six members of the Galway county council discussed, but did not pass, a resolution calling upon Dáil Éireann to negotiate a truce and upon the British government to remove the ban on meetings of the dáil. A report appeared in the press. A second episode was the sending of a telegram to Lloyd George by Rev. M. O'Flanagan, vice-president of Sinn Féin, after he had been in London in a private effort to negotiate peace, declaring that Ireland was ready to make peace (Macardle, op. cit., pp. 413–14).

The Origin of the Constitutional Dáil

ciple of complete independence being conceded as a preliminary to negotiations. De Valera avoided a direct reply by asking another question: whether the prime minister would refuse to meet representatives of the dáil until the principle of complete independence was first surrendered. No direct answer was forthcoming to this question. Another move made by the unofficial intermediaries at this time was to bring about a meeting in Dublin on 5 May between de Valera and Sir James Craig, premier designate of Northern Ireland, in the hope that some basis for agreement might be found through the council of Ireland clause in the Government of Ireland Act, 1920. This also came to nothing. Lord Justice O'Connor was another channel of communication. After interviews with Carson and Lloyd George he informed Father O'Flanagan in May that Lloyd George was now prepared to give fiscal control to an Irish parliament provided a free-trade agreement was concluded between Great Britain and Ireland. Lloyd George was contemplating a truce for the period of the elections but Sir Henry Wilson dissuaded him. In May he replied indirectly to de Valera's question about preliminary conditions for negotiations: according to an American journalist he declared himself ready to meet the Irish leaders without conditions on his part and without exacting promises from them.[1] Meantime the military drive went on and plans to intensify it were under discussion.

The parliament of Northern Ireland was opened on 22 June 1921 by King George V. He took the opportunity of exercising his influence on the side of peace. He disapproved of the speech prepared for him and in consultation with General Smuts drafted another to which the cabinet agreed. In it he appealed to all Irishmen 'to pause, to stretch out the hand of forbearance and conciliation, to forgive and forget and join in making for the land they love a new era of peace, contentment and goodwill'. That the British government intended to avail itself of the opportunity for the opening of official negotiations was shown by its treatment of de Valera. On the afternoon of the day on which the Northern parliament was opened he was arrested by troops who were either unaware of his identity or of the move afoot. Twenty-four hours later he was released. The reason became evident three days later when he received a letter from Lloyd George in which he was addressed as 'the chosen leader of the great majority in Southern Ireland', proposing a conference in London at which Sir James Craig would also be present.

[1] Macardle, op. cit., pp. 447–51.

After consulting with representatives of the Southern unionists and insisting on a truce—which was concluded on 11 July 1921—as a preliminary to negotiations de Valera intimated his willingness to go to London for discussions 'on what basis such a conference as that proposed can reasonably hope to achieve the object desired'.[1] In London he was presented with the British proposals for a settlement —a modified form of dominion home rule, roughly the scheme subsequently embodied in the Anglo-Irish treaty. De Valera rejected the offer but eventually agreed to give a written reply after consultation with his colleagues in Ireland. This formal reply, sent on 10 August 1921, was a confirmation of his earlier refusal to accept the proposed settlement. Lloyd George's retort was that the British government stood by its proposals and would not acknowledge 'the right of Ireland to secede from her allegiance to the king'.[2] The next move came from the Irish side when de Valera, in informing Lloyd George of the dáil's ratification of his and his colleagues' rejection of the offer, reaffirmed his desire for a settlement which, he said, could be achieved 'on the broad principle of government by the consent of the governed'. There followed an exchange of communications between Lloyd George and de Valera, lasting from 26 August to 30 September, in which the conflicting aims of the two sides were clearly revealed and, at the same time, the desire of each party to avoid the responsibility of bringing about a breakdown in the negotiations. Eventually Lloyd George hit upon a phrase which opened the way for a conference: 'to ascertain how the association of Ireland with the community of nations known as the British Empire can best be reconciled with Irish national aspirations.'[3]

The republican cabinet appointed Griffith, Collins, Barton, Gavan Duffy, and Duggan as 'envoys plenipotentiary from the elected government of the republic of Ireland' to negotiate a treaty. Yet they were instructed to keep Dublin informed of the course of the negotiations. An outline draft for a treaty of external association with the Commonwealth was approved as the basis of a settlement. It proposed that British troops and special police recruited since 21 January 1919 should be withdrawn from Ireland; that the Commonwealth should recognize Ireland as a sovereign, independent state, guarantee its neutrality and support its application for membership of the League of Nations; and that Ireland should agree to become an ex-

---

[1] Macardle, op. cit., pp. 466–74; Frank Pakenham, *Peace by Ordeal*, pp. 76–79.
[2] Macardle, op. cit., pp. 489–94.   [3] Ibid., pp. 500–24.

ternal associate of the Commonwealth. A strong British delegation was selected to meet the Irish representatives: Lloyd George himself; Lord Birkenhead, lord chancellor; Sir L. Worthington Evans, secretary of state for war; Austen Chamberlain, leader of the House of Commons; Winston Churchill, secretary of state for the colonies; and Sir Hamar Greenwood, chief secretary for Ireland. Sir Gordon Hewart the attorney-general acted as a member when constitutional questions were being discussed.

The Irish delegation arrived in London on 8 October 1921. After lengthy negotiations the British produced a draft treaty on 16 November. The Irish countered with the external association proposal. The delegates then returned to Dublin for a cabinet meeting at which it was decided to risk the renewal of the war rather than accept an oath of allegiance or partition. Back in London a serious divergence of view among the Irish delegates manifested itself. Gavan Duffy, Barton, and Childers, the secretary to the delegation, drafted new counter-proposals for presentation to the British ministers. Griffith, Collins, and Duggan were opposed to this course. Eventually Griffith agreed to take the amended proposals to Downing Street but Collins and Duggan refused to accompany the others. The British delegates informed them that on the question of inclusion in the Empire the conference must stand or fall. The next day a further tense meeting was held at which Lloyd George delivered an ultimatum to the Irish delegates. Either they signed that night or the war would be renewed. They promised a reply by nine o'clock that evening but it was not until long after midnight that they returned. At 2.20 a.m. on 6 December 1921 the Irish delegates signed articles of agreement for a treaty between Great Britain and Ireland.[1]

The document contained eighteen articles and an annex. Ireland was to have the same constitutional status in the British Commonwealth as the Dominion of Canada, the Commonwealth of Australia, the Dominion of New Zealand, and the Union of South Africa; was to be styled the Irish Free State; and was to have an executive responsible to an Irish parliament. The position of the new state in relation to the imperial government and parliament was to be the same as that of Canada, and the crown's representative in Ireland was to be appointed in like manner to the governor-general of Canada. Nevertheless Ireland was to be subject to restrictions which were not imposed upon Canada. The size of the Free State army was limited to

[1] For a full account of the negotiations see Frank Pakenham, *Peace by Ordeal* (1935).

the proportion of the British army which the population of Ireland bore to the population of Great Britain;[1] the British government was to retain certain harbour and defence facilities which might be expanded in time of war or strained relations with a foreign power; the Irish parliament was forbidden to endow any religion or to discriminate against any individual on account of religious belief; the Free State was to assume liability for an equitable share of the national debt and of war pensions but not for pensions payable to members of the police forces recruited in the preceding two years; and the Free State was to pay compensation to officials retiring as a result of the change of government. An oath to be taken by members of the Irish parliament was laid down. For one month after the passing of the British act for the ratification of the agreement the authority of the Irish Free State government was not to extend to Northern Ireland. If within that time the Northern parliament so requested, Northern Ireland was to remain permanently excluded and was to retain the status it had secured under the Government of Ireland Act, 1920. In that case a boundary commission was to be set up to determine the boundary between the two states in accordance with the wishes of the inhabitants, 'so far as may be compatible with economic and geographical conditions'. Provision was also made for possible arrangements between the two Irish governments. Until such time as the Irish government by arrangement with the British should undertake the defence of the Irish coast imperial forces were to be responsible, but the Irish government was free to provide for the protection of its revenue and fisheries. Finally, provision was made for the transition to the new system. The one concession which the British had made to the Irish claims to sovereign independence had been to allow the word 'treaty' to appear in the title of the agreement. Thereafter they scrupulously avoided even a reference to Dáil Éireann. A meeting of the members of parliament for Southern Ireland elected under the Government of Ireland Act, 1920, was to be summoned and a provisional government constituted. Provided the members of this government signified in writing their acceptance of the treaty the British government undertook to transfer to it the machinery of government in Ireland. The treaty was to be submitted for ratification forthwith to the British parliament and to the parliament of Southern Ireland.

The Anglo-Irish treaty was approved by the British parliament on

[1] This provision was never enforced.

16 December 1921. In Ireland the republican cabinet split on the issue of the treaty, four members being in favour of acceptance (Griffith, Collins, Cosgrave, and Barton) and three against (de Valera, Brugha, and Stack). The dáil was summoned to meet on 14 December 1921 and a long and bitter debate ensued. It was not until 7 January 1922 that the vote was taken—sixty-four for approval and fifty-seven against. By the narrow majority of seven the Anglo-Irish treaty had completed the first stage of its ratification on the Irish side. In the course of the treaty debate de Valera submitted a counter-proposal for a settlement. This alternative scheme, which was known as Document no. 2, was a redraft of the earlier proposal for external association. It provided that on matters of common concern such as defence, peace and war, and political treaties Ireland should be associated with the states of the British Commonwealth. For the purposes of the association Ireland would recognize King George V as head of the association.

De Valera tendered his resignation as president of the dáil on 6 January. On 9 January Griffith was elected in his place and formed a new government. Griffith then proceeded in his capacity as 'chairman of the Irish delegation of plenipotentiaries' to summon the assembly specified in the treaty—the parliament of Southern Ireland. The elections for this assembly and for the Northern House of Commons had been treated by the republicans as elections for the second dáil. But since the successful republicans in the Northern election with one exception had also secured seats in the twenty-six counties the parliament of Southern Ireland would have been almost a replica of the dáil if all the members had attended. In the outcome the anti-treaty group ignored the summons so that the assembly which met at the Mansion House, Dublin, on 14 January was composed of sixty pro-treaty members and the four representatives of Dublin University. This body performed the two tasks assigned to it: it passed a motion approving the treaty and it elected a provisional government. There were thus two governments in existence, one the government of the Irish republic, now composed of pro-treaty members, and the other the provisional government to which the British government was pledged by the treaty to hand over the machinery of government in Ireland. Actually there was considerable overlapping of personnel; Collins, minister for finance in Dáil Éireann, became chairman of the provisional government and five others held office in both ministries (Cosgrave, Duggan, O'Higgins, Hogan, and McGrath).

In February the Irish Free State (Agreement) Bill was introduced in the House of Commons. Its purpose was to give the force of law to the treaty, to provide for an election in Southern Ireland, and to authorize the making of orders in council transferring to the provisional government the powers and machinery necessary for the discharge of its duties. Within four months of the passing of the act the parliament of Southern Ireland was to be dissolved and elections held for a house of parliament to which the provisional government would be responsible.

The preparation of a constitution was entrusted by the provisional government to a committee under the chairmanship of Collins. The other members were Darrell Figgis, vice-chairman; Hugh Kennedy, legal adviser to the provisional government; James Murnaghan, professor of Jurisprudence in University College, Dublin; Alfred O'Rahilly, professor of Mathematical Physics in University College, Cork; John O'Byrne, a barrister; James G. Douglas, a Dublin businessman and a Quaker; C. J. France, an American lawyer; and James McNeill, a retired Indian civil servant. The committee compiled a volume of select constitutions of the world on which to base its own constitution making. Being unable to arrive at a unanimous conclusion it submitted three drafts from which a final draft constitution was prepared by the provisional government. Griffith took this document to London in May 1922. The provisional government was under no legal obligation to submit the draft constitution to the British government, but it was anxious to test the British reactions to its interpretation of the treaty before publishing the draft constitution. The British ministers regarded the draft constitution as unacceptable and it was modified to meet their views. The provisional government's stand in the subsequent debates on the constitution suggests that the sections which were added or amended were the articles which stated the Irish Free State's membership of the Commonwealth; the articles concerning the parliamentary oath; the articles which authorized the withholding of the royal assent to bills; the article which permitted appeals to the judicial committee of the privy council; and the articles which contained references to the crown and its representative. Negotiations were also entered into in London with spokesmen of the Southern unionists who were seeking guarantees for the unionist minority in the composition and powers of a second chamber of the legislature. An agreement on this matter was reached in June 1922; and a further obligation was thus incurred before the draft constitution was submitted to the constituent assembly.

The general election for the constituent assembly was delayed until 16 June by the obstructionist tactics of the anti-treaty group. The draft constitution was published on the morning of the election. The outbreak of civil war prevented the meeting of the assembly until 9 September and resulted in the anti-treaty deputies not taking their seats. On 18 September Cosgrave introduced the Constitution of the Irish Free State (Saorstat Éireann) Bill, 1922. He divided it into three parts: (a) the articles which had been agreed upon with the British government, (b) the articles which covered the agreement reached with the Southern unionists, (c) the remaining articles. He indicated that the government intended to stand by the first two groups; on the third there might be a free vote in the assembly. On 25 October the bill was passed without substantial alteration.

The final steps were then taken on the British side. When parliament reassembled in November after a general election two bills were immediately introduced: the Irish Free State Constitution Bill, 1922, and the Irish Free State (Consequential Provisions) Bill, 1922. Since the constitution had been examined and approved beforehand by the British government the acceptance of it in parliament occasioned no difficulty. Both bills received the royal assent on 5 December and on the following day the Irish Free State constitution was brought into operation by royal proclamation.

The manner in which the constitution came into being made possible the emergence of two conflicting views on its legal origin, each of which obtained judicial recognition. The British interpretation was that the constitution derived its validity from a British statute. This view received authoritative expression from the judicial committee of the privy council which held that

> ... the constituent act and the constitution of the Irish Free State derived their validity from the act of the imperial parliament, the Irish Free State Constitution Act, 1922. This act established that the constitution, subject to the provisions of the constituent act, should come into operation on being proclaimed by His Majesty, as was done on 6 December 1922. The action of the house of parliament was thereby ratified; apart from such ratification that body had no authority to make the constitution.[1]

In Irish constitutional theory the validity of the constitution was regarded as deriving from the act of the dáil. This was the view expressed by Chief Justice Kennedy of the Supreme Court of the Irish Free State in the case of *The State (Ryan and Others)* v. *Lennon*. He

[1] *Moore* v. *Attorney-General for the Irish Free State*, [1935] A.C. 485, p. 497.

declared: 'The constitution, or bunreacht, is the fundamental structure upon which the state was set up by the third Dáil Éireann sitting as a constituent assembly. The dáil thereby formulated the system or principles, and created the organs, of government of the state.'[1] The Irish case was forcefully stated in the dáil by a pro-treaty member during the debate on the removal of the parliamentary oath in 1932: 'On this side of the house . . . we never pretended that the authority of this oireachtas was derived from any act in Westminster. We held that it was derived from the decision of the people of this country. . . . The statute of Westminster may have effect as far as the other dominions are concerned. We never claimed that any act of any British parliament was the basis of the liberties of the people of this country.'[2]

[1] *The State (Ryan and Others)* v. *Lennon,* [1935] I.R. 170, p. 203.
[2] *Dáil Debates,* xl. 727.

V

THE COMPETENCE OF THE DÁIL

THE Irish Free State constitution reflected the conflicting aims of the parties to the agreement from which it originated. The British signatories of the Anglo-Irish treaty had stood firm on their offer of dominion status; the Irish signatories had been forced to abandon their claim to the status of an independent republic. The constituent assembly which had enacted the constitution was obliged to accept Ireland's membership of the British Commonwealth of Nations and the obligations and restrictions of dominion status;[1] it was obliged to subordinate the constitution to the Anglo-Irish treaty which was given the force of law; but it also went as far as it dared towards satisfying its own national aspirations.[2] The spirit in which it enacted the constitution is revealed by the words in the preamble to the Constitution Act, 'all lawful authority comes from God to the people'. In the constitution itself the doctrine of popular sovereignty was unequivocally asserted,[3] and the 'sole and exclusive' power of making laws for the peace and good government of the state was vested in the oireachtas.[4] This declaration of legislative supremacy may seem inconsistent with the provision of the means by which the electorate might participate directly in the work of legislation, but it was designed to guard against any legislative encroachment by the imperial parliament.[5] The competence of the dáil in theory and in practice was conditioned by these contradictory elements in the constitution.

The framers of the constitution showed none of the distrust of the legislature which was so marked a characteristic of the new, post-war European constitutions. On the contrary, they sought to elevate the status of the oireachtas, to strengthen its hands *vis à vis* the executive. But within the oireachtas power was not equally shared between the

---

[1] For a discussion of the respects in which the Free State possessed a status of inequality to the United Kingdom see K. C. Wheare, *Statute of Westminster and Dominion Status* (1949), pp. 112–21, 258–76.

[2] Darrell Figgis, *The Irish Constitution Explained.*

[3] 'All powers of government and all authority legislative, executive, and judicial in Ireland, are derived from the people of Ireland.'

[4] *Constitution of I.F.S.*, art. 12.   [5] *Dáil Debates*, i. 779.

two houses; all real power was concentrated in the dáil. The executive council was to be responsible to the dáil alone;[1] all its members were to be drawn from the dáil;[2] the date of the reassembly of the oireachtas and of the conclusion of the session of each house was to be fixed by the dáil, subject to the proviso that the sessions of the senate were not to be concluded without its own consent;[3] exclusive control over money bills was vested in the dáil;[4] and the dáil was empowered to override the wishes of the senate in ordinary bills.[5] The dáil was intended to be, as Cosgrave once described it in the house, the most important institution of the state.[6]

Nevertheless, the competence of the dáil was restricted. Like every other institution in the state it was subject to the overriding authority of a written constitution which, after an initial period, was to be unalterable by ordinary legislation and which vested in the High Court the power of pronouncing on the constitutional validity of any law.[7] Many of the conventions of British constitutional practice were embodied in specific provisions of the constitution: for example, annual sessions and ministerial responsibility. The nature of the executive, legislative, and judicial organs of state was prescribed;[8] the franchise, the method of election, and the proportion between the number of members of the dáil and the population were fixed;[9] and the form of the parliamentary oath was laid down.[10] The scope of the legislative activity of the dáil was limited by the incorporation of a number of articles in the constitution defining the fundamental rights of citizens. The liberty of the individual and the dwelling of each citizen were declared inviolable; freedom of speech and of conscience were guaranteed; the right to hold meetings and to form associations or unions was established; and the obligation of providing free elementary education for all citizens was imposed.[11] In addition a restraint was placed upon the dáil by the clause in the constitution which prohibited the enactment of any law repugnant to the provisions of the Anglo-Irish treaty,[12] and by the articles of the constitution which forbade the endowment of any religion, the discrimination between citizens on account of religious beliefs, and the enactment of retroactive legislation.[13]

[1] *Constitution of I.F.S.*, art. 51.   [2] Ibid., art. 52.
[3] Ibid., art. 24.   [4] Ibid., art. 35.   [5] Ibid., art. 38.
[6] *Dáil Debates*, xx. 317.   [7] *Constitution of I.F.S.*, art. 65.
[8] Ibid., arts. 12, 31, 51, 60, 64.
[9] Ibid., arts. 14, 17, 27, 32, 33.   [10] Ibid., art. 17.   [11] Ibid., arts. 6–10.
[12] Irish Free State (Saorstát Éireann) Act, clause 2.
[13] *Constitution of I.F.S.*, arts. 8, 9, 43.

The Competence of the Dáil

The constitution also provided for the direct participation of the sovereign people in the work of legislation through the referendum and the initiative. These constitutional devices which had been incorporated in most of the new European constitutions[1] had been advocated by one of the Sinn Féin papers in April 1919.[2] To the framers of the Irish constitution they seemed particularly well suited to a country where the majority of the people had for so long been opposed to the law and the government. Through them, it was hoped, the reality of democratic control would be brought home to the electors.[3]

The referendum was the means by which the people were to exercise their legislative right in a negative way. A bill which had been passed by both houses of the oireachtas might be suspended for ninety days on the written demand of two-fifths of the members of the dáil or of a majority of the members of the senate presented to the president of the executive council within seven days of its passing. The bill would be submitted to a referendum if, within this period of ninety days, a resolution was carried by three-fifths of the members of the senate, or if a petition was signed by one-twentieth of the voters on the electoral register demanding a referendum. Money bills and bills declared by both houses to be urgently necessary for the public safety were exempted from this procedure.[4] Amendments to the constitution were also to be submitted to a referendum after a period of eight years from the coming into operation of the constitution and were not to become law unless the votes of a majority of the voters on the register or two-thirds of the votes recorded were cast in favour of the amendments.[5] The initiative was designed to provide the opportunity for positive action by the people, but while the operation of the referendum was mandatory the establishment of the initiative was permissive. The oireachtas was empowered to provide for the initiation by the people of proposals for laws or constitutional amendments. If it failed to do so within two years it was required, on the petition of not less than seventy-five thousand voters on the register of whom not more than fifteen thousand were voters in any one constituency, either to make provision for the initiative or to submit the question for decision by a referendum. Any legislation passed by the oireachtas providing for the initiative was to lay down that pro-

---

[1] A. Headlam-Morley, *The New Democratic Constitutions of Europe*, pp. 132–47.
[2] *New Ireland*, 19 Apr. 1919.   [3] *Dáil Debates*, i. 1211, 1213.
[4] *Constitution of I.F.S.*, art. 47.   [5] Ibid., art. 50.

posals for legislation might be initiated on a petition signed by fifty thousand voters on the register, that if the oireachtas rejected such a proposal it should be submitted to a referendum; and that if the oireachtas enacted it, it should be subject to the same provisions as ordinary legislation.[1]

In the outcome the dáil of the Irish Free State failed to develop on the lines laid down for it by the framers of the constitution. The failure of the scheme for extern ministers and the development of what was virtually a two-party system resulted in the emergence of a cabinet form of government on the British model and in the consequent subordination of the legislature to the executive. The sovereignty of the people came in practice to be exercised through their elected representatives. Neither the referendum nor the initiative was ever invoked. The senate never became securely enough established in public esteem to risk the odium which might have resulted from its assertion of the right to insist on the referendum. An attempt by a minority in the dáil to secure a referendum on the Electoral (Amendment No. 2) Act, 1927, failed through lack of the required support. The initiative also was never put into operation. The oireachtas did not avail itself of the power to establish it in the first two years. At the Fianna Fáil party convention in November 1927 de Valera announced the intention of the party to organize the extra-parliamentary demand for the initiative in accordance with article 48 of the constitution as the first step towards abolishing the parliamentary oath. A petition signed by ninety-six thousand electors was prepared, but when de Valera sought to present it in the dáil on 3 May 1928 Cosgrave objected on the ground that the oireachtas had not laid down the procedure to be adopted in such circumstances. Deputy Thrift proposed that the matter should be referred to a joint committee of both houses,[2] but before any action could be taken the government introduced a bill to amend the constitution by deleting the provision for both the referendum and the initiative. Although the abolition of the referendum and the initiative at this point was obviously intended to thwart the opposition's attempt to violate a clause in the Anglo-Irish treaty, abolition had been recommended by a sub-committee of the cabinet as early as 1924.[3] As an additional safeguard the government secured from both houses a declaration that the bill was necessary for the public peace and safety so that the

[1] *Constitution of I.F.S.*, art. 48.
[2] *Dáil Debates*, xxiii. 806–7, 1509–25, 2537–8, 2545.   [3] Ibid. xxxiii. 1916.

opposition would be unable to demand a referendum on it. The constitutional requirement that amendments to the constitution should be automatically submitted to a referendum after 5 December 1930 remained unaffected by this bill, but in 1929 the period during which constitutional amendments could be enacted like other bills was extended to 5 December 1938. When faced with abolition in 1934 the senate attempted to have the referendum made operative at once for constitutional amendments, but its bill for this purpose was shelved by the dáil. The result was that when a new constitution was introduced in 1937 it could have been carried as an ordinary legislative measure. But before the Draft Constitution Bill had reached its final stage the Plebiscite (Draft Constitution) Act was passed providing for a plebiscite on the new constitution to be held on the same day as the next general election for the dáil.

The competence of the Irish Free State dáil may be considered from another point of view, namely its right to be regarded as a legitimate assembly. The whole basis of the dáil's authority was challenged by a large minority in the country. The assembly which enacted the constitution was known variously as the provisional parliament, the constituent assembly, or the third dáil. It was summoned by a proclamation of the provisional government in accordance with the terms of a British act, the Irish Free State (Agreement) Act, 1922, after a general election in the twenty-six counties decreed by the second dáil on 20 May 1922.[1] At the opening meeting Laurence Ginnell, one of the anti-treaty deputies, created a scene. Claiming that he had been elected in pursuance of a decree of Dáil Éireann he refused to sign the roll until he was informed whether the assembly was Dáil Éireann or what he called a partition parliament.[2] Later in the proceedings the president of the executive council categorically stated that the assembly was the dáil.[3] The government, however, opposed a labour motion asserting the competence of the dáil to legislate as it pleased. While admitting that the dáil had the power to repudiate the treaty, government spokesmen contended that by the terms of the Free State Agreement Act they were bound to enact the constitution before considering any general legislation.[4] Nevertheless, they maintained that the constituent assembly was the legitimate heir of the republican dáil. In the enumeration of parliaments it was styled the third dáil and its successor, the first to be summoned under the new consti-

---

[1] *Dáil Official Report, 1921–2*, p. 480. [2] *Dáil Debates*, i. 8–13.
[3] Ibid. i. 193. [4] Ibid. i. 424–37, 2040.

tution, was styled the fourth. The retention of the name dáil is in itself an expression of their determination to emphasize the continuity with the revolutionary period. Although on its first mention in the constitution the popular house of the oireachtas was named the chamber of deputies, this title was not used elsewhere in the constitution nor was it ever generally employed. These attempts to identify the Free State dáil with its republican predecessor failed to satisfy the anti-treaty party whose attitude had been hardened by the bitterness engendered by the civil war. Their contention was that the second dáil was still in existence. On 25 October 1922 they held what was described as a secret session of Dáil Éireann. The former deputy speaker of the dáil presided and a clerk of the house was appointed. A resolution was passed declaring that since the speaker and the other executive officers had refused to summon the dáil and with the connivance of other members of the dáil had endeavoured to subvert the republic they, the faithful deputies of Dáil Éireann, called upon the former president, Éamon de Valera, to resume the presidency and to nominate a council of state and executive ministers to assist him in carrying on the government until such time as the parliament of the republic was allowed to assemble or the people were permitted by a free election to decide how they should be governed. Pending the next meeting of the dáil the council of state was empowered to sanction such ministers and executive officers as the president might nominate. In accordance with this decision a council of state of thirteen members was established and de Valera appointed a ministry of five members.[1]

The republican second dáil and its executive survived the split in the anti-treaty party in 1926 and have remained in existence ever since. On 8 December 1938 the executive announced that it had delegated 'the authority reposed in us to the army council'. Since then the position, as stated by J. J. O'Kelly, president of the council of state, has been that 'though the executive council has since held few meetings and its membership has been considerably reduced by death both the army and Sinn Féin as military and constitutional arms continue to give their allegiance to the second dáil'. To the members of these bodies and to their adherents the constitutional dáil has always been a usurping body.[2]

The decision of a majority in the anti-treaty party to form the new

[1] *Poblacht na hÉireann*: War news, no. 78, 26 Oct. 1922; *Dáil Debates*, xliv. 224–7.
[2] Ibid. xliv. 229, and information kindly supplied to the author in January 1955 by Miss Maire Comerford.

Fianna Fáil party and to abandon abstentionism did not involve their full acceptance of the Free State dáil. Leading members of the party made their attitude clear. Lemass described Fianna Fáil as 'a slightly constitutional party';[1] de Valera declared: 'I still hold that our right to be regarded as the legitimate government of this country is faulty, that this house itself is faulty';[2] and Lemass, after he had become minister for industry and commerce in the first Fianna Fáil government, said '... the title of this dáil to legislate for this country is faulty, and it is faulty because of this reason, that it is not open to every section of our people to get representation here'.[3] As soon as the party came into power it set about undermining the treaty settlement. In the process the power of the dáil was augmented. Although Fianna Fáil would undoubtedly have adopted this policy in any case its position was strengthened by the fact that the Statute of Westminster had been carried the previous year. An act was passed abolishing the parliamentary oath and deleting the sections of the Constitution Act which gave the treaty the force of law and prohibited the enactment of legislation repugnant to any of its provisions. The governor-general, McNeill, was replaced by a party member who was prepared to efface himself. The power of recommending the appropriation of money was transferred from the governor-general to the executive council. The governor-general's right to withhold the royal assent to bills or to reserve them for consideration in London was abolished. The right of appeal to the judicial committee of the privy council was abrogated. When the senate was abolished as the penalty for its opposition to the government's policy the dáil became the sole legislative body. The abdication crisis in Britain provided the opportunity for the removal of the king from the constitution, for the abolition of the governor-generalship, and for the introduction of the external association scheme.[4] Finally, the policy was rounded off by the enactment of a new constitution.

The dáil which emerged in 1937 from these constitutional changes was freed from the restrictions which had been placed upon its predecessors by the Anglo-Irish treaty and by the general implications of dominion status. It became the principal legislative chamber of a 'sovereign, independent, democratic state',[5] under a constitution which, like the post-1919 European constitutions,[6] was declared to

---

[1] *Dáil Debates*, xxii. 1615.   [2] Ibid. xxviii. 1398.   [3] Ibid. xli. 217.
[4] See pp. 157-8.   [5] *Constitution of Ireland*, art. 5.
[6] Headlam-Morley, op. cit., pp. 89-90.

have been given to themselves by the people and which was approved by a majority vote in a plebiscite. The state remained associated externally with Great Britain and the Commonwealth[1] but no functions were conferred on the crown in internal affairs. The sphere of the dáil's activity was potentially widened territorially by the assertion in the constitution that the national territory consisted of the whole island.[2] Although the constitution provided for the institution of a senate the preponderance of the dáil was maintained, the powers of the new senate being even more restricted than those of the old. On the other hand the sovereignty of the people was reasserted,[3] and the restrictions inherent in a written constitution continued to be operative. The new constitution, like the old, contained provisions which directly and by implication limited the legislative competence of the dáil. The endowment of any religion was prohibited[4] and the enactment of retroactive legislation[5] or of a law providing for a dissolution of marriage was forbidden.[6] No law was to be passed abolishing the right to the private ownership of property.[7] Any law enacted by the oireachtas which was repugnant to the constitution was to be invalid,[8] the High Court was empowered to pronounce on the validity of any law having regard to the provisions of the constitution,[9] and no law was to be enacted excepting from the appellate jurisdiction of the Supreme Court cases which involved questions as to the constitutional validity of any law.[10] In addition, the president was given the right, after consultation with the council of state, to secure the decision of the Supreme Court on the constitutional validity of any bill other than a money bill, a bill to amend the constitution, or a bill declared by the government to be urgently necessary for the public peace and security.[11] The fundamental rights of citizens were set forth at greater length in the new constitution than in the old, though so too were the exceptions and qualifications governing the enjoyment of those rights.[12] A section of the new constitution, which had no counterpart in the old, contained directive principles of social policy intended for the general guidance of the oireachtas.[13] While application of these principles was not to be cognizable by any court of law their presence in the constitution might be regarded as impos-

---

[1] *Constitution of Ireland*, art. 29. 4. 2°.
[2] Ibid., art. 2.
[3] Ibid., art. 6. 1.
[4] Ibid., art. 15. 5.
[5] Ibid., art. 44. 2. 2°.
[6] Ibid., art. 41. 3. 2°.
[7] Ibid., art. 43. 1. 2°.
[8] Ibid., art. 15. 4. 2°.
[9] Ibid., art. 34. 3. 2°.
[10] Ibid., art. 34. 4. 4°.
[11] Ibid., art. 26.
[12] Ibid., art. 40–44.
[13] Ibid., art. 45.

ing a certain moral restraint upon the dáil. Provision was made in the constitution for the means by which the sovereign people might exercise their right 'in final appeal, to decide all questions of national policy'.[1] A majority of the members of the senate and not less than one-third of the members of the dáil might present a joint petition to the president within four days of the passing of a bill requesting him not to sign and promulgate the bill on the ground that it contained a proposal of such national importance that the will of the people thereon ought to be ascertained. If after consultation with the council of state the president accepted the recommendation of the petition the fate of the bill was to be decided within eighteen months either by a referendum or by a general election.[2] The bill was to be taken as vetoed by the people if a majority of the votes at the referendum were cast against its enactment, provided that the majority amounted to not less than $33\frac{1}{3}$ per cent. of the voters on the register.[3] If a general election was held the bill was not to become law unless it was approved by a resolution of the newly-assembled dáil.[4] Finally, after the first two years, amendments to the constitution were only to become effective after they had been approved by the people. Every proposal for an amendment was to be initiated in the dáil as a bill. After it had been passed by both houses of the oireachtas it was to be submitted to a referendum in which a simple majority vote in its favour was to be sufficient to complete its enactment.

In its day-to-day working the dáil has been largely unaffected by the introduction of the new constitution. It had become under the Free State constitution and it has remained the preponderant part of the legislature. But at the same time it has been from the beginning very much the instrument of the government it has created. Contrary to the intentions of the Free State constitution-makers the cabinet system of government has taken firm root, with the result that the time of the dáil is almost entirely monopolized by government business. All important legislation originates with the government and is normally passed by the dáil without substantial amendment; the sphere of the private member is rigidly confined. Yet the narrowness of government majorities and the relatively high proportion of independent members, both the outcome of proportional representation, have rendered governments less independent of the legislature than under the majority system of voting. Few governments have

[1] *Constitution of Ireland*, art. 6. [2] Ibid., art. 27.
[3] Ibid., art. 47. 2. 1°. [4] Ibid., art. 27. 5. 1°.

lasted for their full term of office; there have been instances of governments being defeated in the dáil and of dissolutions being secured in order to avoid defeat. To some extent, then, the government which is in so many respects the master of the dáil has remained its servant and is less directly responsible to the electorate than in states where the majority system of voting prevails.

VI

PARLIAMENTARY ELECTIONS

THE law governing elections to Dáil Éireann is set forth in provisions of the two constitutions and in a number of statutes of which the most important are the Electoral Act, 1923, and the Prevention of Electoral Abuses Act, 1923. Elections to the republican dáil had been conducted under the existing British law. One of the first changes effected by the constituent assembly was embodied in a resolution, adopted on 19 September 1922, which authorized the preparation of a new electoral register on which women would be entered on the same terms as men.[1] This provision was included in the Free State constitution and repeated in the constitution of 1937 so that the franchise, since the institution of the state, has been enjoyed by all citizens over twenty-one who are not legally incapacitated. Both constitutions prohibit plural voting of any kind and provide that voting shall be by secret ballot.

The electoral system prescribed in the two constitutions is more complicated than the franchise. Proportional representation in parliamentary elections had been introduced into Ireland by the Government of Ireland Act, 1920. It enjoyed great vogue in the post-war years; most of the new states and constitutions adopted it almost as a matter of course. Apart from its current popularity there was a further reason for the adoption of proportional representation by the framers of the Free State constitution: it was part of the agreement entered into with the spokesmen of the Southern unionists at the time of the treaty negotiations.[2] The essence of proportional representation is that the country is divided into large constituencies each returning several members. Electors are entitled not merely to vote for their favourite candidate, as under the majority system of voting, but as well, if they so wish, to indicate their order of preference for the other candidates. The effect is that minorities and special interests are enabled to secure representation to an extent that is impossible under the simple majority system. The form of proportional representation adopted in the Irish Free State was laid down in the Electoral Act of 1923. It is the type known as the single transferable vote. At an

[1] *Dáil Debates*, i. 410–14.   [2] Ibid. i. 355.

election the voter indicates his first preference by placing the number 1 opposite the name of his favourite candidate. He may also, if he wishes, place the numbers 2, 3, and so on opposite the names of the other candidates in the order of his preference.

To obtain the result the returning officer finds the quota, that is the number of votes necessary to ensure the election of a candidate. This figure is computed by reference to the number of votes cast and the number of seats to be filled. It is obtained by counting the total number of valid ballot papers, the total poll, dividing this number by one more than the number of vacancies to be filled, and adding one to the result. For example, if there are 100 votes cast and one member to be elected, 51 votes will ensure his election, $\frac{100}{1+1}+1 = 51$; if there are three members to be elected the quota will be $\frac{100}{3+1}+1 = 26$,[1] numbers which can be obtained, respectively, by only one and three candidates. Candidates who have secured a number of first preference votes equal to or greater than the quota are then declared elected. The next step is to transfer the surplus votes of the successful candidates. All the votes of the candidates having the largest surplus are re-sorted and placed in pigeon-holes under the names of the candidates marked as second choice on them. The returning officer then takes the same proportion of votes from each pigeon-hole and credits that proportion of the total in his pigeon-hole to each candidate. The proportion is the fraction $\frac{S}{T}$ where S is the successful candidate's surplus and T the number of transferable votes received by him. Thus, if the quota is 9,000 and A received a total of 18,000 votes there is a surplus of 9,000 to be distributed. If it is found on re-sorting A's 18,000 votes that B has been marked as the second choice on 9,000 papers, C on 6,000, and D on 3,000, the returning officer takes $\frac{9,000}{18,000} = \frac{1}{2}$ from each bundle and credits B with 4,500 additional votes, C with 3,000, and D with 1,500. If this brings any of them up to the quota they are declared elected, and if it gives them surpluses these surpluses are in turn distributed. A voter does not know whether his particular ballot paper has been transferred to his second choice or retained as part of his first choice's quota. Papers

[1] J. Hogan, *Election and Representation*, p. 12.

on which no second choice is shown are used to form part of the first choice's quota. Where a candidate already declared elected on the first count appears as a second choice on the papers of the candidate whose surplus is being distributed he is passed over and the third choice is taken. When the surplus of the candidate with the highest number of votes has been distributed in this manner the surpluses of other candidates are similarly dealt with in turn. If the remaining number of places has not been filled after this process the returning officer eliminates the candidate at the bottom of the poll and transfers his votes to the candidates indicated as next preferences by his supporters.[1]

This process goes on until either the number of candidates having secured the quota equals the number of seats still to be filled, or the number of candidates not eliminated equals the number of seats still to be filled, in which case they are elected. It is thus possible for a candidate to be elected without having secured the quota, and in each election a considerable number are so elected—forty-eight in June 1927, for example.[2]

One of the main criticisms directed against proportional representation is that it tends to multiply the number of parties and consequently to make for unstable governments since no one party has a secure majority. Two circumstances offset this tendency in Ireland: the treaty issue dominated political life so completely for so long that the parties, in the last resort, fell into two groups not widely different from the usual two party system found where simple majority voting is practised; and in the second place the proportional representation operating in Ireland is a local adaptation[3] designed to produce a stable government as well as a representative assembly.[4] The greater the number of members returned by a constituency, the more nearly does the result approach strictly proportional representation. If the whole country were treated as a single constituency returning 100 members, 1 per cent. of the votes would be sufficient to secure the election of a candidate. But if the country were divided into ten constituencies each returning ten members, a candidate would need 10 per cent. of the votes to secure election. When the number of seats in a constituency falls below five the failure of seats gained to correspond with votes cast becomes more marked, and in a three-member

---

[1] S. R. Daniels, *The Case for Electoral Reform* (1938), pp. 45–54.
[2] *Irish Times*, 15 June 1927.
[3] *Dáil Debates*, lxvii. 1342.   [4] Ibid. cviii. 924.

constituency any party which polls more than 50 per cent. of the votes is sure of obtaining two of the three seats.[1] The Free State constitution fixed the proportion of members to population at not less than one for every 30,000 or more than one for every 20,000; the constituencies were to be defined by law and revised every ten years.[2] In the 1937 constitution these provisions are repeated, except that the revision of constituencies is to take place at twelve-yearly intervals.[3] In accordance with these provisions the constituencies were prescribed by the Electoral Act of 1923 and revised by acts of 1935 and 1947.[4] As the accompanying table shows the consistent tendency has been to increase the number of three-member constituencies. The justification offered on each occasion was the necessity of providing the country with a viable government.[5] The constitution of 1937 guards against any further weakening in proportional representation by forbidding the enactment of any law whereby the number of members to be returned by any constituency shall be less than three.[6]

Number of Members and Constituencies

Electoral act	Number of constituencies	\multicolumn{6}{c}{Constituences returning}	Total number of members
		9	8	7	5	4	3	
1923	30*	1	3	5	9	4	8	153
1935	34	..	..	3	8	8	15	138
1947	40	..	..	..	9	9	22	147

* Includes the two university constituencies, each of which returned three members.

It follows that the Irish electoral system, while being more advantageous to small parties than the majority system would have been, has always favoured the larger parties. This is illustrated by the accompanying table which presents the results of a general election under each of the electoral acts. Though the discrepancies are nothing like so great as under the majority system of voting it is clear that the large parties are over-represented and the small parties under-represented.

[1] Hogan, op. cit., p. 13.
[2] *Constitution of I.F.S.*, art. 26.
[3] *Constitution of Ireland*, art. 16.
[4] Electoral (Revision of Constituencies) Act, 1935, and Electoral (Amendment) Act, 1947.
[5] *Dáil Debates*, li. 1333; cviii. 924.
[6] *Constitution of Ireland*, art. 16. 2. 6°.

Parliamentary Elections

	Parties	Votes polled	Seats obtained	Seats in proportion to votes	Cost in votes per seat obtained
1932*	Fianna Fáil	566,475	72	66	7,868
	Cumann na nGaedheal	449,810	56 (+1)	53	8,032
	Labour	98,285	7	11	14,041
	Farmers	41,302	5	5	8,260
	Independents and others	117,333	9	14	13,037
1937	Fianna Fáil	599,524	68 (+1)	62	8,817
	Fine Gael	461,258	48	47	9,609
	Labour	132,657	13	14	10,203
	Independents and others	131,488	8	14	16,436
1948	Fianna Fáil	553,917	68	62	8,146
	Fine Gael	262,202	31	25	8,458
	Labour†	149,089	19	16	7,847
	Clann na Talmhan	71,686	7	9	10,241
	Clann na Poblachta	173,166	10	19	17,317
	Independents	112,816	12	13	9,401

* Three seats uncontested. The speaker was returned automatically on each occasion.
† Includes labour and national labour.

The advantage enjoyed by the larger parties in the three-member constituencies is shown by the fact that in the 1937 election of the 45 seats in these constituencies Fianna Fáil secured 24, Fine Gael 16, labour 3, and independents 2; and in the 1948 election of 66 seats Fianna Fáil secured 31, Fine Gael 15, labour 9, Clann na Poblachta 4, Clann na Talmhan 3, and independents 4.

Until recently by-elections also played into the hands of the larger parties. When a vacancy occurs the constituency votes for the return of one member under the system of proportional representation. It frequently happened that a large party gained the seat at the expense of one of the smaller parties which had won it in a general election. Cosgrave once suggested that a fairer method of filling a vacancy would be to allow the party which had nominated the original deputy to select his successor and have him co-opted by the dáil.[1] The frequent success of the larger parties tended to rob by-elections of the value they possess under the majority system of giving effect to

[1] *Dáil Debates*, ii. 2457.

changed trends in public opinion. Co-operation among the parties which formed the coalition government in 1948 has introduced a new element into the situation at by-elections. It would now be possible for them to organize their second preference votes in such a way as to ensure the defeat of the largest party in the state, Fianna Fáil.

Apart from the revisions of constituencies various minor changes have been effected from time to time in the laws relating to parliamentary elections. In the Free State constitution the day of a general election was declared a public holiday but this provision was revoked by a constitutional amendment of 1927. Another constitutional amendment of the same year provided for the automatic re-election to the dáil of a ceann cómhairle (speaker) who had not signified his intention of resigning. University representation in the senate had been promised to the spokesmen of the Southern unionists but when the constitution was being enacted representation in the dáil was substituted.[1] The two universities were empowered to return three members each. The Fianna Fáil government abolished university representation in the dáil in 1936 but gave the universities representation in the senate under the 1937 constitution. The duration of the dáil has also been altered. It was originally fixed at four years. In 1927 the life of the dáil was increased to five years, with a possible maximum of six. The constitution of 1937 extended the maximum period to seven years but permitted the fixing of a shorter period by law. The five-year limit has been retained though in 1934 the government attempted to raise the possible duration of the dáil to six years.[2] In the same year another minor change affecting the conduct of elections was made. An act was passed requiring returning officers in all constituencies to send cards to each voter telling him where to vote and giving him his number on the electoral register.[3]

Though proportional representation has not made for unstable government it has been responsible for a large number of general elections in which normally every seat is contested. As the accompanying table shows there were eleven general elections in the $26\frac{1}{4}$ years between the signing of the Anglo-Irish treaty and the establishment of the Republic of Ireland. On four occasions a government held a second general election within a year of the previous one in an attempt, which proved successful each time, to strengthen its position.

[1] *Dáil Debates*, i. 1152–3.
[3] Electoral (Polling Cards) Act, 1943.
[4] Ibid. lxxxix. 1638, 2101, 2357.

Parliamentary Elections

The second table shows the number of candidates nominated and the result of each election.

Dáil	Nomination day	Election	First meeting	Dissolution	Duration Yrs. Mhs.
1	4 Dec. 1918	14 Dec. 1918	21 Jan. 1919	16 Aug. 1921	2 7
2	13 May 1921	No election	16 Aug. 1921	8 June 1922*	0 10
3	6 June 1922	16 June 1922	9 Sept. 1922	9 Aug. 1923	0 11
4	18 Aug. 1923	27 Aug. 1923	19 Sept. 1923	23 May 1927	3 8
5	1 June 1927	9 June 1927	23 June 1927	25 Aug. 1927	0 2
6	3 Sept. 1927	15 Sept. 1927	11 Oct. 1927	29 Jan. 1932	4 3
7	9 Feb. 1932	16 Feb. 1932	9 Mar. 1932	2 Jan. 1933	0 10
8	11 Jan. 1933	24 Jan. 1933	8 Feb. 1933	14 June 1937	4 4
9	23 June 1937	1 July 1937	21 July 1937	27 May 1938	0 10
10	7 June 1938	17 June 1938	30 June 1938	31 May 1943† 26 June 1943	5 0
11	9 June 1943	22 June 1943	1 July 1943	10 May 1944‡ 5 June 1944	0 11
12	19 May 1944	30 May 1944	9 June 1944	12 Jan. 1948	3 7
13	21 Jan. 1948	4 Feb. 1948	18 Feb. 1948	7 May 1951	3 2

* Last meeting.   † and ‡ Election proclaimed.

Dáil		1922	1923	1927 (1)	1927 (2)	1932	1933	1937	1938	1943	1944	1948
Cumann na nGaedheal	a	65	109	97	88	101	85	95	74	87	57	82
Fine Gael (Pro-treaty)	b	58	63	47	62	57	48	48	45	32	30	31
Republican (Anti-treaty)	a	57	85	..	..	..	..	..	..	..	..	..
	b	35	44	..	..	..	..	..	..	..	..	..
Sinn Féin	a	..	..	15	..	..	..	..	..	..	..	..
	b	..	..	5	..	..	..	..	..	..	..	..
Fianna Fáil	a	..	..	87	88	104	103	100	92	105	100	118
	b	..	..	44	57	72	77	69	77	67	76	68
Labour	a	18	44	50	28	31	19	23	30	71	29	59
	b	17	14	22	13	7	8	13	9	17	8	19
Farmers	a	12	64	38	20	9	..	..	..	..	..	..
	b	7	15	11	6	4	..	..	..	..	..	..
Independents	a	21	75	59	32	34	13	36	11	47	25	38
	b	11	17	16	13	13	9	8	7	8	9	12
National league	a	..	..	30	6	..	..	..	..	..	..	..
	b	..	..	8	2	..	..	..	..	..	..	..
Clann Éireann	a	..	..	7	..	..	..	..	..	..	..	..
	b	..	..	0	..	..	..	..	..	..	..	..
Centre party	a	..	..	..	..	..	26	..	..	..	..	..
	b	..	..	..	..	..	11	..	..	..	..	..
Clann na Talmhan	a	..	..	..	..	..	..	..	..	44	31	17
	b	..	..	..	..	..	..	..	..	14	11	7
National labour	a	..	..	..	..	..	..	..	..	..	9	..
	b	..	..	..	..	..	..	..	..	..	4	..
Clann na Poblachta	a	..	..	..	..	..	..	..	..	..	..	92
	b	..	..	..	..	..	..	..	..	..	..	10
Total number of candidates nominated		173	377	383	262	279	246	254	207	354	351	406
Number of seats		128	153	153	153	153	153	138	138	138	138	147

a. Candidates nominated.   *b.* Candidates elected.

Both constituencies prescribe that a general election for Dáil Éireann shall be held not later than thirty days after a dissolution. As far as practicable polling is to take place on the same day throughout the country. The dáil must meet within thirty days from the polling day.[1]

The first of the post-treaty general elections was held in June 1922. The British act which gave legal sanction to the treaty[2] provided that within four months of the passing of the act the parliament of Southern Ireland was to be replaced by a constituent assembly which would enact a constitution. The election was postponed for three months by agreement between the rival groups at the árd fheis of Sinn Féin in February 1922. But this did not satisfy the opponents of the treaty who contended not only that a postponement of at least six months was necessary to allow existing passions to subside, but also that in the last resort there were 'rights which a minority may justly uphold, even by arms, against a majority'.[3] The action of the military wing of the anti-treaty group in repudiating the authority of the dáil and in seizing the Four Courts in Dublin intensified the tension.[4] In May Collins and de Valera concluded an election pact in an attempt to stave off the civil war which was becoming increasingly threatening. This compact, from which Griffith stood aloof, provided for a national coalition panel with pro- and anti-treaty candidates represented on it in proportion to the existing strength of the groups in the dáil. It also stated that other interests and groups were free to contest the election equally with the panel candidates.[5] Once the pact had been signed the second dáil unanimously passed a motion fixing the date for an election in the twenty-six counties.[6] Though Collins virtually repudiated the pact before the election it resulted in the unopposed return of 33 panel candidates. In the remaining constituencies the seats were contested by 47 opposition candidates, 12 of them nominated by a farmers' organization, 18 by the labour party, and 17 by independent groups. Widespread intimidation prevented others from standing.[7] The election itself was marked by further instances of intimidation. In south-east Mayo the agents of two independent candidates were kidnapped and their papers were burnt. At Donaghmore in Leix the presiding officer, a former mem-

---

[1] *Constitution of I.F.S.*, art. 28; *Constitution of Ireland*, art. 16.
[2] Irish Free State (Agreement) Act, 1922.
[3] *Irish Independent*, 2 May 1922.   [4] *Irish Times*, 29 Mar. 1922.
[5] *Irish Independent*, 22 May 1922.
[6] *Dáil Official Report, 1921–2*, p. 480.   [7] *Irish Times*, 7 June 1922.

ber of the Royal Irish Constabulary, was ejected from the booth by armed men. There were cases of interference with agents in co. Tipperary. Protestant electors in the Sligo-East Mayo area received a warning by post: 'The border men expect that the unionists will kindly stay at home next Friday, as they did in the 1918 election. If they do not, it will mean some night duty for us next week. Please convey instructions to your neighbours.' Ballot boxes in the senate room of the National University in Dublin were seized by armed men but the count had been completed at the time of the incident.[1] At one country polling station the presiding officer was compelled, at the point of the revolver, to fill the ballot papers for every name on the register.[2] Personation was carried to extraordinary lengths. The election was conducted on an old electoral register. Yet 100 per cent. polls were nothing unusual. Ernest Blythe quoted a case in the dáil of a district where there was not only a 100 per cent. poll but where every paper in the box had its first preference vote for the same candidate, a fact which, as he said, 'showed the peculiar unanimity of the people in that district dead and alive'.[3] Another deputy declared[4] that some of the successful candidates should be classified as representing Glasnevin.[5] Johnson, the leader of the labour party, summed the matter up by saying: 'It is hypocrisy to refer to the elections as a test of the will of the people . . . the elections were a farce and utterly useless as any test upon these questions.'[6] The corrupt practices were probably not confined to one side but the more violent of them, at any rate, were directed against treaty supporters. Nevertheless, the result was a victory for the pro-treaty group.

The assembly thus elected was described as the house of parliament to which the provisional government is responsible, the constituent assembly or the third Dáil Éireann. It enacted the constitution and was empowered, by article 81 of the constitution, to continue in existence as the lower house of the new bicameral legislature for not longer than a year from the date when the constitution came into operation. It was obviously desirable that a more representative assembly should be brought into being as soon as possible. By the summer of 1923 the essential preliminaries to a general election had been completed. The civil war had been brought to an end; some semblance of order had been restored in the country; and an Electoral

---

[1] *Irish Times*, 17 June 1922.
[2] *Dáil Debates*, i. 1846.
[3] Ibid. i. 1847.
[4] Ibid. i. 1853.
[5] A Dublin cemetery.
[6] *Dáil Debates*, i. 1850.

Act and a Prevention of Electoral Abuses Act had been passed. The third dáil was dissolved on 9 August and a general election held on 27 August. The more settled state of the country and the legislation against corrupt practices had their effect in producing an election in some ways more normal than the last. Complaints of corruption were made but it was clearly on nothing like the scale of the previous election. On the other hand the campaign was conducted with an intense bitterness which was the inevitable outcome of civil war. If the supporters of the treaty had been the victims of intimidation in 1922 it was the republicans who were at a disadvantage in 1923. They contested the election under the name of Sinn Féin, but some of their leaders had been killed or executed and others were imprisoned or 'on the run'. De Valera himself was arrested by Free State troops as soon as he began to address an election meeting at Ennis, co. Clare.[1] The election resulted in the return of the pro-treaty Cumann na nGaedheal party with a majority over any other party but not an overall majority.

The next general election fell due in 1927 under the constitutional provision limiting the duration of the dáil. The election campaign was remarkable for the number of parties contesting seats and for the great duel between the Cumann na nGaedheal and Fianna Fáil parties conducted through the medium of press advertisements. Although political passions were still sharp they were less intense than they had been in 1923. The newly-formed Fianna Fáil party fought the election largely on the issue of the parliamentary oath. The government relied on its record of achievements. In the outcome the extent to which its legislative activity had antagonized various groups was reflected in a considerable drop in its members.

This circumstance in itself made likely another election within a short time but the events following on the assassination of the vice-president Kevin O'Higgins precipitated it within three months. One of the bills introduced by the Cosgrave government as a result of the assassination was an Electoral Amendment Bill to compel every candidate for election to the oireachtas to swear an affidavit that he would, if elected, take the oath. This threatened to exclude permanently the abstentionist followers of de Valera who were already moving in the direction of constitutional action. The result was that they took their seats in the dáil on 12 August 1927. Four days later the leader of the labour party, with the backing of the national league

[1] *Irish Times*, 16 Aug. 1923.

and Fianna Fáil, moved a vote of no confidence in the government. Though the government was saved from defeat by the casting vote of the ceann cómhairle it was in too insecure a position to carry on; on 25 August Cosgrave obtained a dissolution of the dáil.

The ensuing election was fought with all the acrimony that had been reawakened by the assassination and by the government's reaction to it. Shortage of funds compelled the parties to put up fewer candidates; the rump Sinn Féin party disappeared from the lists altogether. The Cumann na nGaedheal party denounced the revolutionary aims of Fianna Fáil, and Fianna Fáil replied by accusing its opponents of pro-English imperialist sentiments. The election increased the strength of the two larger parties at the expense of the smaller ones. With the support of the farmers' party and some independents the Cumann na nGaedheal party was able to form a government.

The next general election was due in the autumn of 1932. For two reasons the government decided to hold it some months earlier; the Eucharistic Congress was to take place in Dublin in June and the Imperial Economic Conference in Ottawa in July. So that a government might be firmly installed before these events the dáil was dissolved on 29 January 1932 and the general election held on 16 February. The election campaign was lively but peaceful. W. A. Redmond, the former leader of the national league, joined the Cumann na nGaedheal party and so, for all practical purposes, did the farmers' party—a development which Fianna Fáil described as 'the alliance of a dog with his fleas'. Cumann na nGaedheal once again was content to depend on its past record and on gloomy forebodings about the likely effects of its rival's accession to power. Fianna Fáil, on the other hand, presented a vigorous programme which included the abolition of the oath, the retention of the land annuities, and the establishment of new industries as well as the release of political prisoners. It was rewarded by success in the election. The party won sufficient seats to enable it to form a government with the backing of the labour party.

There followed the opening of the attack on the treaty settlement and the beginning of the economic war with Great Britain. The desire for a clear mandate on this policy and for a majority independent of labour support induced de Valera to appeal to the country again in January 1933, before his opponents had fully mobilized their forces. The brief election campaign was conducted in a tense atmosphere. The I.R.A.'s contribution was summed up in its slogan, 'No free speech for traitors.' Organized interruptions at opposition meetings brought retaliation from the Army Comrades Association which was acting as the opposition's private police force. There was thus a good deal of violence and a flood of rumours and threats. The result of this election was a victory for the government which gained five seats while the principal opposition party lost nine.

General elections since 1933 have been occasioned by different circumstances and have evoked varying degrees of public interest but they have all been held in a more normal political atmosphere than the earlier elections. The election of 1933 cleared the way for the full adoption of the Fianna Fáil programme which culminated in the drafting of the new constitution. On the day on which the draft constitution was finally approved the dáil was dissolved and a plebiscite on the constitution was held concurrently with the general election on 1 July 1937. The result was a return to the position of 1932: the government lost its clear majority and was left dependent on labour support. On 25 May 1938 it was defeated by one vote on a motion relating to arbitration in civil service disputes.[1] Two days later the presidential commission (which was acting till a president was chosen) dissolved the dáil on the advice of the taoiseach. The general election, held on 17 June 1938, was quite uneventful, but it did result in the establishment of a government that was able to survive for the full legal term of the dáil. By 1943, when the next general election was due, the World War was at a critical stage. For this reason a postponement of the election was suggested,[2] but the majority favoured adherence to the normal practice. With all parties agreed on the vital question of neutrality there was little scope for a lively contest. The development of greatest ultimate significance was the proposal for a national government put forward by the Fine Gael party. Once again Fianna Fáil emerged as the strongest party, but with its numbers considerably reduced; both large parties lost heavily to smaller parties. As had happened in a similar situation on three previous occasions there was another general election within a year. The government was defeated by one vote on a Transport Bill[3] and dissolved the dáil in May 1944. The campaign was again remarkable for the reticence of all parties on grave current problems, but the election restored the position of the government and brought the Fine Gael party to its lowest ebb. In 1946 a new party called Clann na Poblachta

[1] *Dáil Debates*, lxxi. 1865–8. [2] Ibid. lxxxix. 732–88.
[3] Ibid. xciii. 2466–7.

was formed under the leadership of Seán MacBride. Its first opportunity of testing its strength came in October 1947 when three by-elections were held: in co. Dublin, Waterford, and S. Tipperary. Knowing that the new party had won adherents from among his own followers de Valera made the results of these by-elections a matter of confidence. He announced that if the government was defeated in any of the three there would be a general election. Clann na Poblachta was successful in two of the contests and the result was a general election in February 1948 in which the government's majority was considerably reduced. This was not an unprecedented situation but on this occasion the opposition parties combined to secure the defeat of de Valera and the election of J. A. Costello to the leadership of a coalition, or as it was officially styled, an inter-party government.

As the accompanying table shows the size of the poll at these general elections has remained fairly uniform since the establishment of settled conditions in the country. It shows, too, that the number of spoiled votes has been remarkably low considering the complication of proportional representation. For purposes of comparison a table has been added showing the percentage poll at British elections in the same period.

A parliamentary election can be contested by any citizen without distinction of sex, who has reached the age of twenty-one and who is not under any legal disability.[1] Between 1927 and 1933 candidates were required on nomination to swear an affidavit that they would take the parliamentary oath if elected. A candidate for election must be nominated in writing by two registered electors of the constituency, as proposer and seconder, and by eight other registered voters. He is required to lodge a deposit of £100 which is forfeited if he does not succeed in polling at least one-third of the quota. Prior to 1933 failure to take the parliamentary oath also involved forfeiture of the deposit. Each candidate must submit to the returning officer a statement of his election expenses the limit of which is fixed by law. The method of selecting candidates is virtually the same in each of the principal parties. When an election is impending the national executive of the Fianna Fáil party meets and examines the figures for the previous and other elections. On the basis of these figures it decides on the number of candidates that should be put up in each constituency. Its findings are communicated to the local organizations in each constituency where a convention is convened for the selection of candidates.

[1] *Constitution of Ireland*, art. 16. 1. 1°.

Irish General Elections

Election	Percentage of electorate which voted	Percentage of votes invalid
1922	62	3·08
1923	61	3·66
1927 (1)	68	2·6
1927 (2)	69	1·86
1932	77	1·6
1933	81	1·05
1937	76	2·1 *
1938	79	1·2
1943	74	1·2
1944	68	1·04
1948	74	0·98

British General Elections

Election	Percentage of electorate which voted
1922	71
1923	71
1924	77
1929	76
1931	80
1935	75
1945	76
1950	84

* The marked increase in the number of spoiled votes in 1937 may be due to confusion among voters arising from the fact that a plebiscite on the new constitution was held concurrently with the general election.

If time and other circumstances permit each branch or cumann of the party has the right to submit to the constituency organization the names of suggested candidates, not exceeding the number fixed by the national executive. Each name must be accompanied by the written consent of the suggested candidate and by his signed pledge of loyalty to the party. A list of all persons suggested as candidates is then sent to the national executive which has the right to add a name or names to it. A copy of this ratified list must be circulated to all the branches in the constituency prior to the summoning of the convention. If these provisions have been complied with no person whose name is not on the list is eligible for selection by the convention, but if it is not possible to carry them out candidates may be proposed by delegates at the convention. The names of those recommended for nomination as candidates are then submitted to the national executive for ratification and at this stage also it may add further names. The national executive is empowered, in special circumstances, to dispense with a constituency convention or to substitute for it a number of district conventions. In practice the final decision is normally left to the local organization which is presumed to know local conditions and the chances of success best. Even on the matter of fixing the number of candidates the executive is ready to listen to the advice of the local organization. Undue interference from headquarters is resented. Carpet-baggers are suspect; the full support of the national executive or of the leader of the party will not in itself ensure election as a candidate.

Fine Gael candidates are chosen in much the same way. The national council decides on the number of candidates to be put up in each constituency.[1] Candidates are selected by a convention in the constituency and submitted to the national council for approval. The constituency organization may question the wisdom of the national council's decision on the number of candidates and the national council may, in exceptional circumstances, reject a local choice. In the labour party candidates are selected by a constituency selection conference convened by the administrative council. The final ratification of all candidates rests with the administrative council which may also select candidates itself in cases of emergency or where no adequate machinery exists locally. In all three parties the constituency is expected to bear the expense of the election.

There is no essential difference between election campaign methods in Ireland and in any other democratic state. In Ireland, as in Britain, an attempt to examine the means by which candidates appeal to the electorate is rendered difficult by the ephemeral nature of election literature. It is designed to meet an immediate need, to fit a particular set of circumstances. None of the major Irish parties has felt called upon to preserve samples of it systematically. In some cases its existence might even be a source of embarrassment. Only one party was able to produce copies of election posters. Election addresses disappear with extraordinary rapidity. But from what material there is available, from the newspapers and from information supplied by party officials, it is possible to piece together a reasonably complete

[1] *Irish Times*, 2 Sept. 1927.

picture. The general policy of the party is decided at headquarters but, unlike the British parties, the Irish parties do not normally issue an election handbook for candidates. With general elections occurring so frequently and often so unexpectedly expense and time militate against the practice. The Cumann na nGaedheal party did produce a handbook entitled *Fighting Points for Cumann na nGaedheal Speakers and Workers* for the general election of 1932. It was a 160-page printed booklet roughly half of which was devoted to the achievements of the party and half to points against Fianna Fáil. A later handbook had detachable pages so that information of interest to a particular locality might be supplied without sending the whole book. In subsequent elections the head office of the party dispatched roneoed sheets to the local organizations or prepared a special election number of the party paper. The Fianna Fáil party has not provided its candidates with election handbooks in recent elections. Instead it has published special pamphlets and booklets, illustrated with photographs of historical interest relating to the party or of national activities promoted or encouraged while the party was in power. These productions serve the twofold purpose of supplying candidates with facts and figures and of providing propaganda suitable for distribution to the public. The labour party issues an election manifesto from which candidates and speakers can draw during the campaign.

The appeal to the electorate is both visual and vocal. Every candidate has the right to send one communication by post free of charge to each elector. For this purpose, and for distribution, electoral addresses are prepared. Usually they are a joint appeal on behalf of all the party candidates standing in the constituency, but it is recognized that a candidate may issue his own address provided he mentions his colleagues in it. The addresses conform to a fairly uniform pattern. Though the candidates are free to compile them themselves it is only occasionally that some point of special local interest is added to the facts supplied from headquarters. In some cases identical wording is used by candidates in different constituencies. The front page of a four-page folder contains photographs of the party candidates and brief biographical notes. Inside, the main points in the party programme are set forth, and at the end there is an appeal for the votes of the elector. Similar appeals from individual candidates or groups of candidates appear in the newspapers, but the direction of the main press campaign is in the hands of the central organizations. It takes two forms: advertisements, usually accompanied by an appeal for subscriptions, and formal addresses, under the name of the leader, setting out the party's aims. Only the two large parties have been able to use press advertisement on an extensive scale and even with them the volume varies with the state of their funds. It first attained significant proportions in the general elections of 1927. The record and intentions of the opposing party were attacked under such captions as: 'Where millions of your money go'; 'Government by panic and propaganda'; 'Economy by torch and petrol can'; 'Dev. in the dumps and Dev. on the warpath: when Dev. is sick—Dev. a saint would be; when Dev. was well—the d—l a saint was he.' Unusual and varied layouts were employed and so much political propaganda was packed into them that the *Irish Statesman* commented, '... the election advertisements were much better reading than the election speeches'. The Cumann na nGaedheal party, during the second election of 1927, inserted advertisements in practically every newspaper in the country. Advertisements appeared in the daily morning press each day up to the day of the election. In all about 300 appeared, including seven full-page and 126 half-page advertisements, and not a single one was repeated.[1] In the general election of 1932 a similar campaign was conducted but since then there has been a marked decline. Fine Gael no longer uses the provincial press but Fianna Fáil inserts advertisements in the local papers, the national dailies, and in trade and other journals. The headquarters of the labour party confines itself to the national dailies but the candidates use the local press serving their constituencies.

The use of posters is another device employed at election times. Considerable ingenuity has been displayed in this form of propaganda. During the 1932 campaign the Cumann na nGaedheal party devised a poster in the form of a circus playbill, headed, 'Devvy's Circus: Absolutely the greatest road show in Ireland today', and starring 'The world-famous illusionist, oath-swallower and escapologist. See his renowned act escaping from the strait jacket of the republic.'[2] Political cartoons on posters have also appeared. Cumann na nGaedheal was responsible for two in the autumn election of 1927. The first depicted a hen with the head of de Valera standing beside an egg, broken at the end and marked 'The empty formula'. The caption read: 'The hen that took five years to lay an egg and then it was empty.' In the second de Valera was shown as an artist with a painting

[1] B. W. O'Kennedy, *Making History: the Story of a Remarkable Campaign*.
[2] D. O'Sullivan, *Irish Free State and its Senate*, p. 284.

suggesting fire and destruction. The title of the painting was 'The civil war', and its price ticket was marked '33 million pounds'. The caption was: 'Presented by the artist to the nation. De Valera is now working on another canvas(s) but what about the price?'[1] About the same time Fianna Fáil displayed a poster entitled, 'On the rocks'. It showed a ship called the Irish Free State securely wedged on the rocks of bankruptcy, unemployment, extravagance, adverse trade balance, and dumped goods. The ship was piloted by Cosgrave who was represented as saying, 'Well anyway I have given you stability'. Underneath was the exhortation, 'Change the pilot'. Another Fianna Fáil poster was entitled, 'Fianna Fáil is winning'. It portrayed de Valera as a jockey on the horse Fianna Fáil which was moving rapidly towards the winning post. Cosgrave was mounted on a seedy animal called Cumann na nGaedheal which had stopped. A frock-coated figure labelled 'Secret fund committee' was feeding Cosgrave's horse out of a tall hat which bore the words 'Unionist oats'. The horse was being pushed from behind by Heffernan and Redmond[2] from whose pockets protruded papers marked, respectively, 'Government job' and 'Government briefs'.

It is now felt that posters of this type may amuse supporters but are hardly likely to win over waverers. They have consequently been replaced by a quieter type. On the whole, however, posters have figured less prominently in Irish than in British elections. In the rural areas which make up the bulk of the Irish constituencies the effective display of posters is difficult. A less common form of appeal is the election window—a shop window elaborately decorated to attract a crowd which may thus be made conscious of the party's aims. Finally, reference must be made to an all too frequent practice during Irish election campaigns—the painting of slogans on dead walls.

The verbal appeal to the electors is made primarily by means of public meetings. In a preponderantly catholic country the simplest way of collecting an audience is to organize a meeting at the church gates after last mass on Sundays. Such meetings are usually addressed by the local candidates and their supporters. Each party then organizes larger meetings which are attended by the leader of the party or by some other prominent member, in addition to the local candidates. The leaders and their principal colleagues are thus obliged to undertake strenuous tours throughout the country during an election cam-

[1] *Freeman*, 24 Sept. 1927.
[2] Leaders respectively of the farmers' party and the national league.

paign. The climax of the campaign is marked by great eve-of-poll rallies in Dublin at which the strongest men in each party have their last opportunity of soliciting the support of the electors. The appeal through public meetings is supplemented by a door-to-door canvass, by short broadcasts from committee rooms, and by loudspeaker vans. Radio broadcasts were not permitted until 1954. It was felt that if scripts were not censored offence might be given through references to the civil war period and that if they were censored the government in power would be exposed to charges of partiality.

An ingenious device resorted to by one party had unforeseen repercussions. An aeroplane fitted with a microphone was hired to make a country-wide flight on polling day. In each constituency it swooped down on the principal towns roaring forth its exhortation to the electors to give their first preference votes to the local party candidate. Unfortunately for the party it so happened that in a number of towns fairs were in progress. By the time the plane had gone on its way the owners of the panic-stricken animals were imbued with political convictions which boded ill for the party that had been trying to woo them.

VII

THE COMPOSITION OF THE DÁIL

BETWEEN 1922 and 1948 the total membership of the dáil varied between 128 and 153. To the third dáil or constituent assembly which met in September 1922 128 members were elected. The Electoral Act, 1923, fixed the membership of the dáil at 153. In accordance with the provisions of the Free State constitution the constituencies were revised in 1935 and the membership of the dáil was reduced to 138.[1] A further revision, as required by the terms of the new constitution, took place in 1947 when the dáil was increased in size to 147 members.[2] In the early years of the Free State the actual membership was less than the nominal figure: the abstentionist policy of the republicans deprived the dáil of its full complement until 1927. In the following analysis, however, all the members are included whether they took their seats or not.

In spite of the frequency of general elections the total number of individuals who were members of the dáil between 1922 and 1948 was only 518. This figure is indicative of the relatively low turnover of members at general elections or, alternatively, of the high expectancy of long parliamentary life. Table I shows the number of new members elected at each general election.

TABLE 1

New Members Elected at Each General Election

General election	1922	1923	1927 (1)	1927 (2)	1932	1933	1937	1938	1943	1944	1948
Total number of new members	32	78	63	30	38	23	23	12	32	12	33
Percentage of total membership	25	51	41	20	25	15	17	9	23	9	22

Clearly, with two exceptions, the influx of new members follows a remarkably consistent pattern. At the general elections of 1923 and June 1927 an unusually large number of inexperienced candidates were elected. The 1922 dáil was composed in the main of persons who had been active in the revolutionary period but with the return of

[1] Electoral (Revision of Constituencies) Act, 1935.
[2] Electoral (Amendment) Act, 1947.

peaceful conditions more diverse interests sought representation. New parties emerged and new blood was infused into the expanded dáil. Yet in spite of the high percentage of new members returned at the first two elections under the Free State constitution, the average percentage of new members over the whole period—23—is lower than in the house of commons, where the average percentage for the seven general elections between 1918 and 1935 was a little under 30,[1] or in the Canadian House of Commons where the percentage has rarely fallen below 40.[2]

The low turnover means that a high percentage of the members served for lengthy periods in the dáil. This service was not always continuous: at each general election a considerable number of members were not re-elected as Table 2 shows.

TABLE 2

Members Not Re-elected at Each General Election

General election	1922	1923	1927 (1)	1927 (2)	1932	1933	1937	1938	1943	1944	1948
Members not re-elected	33	47	72	39	51	41	54	22	40	22	32
Percentage of total members	26	37	47	25	33	27	35	16	29	16	23

These figures include members who died in the inter-election periods and members who retired permanently from politics, but of the remainder a high proportion re-entered the dáil at later elections, sometimes after a protracted interval. For example, one member of the second dáil (1921) did not reappear in the house until 1943.

An analysis of the parliamentary experience of members in the 1948 dáil shows the long service of many members (p. 88).

Ten members of the 1948 dáil sat in the revolutionary dáil: five of them served in both the first dáil and the second and five in the second only. Twenty-two per cent. had over twenty years experience, 50 per cent. over ten years, and 66 per cent. over four years. Of the total members 105 or 71 per cent. had first entered the dáil prior to the preceding general election (1944). Only 26 of these members—a quarter—had ever suffered defeat at the polls after their first election.

As Table 4 (p. 88) shows parliamentary experience was rarely confined to a single dáil. Only in 1923 when the independents were strong and the parties fluid was the number considerable.

[1] J. F. S. Ross, *Parliamentary Representation* (1948), p. 39.
[2] Norman Ward, *The Canadian House of Commons* (1950), p. 115.

Table 3

Parliamentary Experience of Members in 1948 Dáil

Years in dáil	Number of members	Percentage of total membership
29	2	1
25–28	8	5
20–24	22	15
15–19	29	20
10–14	12	8
4–9	24	16
Under 4	17	12
No previous experience	33	22
	147	100

The percentages are given to the nearest 1 per cent. and do not necessarily total 100.

Table 4

Members who Sat in One Dáil Only

Dáil	1922	1923	1927 (1)	1927 (2)	1932	1933	1937	1938	1943	1944	1948
Members of single dáil	10	37	16	10	7	11	3	3	5	6	..
Percentage of total membership	8	24	10	7	5	7	2	2	4	4	..

Personal information about members of parliament is more difficult to secure in Ireland than in Great Britain or the dominions. There is no Irish *Who's Who* and no parliamentary handbook. The following conclusions are based on evidence collected from such biographical works as exist and from obituary notices and other press reports supplemented by information from party leaders, party officials, individual deputies, and others. It is not complete on all points; in particular, Irish public men appear to have an almost feminine aversion to disclosing their age. In some cases, then, figures must be taken as representing a minimum in a particular classification and not necessarily the absolute total.

The pre-parliamentary experience of members has been fairly uniform. Table 5 shows that most of the members entered the dáil through well-defined channels.

As we have seen the republican dáil was composed entirely of participants in the revolutionary struggle. Many of them continued in politics after the conclusion of the Anglo-Irish treaty; others with a similar background were returned at subsequent elections. Aspirants

TABLE 5
Pre-parliamentary Experience of Members

Dáil	1922	1923	1927 (1)	1927 (2)	1932	1933	1937	1938	1943	1944	1948	Total 1922–48
Participants in revolutionary movement	102	94	82	88	87	89	77	73	65	72	63	251
Percentage of total membership	80	61	54	58	57	58	56	53	47	52	43	48
Participants in local government	33	45	82	92	91	91	97	90	93	93	83	265
Percentage of total membership	26	29	54	60	59	59	70	65	67	67	56	51
Old nationalists	2	5	13	10	10	8	5	5	4	3	2	20
Percentage of total membership	2	3	8	7	7	5	4	4	3	2	1	4
Ex-unionists	4	10	12	12	10	8	5	5	2	1	..	16
Percentage of total membership	3	7	8	8	7	5	4	4	1	..	..	3
Former M.P.s	2	4	5	4	2	1	2	2	2	1	2	8
Percentage of total membership	2	3	3	3	1	..	1	1	1	..	1	2

to parliamentary honours were never slow to emphasize their services during the revolutionary period for, as Table 5 reveals, a revolutionary past was a sound political asset. At least 48 per cent. of all those who sat in the dáil between 1922 and 1948 had taken part in the revolution. Experience in local government was another common preliminary to parliamentary service. It was less widespread among members at the beginning of the period than later, probably because so many of them at that time were new to public life. Yet at least 51 per cent. of all the members participated in local government. A very much smaller group among the members had a different political background; it was composed of the remnants of the pre-revolutionary political parties. Table 5 shows the number of former nationalists and unionists in each dáil. Since neither of these parties revived the numbers steadily declined after reaching their maximum during the party fluctuations of the late 'twenties and early 'thirties. This group contained the only members who had previous parliamentary experience; a few from each party had sat in the House of Commons prior to the revolution. Labour members also had a distinctive background. Some of them, it is true, took part in local government but it was in trade union circles that they served their real apprenticeship. In having this sectional background they resembled the farmer deputies most of whom were active in various farmers' organizations. Apart from those who had fought in the Anglo-Irish war there were some members with military service either in the British army or in the Irish army as professionals after 1922 or during the Second World War emergency. Another group of members identified themselves with the activities of the Gaelic Athletic Association. Finally, there were members who inherited a family tradition of politics. This is particularly noticeable among the women members. Of the twelve women who sat in the dáil between 1922 and 1948 three were widows and three sisters of prominent leaders in the revolutionary period and five were widows of former members. Among the male members there were twelve near relatives of leaders and eight sons of members, six of whom sat with their fathers.

Since 1922 the Irish electorate has shown a marked tendency to elect local men to the dáil. From Table 6 it is clear that almost two-thirds of the members were born in the constituency they represented and that a considerably higher proportion were resident in the constituency at the time of their first election. Most of the non-residents were national figures, prominent party men, or former inhabitants of the constituency.

TABLE 6

Birthplace and Residence of Members

Dáil	1922	1923	1927 (1)	1927 (2)	1932	1933	1937	1938	1943	1944	1948	Total 1922–48
Members born in constituency	72	96	104	104	91	87	93	93	87	94	86	331
Percentage of total membership	56	63	68	68	60	57	67	67	63	68	59	64
Members resident in constituency	92	124	124	135	127	119	114	115	115	116	117	440
Percentage of total membership	72	81	81	88	83	78	83	83	83	84	80	85

Attention has been drawn in an earlier chapter to the preponderance of young men in the revolutionary dáil. Since 1922 the dáil has been a steadily ageing body. This is disclosed by Table 7 which sets out the number of members in five-yearly age-groups at the beginning of each dáil.

The Composition of the Dáil

TABLE 7
Age Distribution of Members in Each Dáil

Dáil	1922	1923	1927 (1)	1927 (2)	1932	1933	1937	1938	1943	1944	1948
20–24	2	3	0	0	0	0	0	0	2	2	0
25–29	12	11	6	8	1	1	2	3	0	1	3
30–34	23	19	14	18	11	15	4	4	5	4	10
35–39	16	15	21	22	22	22	20	19	9	11	7
40–44	19	21	23	26	28	25	21	25	20	17	15
45–49	5	14	24	17	19	21	27	27	22	21	27
50–54	14	11	16	16	21	19	14	16	28	25	19
55–59	4	9	6	3	11	15	18	18	16	21	29
60–64	4	6	5	3	4	4	10	9	12	17	16
65–69	0	0	4	3	2	1	2	1	8	4	10
70 or over	2	2	3	3	2	2	1	2	0	1	2
Total ages ascertained	101	111	122	119	121	125	119	124	122	124	138
Ages unascertained	27	42	31	34	32	28	19	14	16	14	9
Total membership	128	153	153	153	153	153	138	138	138	138	147
Average age	40·9	42·5	45·2	43·4	46	45·8	47·6	47·7	50·2	50·5	51·3

The general trend is indicated by the average age of the members in each dáil which has risen over the period from 40·9 to 51·3 years. The manner in which this change has affected the strength of three important age-groups is shown in Table 8.

TABLE 8
Percentage Age Distribution (Based on Ages Ascertained)

Dáil	1922	1923	1927 (1)	1927 (2)	1932	1933	1937	1938	1943	1944	1948
Under 35	37	30	16	21	10	13	5	6	6	6	9
35–44	35	32	36	40	41	38	34	35	24	23	16
45 or over	29	38	48	38	49	50	61	59	70	72	75

These two tables must be considered in conjunction with Table 9 (p. 92). which shows the age distribution of new members in each dáil

The table reveals considerable fluctuation both in the number and in the average age of new members. The rise in the age level of the dáil clearly cannot be attributed to a steady influx of new members drawn from the higher age-groups; it is due, rather, to the long parliamentary experience of so many members.

It remains to analyse the personnel of the dáil according to religion, education, and occupation as a means of gauging the extent to which the house was truly representative of the country. The dáil has always been a preponderantly catholic body but thanks to proportional representation the protestant section of the population has not been

Table 9
Age Distribution of New Members in Each Dáil

Dáil	1922	1923	1927 (1)	1927 (2)	1932	1933	1937	1938	1943	1944	1948
20–24	2	3	0	0	0	0	1	0	2	0	0
25–29	2	7	2	2	1	1	2	1	0	1	1
30–34	6	3	7	3	5	6	2	2	2	1	7
35–39	3	7	6	6	3	3	6	2	6	1	3
40–44	3	8	9	3	5	1	1	2	6	2	6
45–49	2	9	7	3	3	1	3	1	1	2	8
50–54	6	2	10	2	5	1	2	1	4	2	1
55–59	1	4	2	1	1	5	0	0	2	2	3
60–64	0	3	1	0	1	2	1	0	3	0	0
65–69	0	0	1	0	0	1	0	0	2	0	1
70 or over	0	0	3	0	0	0	0	0	0	0	0
Total ages ascertained	25	46	48	20	24	21	18	9	28	11	30
Ages unascertained	7	32	15	10	14	2	5	3	4	1	3
Total new members	32	78	63	30	38	23	23	12	32	12	33
Average age	40·1	41·6	46·1	40·5	43·4	45·6	40	39·2	45·9	45·3	43·2

left unrepresented. Since 1927 there has also been one Jewish member. Table 10 shows that the number of protestants in each dáil has decreased steadily throughout the period.

Table 10
Number of Protestants in Each Dáil

Dáil	1922	1923	1927 (1)	1927 (2)	1932	1933	1937	1938	1943	1944	1948	Total 1922–48
Protestants	9	14	14	13	12	9	7	7	6	4	3	30
Percentage of total membership	7	9	9	9	8	6	5	5	4	3	2	6

This was occasioned in part by changes in the electoral system. The abolition of university representation in the dáil resulted in the disappearance of the four protestants returned by Dublin University, and the increase of three-member constituencies in 1935 and 1947 made it more difficult for minorities to secure representation. But part of the explanation also lies in a decline of political consciousness among protestants. In the early days of the independent state there were protestants who had been accustomed to take part in public affairs but as they died or retired their places were not always filled, partly because of a fall in the protestant population and partly because the means of entry into public life were no longer so readily accessible to protestants. Nevertheless, of the total members between

1922 and 1948 6 per cent. were protestants—a remarkably close approximation to the total protestant strength in the country.[1]

The facts relating to the education of members are set out in Table 11.[2]

TABLE 11
Education of Members

Dáil	1922	1923	1927 (1)	1927 (2)	1932	1933	1937	1938	1943	1944	1948	Total 1922–48
National school	51	64	71	72	67	70	60	61	65	66	56	234
Percentage of total membership	40	42	46	47	44	46	43	44	47	48	38	45
Secondary school	77	88	78	78	86	81	77	77	73	71	90	283
Percentage of total membership	60	58	51	51	56	53	56	56	53	51	61	55
University or professional training	33	29	35	35	37	38	33	33	29	30	32	109
Percentage of total membership	26	19	23	23	24	25	24	24	21	22	22	21

Even when allowances are made for inaccuracies arising out of incomplete information it can safely be said that the members of the dáil have a more varied educational background than the members of the House of Commons where the higher levels of education are so heavily represented.

Certain difficulties were encountered in making an occupational analysis of the dáil. A considerable number of members have had more than one occupation. The commonest instance of this was the shopkeeper who was also a farmer, but there were as well barristers, solicitors, teachers, and others who combined farming with their principal occupation. It was not uncommon to find such pursuits as auctioneering, journalism, or insurance work carried on in conjunction with another occupation. There were also among the members professional men who were not practising their professions either because they were devoting their full time to politics or because they had some other interests and sources of income. Rather than

---
[1] The 1926 census gave the protestant population as 7 per cent. of the total; in 1936 the percentage was 6.
[2] Members who were privately or self-educated have been assigned to the 'secondary' column. In a few cases where direct evidence was not available the classification has been made on presumptive evidence: for example, a small farmer living in his native district has been placed in the 'national' column.

create confusion by including a member in more than one category it has been decided in Table 12 to indicate by a plus sign followed by the number those members who qualified for inclusion in a particular occupation but who were principally engaged in another. It is thus possible to see at a glance, for example, the total number of barristers in each dáil and the number of those barristers who were actually practising. The totals for each group of occupations include only those members principally engaged in one of the occupations in the group. Another difficulty in classifying the members arose from the fact that since the establishment of the independent state there have always been a number of members who had no occupation other than politics and in some cases no source of income other than their parliamentary allowance. They include front bench politicians, retired and independent persons, and persons who had never followed any settled occupation. In Table 12 they have been assigned to a separate group and to them have been added all members holding ministerial office even though the extent to which a minister was obliged to renounce his former occupation varied with the nature of the occupation. Finally, it was found that some members changed their occupations in the course of their parliamentary career. A man might enter the dáil as a farmer and appear some years later as a barrister. In the first eleven columns of Table 12 the members of each dáil are classified according to their occupations at the opening of the dáil, but in the final column all the members between 1922 and 1948 are classified according to their occupations at the time of their election.

The first impression created by Table 12 (pp. 96 ff.) is that the composition of the dáil has changed remarkably little over the whole period. Each of the principal groups maintained roughly the same strength. But a closer examination reveals minor fluctuations. The third dáil (1922) was more akin to the revolutionary dáil than to any elected after the establishment of the Irish Free State. In spite of the emergence of farmers' and labour groups it was largely the preserve of the Sinn Féin party which, although split, was still composed of the same men as before. It is only natural, then, to find the same preponderance of the professions and the same paucity of farmers in the third as in the revolutionary dáil. Again, the third dáil and to a lesser extent the fourth contained an abnormally high percentage of members with no fixed occupation. This is as understandable in the turmoil of the time as is the decline in the number of such members with the return of normal conditions. The slight increase in recent dáils is due in part to an expansion in the size of the government and in part to a growing realization that politics offer a not unprofitable career. The table shows that the professional occupations were more strongly represented in the first ten years than since. The continuity of personnel from the revolutionary dáil was partly responsible, but the main reason was that the universities enjoyed representation in the dáil at the time and the six university members were almost invariably professional men. The upward trend in 1948 can be ascribed to increased professional representation among the new members. The opposite tendency is noticeable in the commercial group. In the first three post-treaty dáils commercial interests figured less prominently than they have done since. So too did members in the agricultural group. The general election of 1923 was the first at which farmers were returned in any numbers. It brought them into a position of prominence from which they have never been dislodged. Even in the miscellaneous group a small but significant fluctuation is discernible. In the early dáils the members of this group formed a slightly larger component of the house than later.

These fluctuations in the main groups reflect some interesting variations in the representation of particular occupations. The revolutionary dáil was remarkable for the small number of lawyers it contained, but since the establishment of the Free State the dáil has come into line with other legislative assemblies in having a strong lawyer group. The increase is attributable not only to the attraction which politics possess for lawyers but also to the appeal which the legal profession has had for members: a number have qualified as barristers after their election to the dáil. The increase in lawyers has been partly offset in recent years by a decrease in the number of doctors who appear to have become less ready to enter politics or less able to win the support of the electorate. The number of university teachers has fallen even more spectacularly. Some of the university teacher members figured prominently in the revolution, others had entered the dáil as representatives of the universities. With the retirement of the former and the unseating of the latter by the abolition of their constituencies this group quickly disappeared from the dáil. The number of journalists in the dáil has also declined sharply since the revolutionary period when, as the publicists of the movement, they occupied a position of great importance. Within the commercial group the changes have been less pronounced. It will be seen, however, that the number of

Table 12
Occupation of Members
A. PROFESSIONAL OCCUPATIONS

Dáil	1922	1923	1927 (1)	1927 (2)	1932	1933	1937	1938	1943	1944	1948	Total 1922–48 occupation on election
Barristers	3+3	2+4	6+4	4+3	11+4	11+6	10+2	9+2	6+3	6+3	8+7	26+6
Solicitors	3+2	3+3	3+2	3+2	6+3	2+2	5	4+1	7	6+1	8	20
Medical doctors	9+1	7+1	8+2	9+1	6+3	5+3	5+2	6+2	4+2	4+2	3+2	27+2
Veterinary surgeon	1	1	1	1	..	..	..	1	..	..	..	1
University teachers	8	6+2	4+1	5+2	5	4	1	4	4	..	..	13
Other teachers	5+6	8	5	5	8	5	5	0+1	2+1	5	8	34
Journalists	6+4	5+2	3+1	4+2	2+2	2+2	1+1	1	..	2+2	2	15+1
Accountants	2	1	..	..	..	2	1	1	..	..	..	3
Engineers	1	2	3	5	1+3	1+3	1+3	1+3	1+2	2+1	2+2	6
Total number	38	35	33	36	39	32	29	26	24	25	31	145
Percentage of total membership	30	23	22	23	25	21	21	19	17	18	21	28

B. COMMERCIAL, FINANCE, AND INSURANCE OCCUPATIONS

Dáil	1922	1923	1927(1)	1927(2)	1932	1933	1937	1938	1943	1944	1948	Total 1922-48 occupation on election
Company directors	..	..	2	4	5+6	6+3	7+1	6+4	6+7	6+4	8+5	19+8
Shopkeepers	12	12+4	19+2	19+4	15+4	18+1	12+1	17+2	16	17	15+2	63
Chemists	1	..	..	..	..	..	..	1	..	1	..	2
Publicans	1	1+1	..	5	4	3	2	2	1	1	3	11+1
Agents	2	2	2	..	..	..	..	..	..	..	..	3
Commercial travellers	..	1	..	2	..	1	1+1	2+1	1+1	1+1	..	2
Shop assistants	..	..	..	1	1	1	..	..	..	..	..	1
Cattle dealers	..	..	..	1	..	..	..	..	1	1	1	1
Cattle salesmen	..	..	..	0+4	1+1	2	0+1	0+1	0+1	0+1	0+1	2+1
Auctioneers	1	3+1	2+1	1	3	2+3	1+4	1+3	1+2	1+2	1+3	7+5
Insurance officials	2	..	..	..	..	2	2+1	2+1	4+1	1+1	1+1	5
Total number	19	19	25	33	30	35	25	31	30	29	29	116
Percentage of total membership	15	12	16	22	20	23	18	22	22	21	20	22

C. AGRICULTURAL OCCUPATIONS

Dáil	1922	1923	1927 (1)	1927 (2)	1932	1933	1937	1938	1943	1944	1948	Total 1922–48 occupation on election
Farmers	14+9	36+9	37+11	41+12	41+13	42+14	47+12	42+16	40+14	39+16	35+17	133+39
Percentage of total membership	11	24	24	27	27	27	34	30	29	28	25	26
Percentage of dáil engaged in agriculture	18	29	31	35	35	37	43	42	39	40	35	33

D. MISCELLANEOUS OCCUPATIONS

	1922	1923	1927 (1)	1927 (2)	1932	1933	1937	1938	1943	1944	1948	Total 1922–48 occupation on election
Secretaries of trade or other association	.	2	3	2	1	2	.	1	1	.	1	4
Trade union officials	11	8	12	7	5	5	8	5	7	6	6+3	27
Clerks	2	1	1	.	.	2	2	2	3	2	3+1	10+2
Local government employees	1	1	1	1+1	1+1	.	0+1	0+1	0+1	1+1	1+2	5+3
Hospital official	.	.	.	.	.	1	.	.	.	1	1	1
Building contractors	2	4	4	2	4	5	1+1	4+1	1+1	2+1	5	11
Hotel proprietors	.	1	.	1	3	1	2	1	1	1+2	1+2	3+2
Cinema proprietors	1	1	.	.	1	.	.	.	.	.	.	2
Ballroom proprietor	.	.	.	.	.	.	.	.	.	.	1	1
Bookmaker	.	.	.	.	.	.	1	1	1	1	1	1
Foundry owners or managers	1	.	.	.	.	.	.	.	.	.	1	2
Carpenters or cabinet makers	1	3	.	.	.	.	.	.	.	.	.	4
Coachbuilders	.	1	.	2	2	2	2	2	1	1	1	3
Upholsterer	.	1	.	.	.	.	.	.	.	.	.	1
Plumber	.	.	1	.	.	.	.	.	.	.	.	1
Bricklayers	1	1	2	2	.	.	1	1	1	1	1	2
Tailors	1	.	1	1	1	1	.	1	.	1	.	3

Compositors or linotype operators	..	..	2	1	1	1	1		1		1	2
Bookbinder	..	..	..	..	..	..	..	..	..	..	..	1
Harness maker	1	..	..	..	1	..	..	..	..	..	..	1
Employee of Electricity Supply Board	..	1	..	..	1	..	..	..	..	..	..	1
Railway employees	1	1	2	1	1	2	2	2	2	2	1	2
Mill operatives	1	1	..	..	..	..	..	..	2	1	1	3
Distiller's assistant	..	1	..	..	..	..	..	..	..	..	..	1
Bonesetter	..	..	..	0+1	..	..	1	1	1	1	1	1+1
Labourers	..	3	1	1	..	..	..	..	..	..	..	4
Total number	24	29	32	22	21	22	21	20	23	22	25	97
Percentage of total membership	19	19	21	14	14	14	15	14	17	16	17	19

E. PERSONS ENGAGED IN POLITICS

Dáil	1922	1923	1927 (1)	1927 (2)	1932	1933	1937	1938	1943	1944	1948	No occupation
Total number	33	30	25	21	22	22	15	19	21	23	27	26
Percentage of total membership	24	20	16	14	14	14	11	14	15	17	18	5

shopkeepers and company directors has increased since 1922. In view of the prominent part taken by publicans in the old parliamentary party it is surprising to find so few among the members of the dáil. Probably a number of members who described themselves as merchants were 'spirit-grocers', that is traders who combined the sale of liquor with a general retail business. Since 1923 the number of farmers has been consistently high. As we have seen there have always been, in addition to those whose sole occupation was farming, a considerable number of members who combined farming with some other occupation. If these are added to the farmers the total exceeds one-third of the house in practically every dáil. Among the occupations included in the miscellaneous group there are no fluctuations comparable to those found in the other groups. It should be noted, however, that in the early dáils, especially in the 1923 dáil, there was a greater variety of occupations, covering a wider range of social groups, than in later dáils.

To what extent was the dáil representative of the country in the period under consideration? It cannot claim to have reflected proportionally all the occupational groups in the population. Only in the agricultural group is there any relationship between the percentage of members in the dáil and the percentage of the total population included in the group. Of all those elected to the dáil between 1922 and 1948 26 per cent. were farmers; the percentage of the population over fourteen years of age engaged in agriculture was 31 in 1926 and 29 in 1936. But the percentage of members in the other two principal groups was very greatly in excess of the percentage of the total population comprised in these groups. While 28 per cent. of the total dáil membership were engaged in professional occupations and 22 per cent. in commercial occupations the percentage of the total population included in these groups was 3 and 4 respectively. As for the various groups of manual and non-manual wage-earners in the population, they have been represented among the members by a mere handful of individuals. Obviously the dáil has always been recruited from a few occupational groups in the country. But it does not follow that it is unrepresentative, or that it is the instrument of a particular class or profession. Éire is essentially an agricultural country. Even its town dwellers are not far removed from the land. Agriculture and commerce are the two basic economic pursuits. Moreover, the professional classes are largely drawn from the higher levels of intelligence in these groups.

Socially and economically, then, the dáil is less varied in composition than it appears on the surface. When the occupational analysis is considered in conjunction with the other facts relating to members—their religion, education, birthplace, and residence—the conclusion may safely be drawn that the representative character of the dáil is reasonably satisfactory.

VIII

THE POLITICAL PARTIES

THERE were no party divisions in the revolutionary dáil; it was the creation of a single political party. Any diversity of view which existed among the members was held in abeyance by the necessity of presenting a united front to the enemy. The signing of the Anglo-Irish treaty both cleared the way and created the circumstances for the emergence of parties: it restored more normal conditions in which the labour movement and the organized farmers were able to enter the political field and it split the republican ranks into two groups which developed eventually into the two main parties in the state. In the general election of 1922 the labour party nominated eighteen candidates and the farmers' party twelve. The labour party had come into being on the adoption of a resolution moved by James Connolly at the Irish trades union congress at Clonmel in 1912. In its early years its political policy was moulded by Connolly in a revolutionary nationalist cast. After 1916, as the revolutionary movement gathered momentum, the labour party was hard pressed to maintain its separate identity. Although, unlike the other separatist groups, it was not absorbed into the reconstituted Sinn Féin it refrained from contesting the general elections of 1918 and 1921, realizing that its future was bound up with the nationalist cause and that, in any case, it was unlikely to secure any substantial measure of support in the circumstances. The farmers' party was an offshoot of the Irish farmers' union which had been founded some time before on the model of the English farmers' union. When the Anglo-Irish treaty was signed the union came out strongly in support of it. Early in 1922, at the annual congress of the farmers' union, a motion was put forward proposing the formation of an independent farmers' party. After a full debate the motion was passed. Since the farmers' union had been organized as a non-political association its rules were changed to enable it to become associated with a political body. Acceptance of the treaty was the foremost plank in the platform of the farmers' party; but, in addition, it had an independent political and economic policy which included the advocacy of free trade and of economy in government expenditure.

At the time of the 1922 general election the pro-treaty and anti-treaty groups of Sinn Féin were still seeking a *modus vivendi*, but on the outbreak of the civil war the split became absolute. Early in 1923 the followers of Griffith and Collins were formed into a party called Cumann na nGaedheal, under the leadership of William T. Cosgrave. By avoiding a too precise declaration of opinion on any issue other than the treaty this party sought to draw to itself all the various elements in the country who were prepared to abide by the treaty settlement.[1] The section of the old dáil which had opposed the treaty regarded the republic proclaimed in 1916 and ratified in 1919 as still in existence. Nevertheless, under the old name Sinn Féin, they contested the general election of 1923. These four parties alone nominated any considerable number of candidates in the 1923 election but there were fifteen other groups, represented by from one to eight candidates, and forty independents. In spite of proportional representation the majority of these small groups made no showing in the election results. Cumann na nGaedheal was returned with a majority and, since the Sinn Féin members did not take their seats in the dáil, the labour party, led by Thomas Johnson, became the official opposition.

The Cumann na nGaedheal party had within itself the seeds of disruption. Even in the government there were two members who held diametrically opposed views on the question of free trade. Acceptance of the treaty was the only bond holding the party together. As soon as a crisis occurred it was hardly likely to withstand the strain unimpaired. It was put to the test in 1924. There were two rival groups among the army officers: one, calling themselves the old I.R.A., wanted to use the treaty settlement as a stepping-stone towards greater freedom; and the other, representing the I.R.B., stood for a full acceptance of the treaty. In March 1924 the I.R.A. group presented an ultimatum to the government and revolted.[2] The government took energetic measures to deal with the mutiny, but Joseph McGrath, the minister for industry and commerce, while disapproving of the officers' action, sympathized with their aim and resigned his office. In the following autumn he and eight other deputies resigned from the party and the dáil and formed a new party called the national party which aimed at amending the treaty settlement in a republican direction. In the ensuing by-elections the new party failed to win a single seat and nothing further was heard of it.

[1] *Freeman's Journal*, 28 Apr. 1923.
[2] T. de V. White, *Kevin O'Higgins*, pp. 158–9; *The Truth about the Army Crisis*.

The crisis over the boundary settlement of 1925 brought another splinter party into being. Professor William Magennis, one of the representatives of the National University, broke with Cumann na nGaedheal and formed a new party called Clann Éireann in 1926. He was joined by two members of the dáil and one member of the senate and drew some support from former members of the defunct national party. At the general election of June 1927 the party stood for the abolition of the oath, a revision of the boundary settlement, and the imposition of tariffs, but none of its seven candidates were elected. Another minor party which went to the polls for the first time in this election was the national league which had been founded in September 1926 by an independent deputy, Captain W. A. Redmond. It was an attempt to revive the old parliamentary party which had been led by his father. In addition to soliciting the support of former nationalists he appealed to such sectional interests as the liquor trade and the ex-service men. Thirty candidates were nominated in June 1927 and eight elected. After figuring in the dramatic 'no confidence' motion of August 1927 the party was practically obliterated in the autumn election of 1927 when it was only able to secure the return of two of its six candidates. It finally disappeared in the turmoils of the 'thirties during which its leader joined the Cumann na nGaedheal party.

The farmers' party fared little better than the other small parties. There was always a good deal of internal friction in the party. Although it retained its identity it had tended from the beginning to side with Cumann na nGaedheal against the labour party. Too vigorous opposition to the government would have been regarded by many of its followers as playing into the hands of the republicans. Besides, its leader, D. J. Gorey, had always gravitated towards Cumann na nGaedheal, and from about 1925 he was in favour of fusion with that party. At a farmers' party meeting in November 1926 two deputies proposed amalgamation with the national league. A conference was held but it broke down over the terms of the union. Early in March 1927 Gorey broached the subject of amalgamation with the government party to one of his colleagues. A few days later he and M. F. O'Hanlon had an informal discussion with leading members of the executive council. On receiving their report the farmers' party appointed representatives to confer with the government. As a result of these negotiations the congress of the Irish farmers' union was called to consider the question of amalgamation.

When the proposal was turned down by the congress Gorey and O'Hanlon resigned from the party before the general election of June 1927.[1] The entry of the Fianna Fáil party into the dáil changed the whole political situation. After the second general election of 1927, when the strength of the farmers' party had fallen to six, it was clear to the new leader of the party, M. R. Heffernan, that the issue was between Cosgrave and de Valera, with the smaller parties counting for little. On the morning of the day on which the new dáil was to meet a conference took place between Cosgrave and a delegation from the farmers' party. Cosgrave said that he would form a government only on being assured of the firm support of the farmers' party, and he proposed an alliance or coalition. In that event he offered to nominate a member of the farmers' party for the post of parliamentary secretary, the holder to be selected by the farmers' party. This member would be invited to the executive council when matters bearing on the policy of the farmers' party were being considered. This proposal was accepted; the farmers' party voted for the election of Cosgrave as president of the executive council; on the evening of the same day Heffernan was selected by his party for the parliamentary secretaryship. From this time the farmers' party sat and voted with Cumann na nGaedheal but it maintained its independent existence as a party: it held its own party meetings, and it remained responsible to its controlling organization—the farmers' union. By the time of the next general election it was obvious that the farmers' party could get little independent support and most of its members who stood for election, including Heffernan himself, did so as Cumann na nGaedheal candidates.

Of more permanent significance than the rise and fall of these small parties were the developments among the Sinn Féin abstentionists. There were early indications that all was not well in the party. A party meeting in Limerick on 7 July 1925 had before it a report from the director of organization disclosing a general state of apathy in the movement.[2] Towards the end of the same year the I.R.A. withdrew its allegiance from the shadow government which had been kept in existence since 1922.[3] The advisability of abandoning the abstentionist policy was debated at length in party conventions in November 1925 and January 1926 without a decision being reached. In an attempt to persuade the Sinn Féin deputies to enter the dáil during

[1] *Irish Times*, 7 May 1927. [2] Ibid., 25 Mar. 1948.
[3] *Dáil Debates*, xx. 830.

the boundary crisis the other opposition parties convened a conference in the Shelbourne Hotel, Dublin, on 8 December 1925.[1] Finally, in March 1926, an extraordinary convention was summoned to consider a motion by de Valera urging the expediency of entering the oireachtas. When it became evident that his policy had not the full support of the party de Valera resigned from the presidency and set about forming a new organization.[2] The inaugural meeting of the Fianna Fáil party was held in Dublin on 16 May 1926. At this meeting, and more fully at the first árd-fheis in November 1926, the programme of the party was expounded. Its immediate political aim was the abolition of the parliamentary oath; its ultimate aim the replacement of the Free State constitution by a new constitution in which the independence of the country would be asserted. The encouragement of the Irish language, the development of native industries assisted by tariffs, and the withholding of the land annuities paid to Great Britain were other points in its programme. The campaign against the oath and the circumstances in which the Fianna Fáil deputies eventually entered the dáil will be described elsewhere.[3] The remnant of the Sinn Féin party, under the leadership of Miss Mary MacSwiney, held uncompromisingly to a republican course but it dropped out of parliamentary election contests after 1927.

The increased tension following on the accession of the Fianna Fáil party to power was responsible for the next development in the history of the parties.

The I.R.A. had been driven underground by the previous government. Now it emerged to launch an offensive against the opposition. The government was loath to take action against an organization with which it had so recently been associated, especially since its policy was designed to lead all sections in the country to the constitutional path. But the I.R.A. adhered so resolutely to methods of violence and created such a state of disorder by the vigour with which it pursued its campaign not only against the opposition but also against the government itself, that the government was eventually obliged, in June 1936, to declare it an illegal organization.

Meantime another extra-parliamentary political organization had come into being to act as the counterpart of the I.R.A. This was the Army Comrades Association, led by Dr. T. F. O'Higgins, a brother of Kevin O'Higgins, the former vice-president. Originally a friendly

[1] *Irish Times*, 9 Dec. 1925; *Dáil Debates*, xliv. 1869.
[2] *Irish Independent*, 12 Mar. 1926.   [3] See pp. 154–7.

The Political Parties

society of ex-officers and men of the Irish Free State army it now expanded its membership to about 30,000 and acted as an auxiliary police force at Cumann na nGaedheal meetings.[1] The influence of continental ideologies was revealed in April 1933 when the Association adopted the uniform of a blue shirt. Three months later its name was changed to the National Guard and O'Higgins resigned the leadership in favour of General Eóin O'Duffy, the recently dismissed chief of police. In the following month the government banned the organization.

The other development was the formation of a new political party in the interests of the large farmers who were suffering the effects of the tariff war with Britain. An independent deputy, Frank MacDermot, became the leader of the national farmers' and ratepayers' league.[2] The name of the party was changed to the national centre party when it was joined shortly afterwards by another prominent independent, James M. Dillon.

A proposal to replace the existing anti-government groups by a single united party was put forward at the end of 1932,[3] but it was not until September 1933 that the efforts to draw them together bore fruit in a conference at which the Cumann na nGaedheal party, the national centre party, and the National Guard were amalgamated to form the united Ireland party with O'Duffy at its head, although he was not a member of the oireachtas. Cosgrave, MacDermot, and Dillon became its vice-presidents and Cosgrave was to act as parliamentary leader. As the National Guard had been suppressed it was reconstituted as a wing of the new party under the name Young Ireland Association. The aim of the united Ireland party was declared to be the unification of Ireland on the basis of dominion status; the settlement of the economic war; the establishment of agricultural and industrial corporations with statutory powers; and the abolition of proportional representation. When the Young Ireland Association was in turn declared an illegal organization it was dissolved and replaced by the League of Youth.

The peculiar arrangement for the leadership of the party proved far from satisfactory. O'Duffy became increasingly sympathetic towards the idea of a corporate state, and his encouragement of farmers who had refused to pay their rates and land annuities did not meet with the approval of his parliamentary colleagues. The first open rift was

[1] *United Irishman*, 15 Oct. 1932. [2] *Irish Times*, 7 Oct. 1932.
[3] Ibid., 28 Dec. 1932; 30 Dec. 1932.

the resignation of Professor James Hogan from the party in September 1934. A few weeks later O'Duffy himself resigned from the chairmanship. A split in the Blue Shirt movement followed; a section remained loyal to O'Duffy, who, in June 1935, formed it into the national corporate party, and a section accepted the leadership of Commandant Cronin who was appointed by the united Ireland party to succeed O'Duffy in command of the Blue Shirts. The chairmanship of the party remained vacant till the election of Cosgrave in March 1935; at the same time Dillon, MacDermot, Cronin, and O'Higgins became vice-chairmen. Dissensions within the party were not yet at an end. When Cosgrave and O'Higgins denounced de Valera's stand over Abyssinia at the League of Nations in September 1935 MacDermot resigned from the party. The conflicts between Cronin and the parliamentary members came to a head in 1936. On 9 October the standing committee of the party, which by this time had come to be known as Fine Gael, decided to terminate the practice of having 'an autonomous self-directed political organization within another political organization'.[1] With the breakdown of the attempt to weld a parliamentary political party to an extraneous near-fascist movement the principal opposition party reverted to its pre-1933 form. As O'Sullivan says: 'New Fine Gael was but old Cumann na nGaedheal writ small.'[2]

The one party which survived all these upheavals was the labour party though neither in outlook nor in organization was it identical with the party founded by Connolly. Throughout the years there has been a steady retreat from the socialism preached by Connolly and James Larkin until the labour party has become almost indistinguishable from the other political groups. Until 1918 the party was known as the Irish trades union congress and labour party, but in that year the name was changed to the Irish labour party and trades union congress, an alteration which foreshadowed a more active and independent participation in politics. The political and industrial branches of the labour movement remained united in a single organization until 1930 when, at a special congress, it was decided to constitute the Irish labour party as a distinct body.[3] The influence of the trade unions, as affiliated members, naturally remained strong, a fact which was to be responsible for a split in the party in 1944. In January of that year the largest union in the country, the Irish transport and

[1] *Irish Independent*, 10 Oct. 1936. [2] *Irish Free State and its Senate*, p. 474.
[3] *Irishman*, 8 Mar. 1930.

general workers union, became disaffiliated from the labour party and James Hickey, a member of the union, resigned from the chairmanship of the party's administrative council. The primary cause of the split was an old-standing feud between William O'Brien, general secretary of the I.T. & G.W.U., and James Larkin senior, whose entry into the party and election to the dáil as an official labour candidate had been opposed by the union. Contributory reasons for the dispute were resentment of the union's efforts to secure a preponderating influence in the affairs of the party, divergence of views between the union and the party on a government-sponsored Trade Union Bill and a transport merger, and O'Brien's acceptance of an appointment to the directorate of the Central Bank, the creation of which had been opposed by the party. A further source of friction was introduced by the union's allegation that the administrative council had admitted persons of communist sympathies to membership of the party.[1] Five of the eight labour members in the dáil belonging to the union severed their connexions with the party and formed a new group under the name of the national labour party on 17 February 1944. The group maintained its separate existence until after the formation of the coalition government in which both labour parties participated. The logical outcome of this co-operation was the re-union of the labour movement which was effected in July 1950.

With the decline in the political ferment which had proved fatal to the original farmers' party, farmers, especially the smaller farmers of the west, began to concentrate again on their sectional interests and grievances. At a meeting in Athenry, co. Galway, on 15 August 1938, attended by delegates from counties Clare, Cork, Donegal, Galway, Kerry, Kildare, Leitrim, Longford, Mayo, Monaghan, Roscommon, and Sligo it was decided to found an organization to represent farmers in the dáil. The name given to the party was Clann na Talmhan to which was added, as a subsidiary title, 'the national agricultural party' after a short-lived amalgamation with some independent members representing constituencies in the eastern counties.[2] The programme of the new party included the fostering of rural life by providing rural amenities, the establishment of national schemes of afforestation, drainage, and land reclamation, and the total derating of the first £20 of the poor law valuation on agricultural

---

[1] *The labour party. Official statement relating to the disaffiliation from the labour party of the Irish transport and general workers union* (1944).
[2] *The Book of Clann na Talmhan* (1944); *Irish Press*, 3 Jan. 1948.

land and a further total derating of each additional £15 of the poor law valuation in respect of each adult worker employed on the holding.[1] The party, under the leadership of M. T. Donnellan, won its first electoral success in the general election of 1943.

The most recent addition to the Irish political parties is Clann na Poblachta which was set up after a conference in Dublin on 6 July 1946. The impulse behind this development was provided by the tardy acceptance of constitutional methods by a group of republicans who had persisted in revolutionary action long after the majority of the original republican party had entered the dáil. They now asserted their intention of working 'for the achievement of republican ideals by purely political means'.[2] In addition to the former members of the I.R.A. who constituted the nucleus of the party a number of dissatisfied adherents of Fianna Fáil were won over. The party's programme was designed to have a wide appeal: it aimed at the reintegration of Ireland as an independent democratic republic, free from any external association, save such as might be freely entered into by the nation; at the establishment of a reign of social justice based on Christian principles; at the securing of international recognition for the republic of Ireland; and at the restoration of the Irish language as the spoken language of the people.[3] After winning two by-elections in the autumn of 1947 it contested the general election of 1948 on an extensive scale and won ten seats.

Only the three principal parties are organized on a country-wide basis; and in them—as in the two smaller parties—the general structure is the same. Each is divided into the constituency organization, the central executive, and the parliamentary party, and each has an annual convention in which the various parts are drawn together. The one feature peculiar to the labour party is the provision for corporate members, that is trade unions and analogous bodies affiliated to the party. The basic unit in the Fianna Fáil and Fine Gael parties is the branch or cumann, centred on the parish or polling station district in rural areas and on the urban area or ward in urban areas. Each branch is registered at headquarters on the payment of an annual affiliation fee of at least 10s. in the case of Fianna Fáil and of £1 in the case of Fine Gael. The function of the branch is to maintain the machinery necessary for fighting an election, to recruit supporters, to raise funds, and to keep the central organization informed of local

[1] *Clann na Talmhan Rules Book.*   [2] *Irish Times,* 7 July 1946.
[3] *Clann na Poblachta Constitution.*

sentiment. The number of branches in the Fianna Fáil party in 1949 was 1,530 and in the Fine Gael party in 1950 just over 1,000. A branch of the labour party may be formed in any district with the approval of the administrative council. The affiliation fee is fixed at £1 if the membership of the branch does not exceed fifty with an additional 10*s.* for each additional fifty members. In the Fianna Fáil party two delegates are selected by each branch to serve on the cómhairle ceanntair which functions in each county electoral area. The corresponding organization in the Fine Gael party is the district executive which is made up of three delegates from each branch and all party members in the area who are county or urban councillors or who are members of corporations or town commissioners. In both parties three additional members may be co-opted. These organizations coordinate and stimulate the activities of the branches in their districts and, in the Fianna Fáil party, arrange conventions for the selection of candidates for local government boards. Next in the hierarchy comes the constituency executive which, in the Fianna Fáil party, consists of three delegates from each cómhairle ceanntair in the constituency, the dáil deputies for the constituency, the constituency delegate to the national executive, and not more than three co-opted members. The Fine Gael constituency executive is made up of the party deputies, the senators, councillors, and town commissioners in the constituency; two delegates from each district executive; and two members nominated by the national council. The constituency executive carries on propaganda and supervises the activities of the subordinate bodies. It summons conventions for the selection of candidates for dáil elections—in the Fine Gael party for the selection of local government election candidates as well—and it is responsible for the conduct of election contests. In the labour party the standard constituency organization is the constituency council, but whenever it is considered necessary the administrative council may establish two or more divisional councils in the area. These bodies are responsible for the selection of candidates for local government elections. The constituency council is empowered to appoint a constituency executive and, in conjunction with one or more councils in adjacent areas, to form a regional executive consisting of not more than four delegates from each constituency council. The supreme governing body in the Fine Gael and Fianna Fáil parties is the annual árd-fheis or convention which is composed of the central executive, the party's deputies, and representatives of the local organizations. In the interval between meetings of the árd-fheis its powers are delegated to a permanent body entitled the national executive in the Fianna Fáil party and the national council in the Fine Gael party. The national executive of Fianna Fáil is made up of the office holders; a committee of fifteen members elected by the árd-fheis; one delegate from each dáil constituency or, where two counties are comprised in one constituency, one delegate from each county; and five co-opted members. The national council of Fine Gael consists of the office holders; one representative nominated by each county or constituency executive, whichever is the smaller; and not more than ten members nominated by the president of the party. These bodies remain in existence for a year; they hold frequent meetings; and they direct the work of the paid officials in the party headquarters. The ultimate control of the labour party is vested in the national conference which consists of delegates appointed by branches and corporate members in proportion to their membership; of one delegate from each constituency council, divisional council, and regional executive; and of the members of the administrative council who have the right to speak but not to vote. The members of the labour party in the oireachtas may attend the national conference but only those of them who are also delegates have the right to vote. As in the other parties the powers of the national conference are exercised throughout the year by a permanent body styled the administrative council which is composed of the office holders, the chairman of the labour party in the dáil, two members of the party in the oireachtas elected by the parliamentary party, and fifteen ordinary members, drawn from Dublin and the four provinces, elected by the national conference.

The importance of the local bodies and the dependence of the Irish parties on voluntary workers is revealed by the smallness of the permanent paid staff in the headquarters of the parties.[1] Paid organizers have been employed by the Fine Gael and labour parties but the Fianna Fáil party dispensed with full-time organizers once the party had been well established. A resolution before the Fianna Fáil árdfheis of 1950 calling for the appointment of whole-time organizers was rejected.

Each party in the dáil has its chairman and whips. Regular meetings are held and party discipline is strictly enforced. No back-bench movement has ever developed; if a deputy departs from the party line he is expelled: Belton was expelled from the Fianna Fáil party in

[1] The Fianna Fáil party has a staff of five.

1927 for entering the dáil at a time when the party policy was to abstain;[1] and Morrissey and Anthony were expelled from the labour party for voting for the Military Tribunal Bill in 1931.[2] The rigidity of the party system has led each side in the dáil to apply to its opponents such expressions as 'a mere registering machine', 'a voting machine', or 'dumb driven cattle'.[3] The party in the dáil is linked to the organizations outside by its membership of the central executive and its representation on the constituency executives. But apart from this deputies are brought into contact with the central office and the constituencies. They are expected to assist in collecting funds and in maintaining the efficiency of the party organization in the constituencies. They must expound the party's policy at public meetings and they are called upon to act as ambassadors in Dublin for their constituencies. This last aspect of a deputy's work has come in for a good deal of criticism in the dáil. It is felt that importuning of government departments by deputies on behalf of their constituents is undesirable.[4] Efforts have been made to check the practice, but it has become so deeply rooted that they have not met with much success.[5]

Party funds are derived from affiliation fees, from subscriptions, collections, and the proceeds of specially arranged social functions. In the main parties each deputy and senator is required to subscribe a fixed amount monthly to the party funds. To fight the general elections of 1927 the Fianna Fáil party drew substantial sums from America,[6] but its principal source of income since has been from a collection made at the church gates on a certain Sunday each year. The total of this national collection in 1949 amounted to £11,951. Fine Gael has recently adopted the same practice. Labour also makes a national collection but it has the additional advantage of the trades unions' financial support.

Each of the principal parties is alive to the advantage of possessing a party newspaper. Fine Gael and its predecessor Cumann na nGaedheal have had a succession of small weekly or monthly papers: *The Freeman, The Star, The United Irishman, Forum*, and *The Fine Gael Digest*. Similarly the labour party has been responsible for such periodicals as *The Irishman, Watchword, Labour News, Torch, The*

---

[1] *Irish Times*, 1 Aug. 1927.   [2] O'Sullivan, op. cit., p. 262.
[3] *Dáil Debates*, iv. 839; xxi. 1909; xli. 806.
[4] Ibid. xcii. 1217; ci. 132–4; *Report of Commission on Vocational Organization, 1943*, p. 341.
[5] *Dáil Debates*, civ. 1851; *Senate Debates*, xxxiv. 268.
[6] *Irish Times*, 5 Sept. 1927; *Dáil Debates*, lxvii. 383.

Irish People, and *The Citizen*. Fianna Fáil was served at first by a weekly called *The Nation*, but with the founding of the *Irish Press* in September 1931 it secured the backing of a national daily newspaper. A monthly *Bulletin* printed for circulation to branches between 1934 and 1941 has recently been resumed under the title *Gléas*.

It remains to inquire into the social and geographical divisions reflected in the Irish political parties. Originally, the social division between the two principal parties was more clear cut than it is today. The pro-treaty party which stood for peace and ordered government won the support of the conservative, propertied class in the country: the large farmers, the leaders in industry and commerce, and the well-established professional men. The anti-treaty party relied chiefly on the small farmers, the shopkeepers, and sections of the artisan and labourer classes. But when the anti-treaty party adopted constitutional methods and formulated a political and economic programme of such wide appeal that it rapidly became the largest party in the state, secure in the support of a new propertied class, the old divisions were notably weakened. An occupational analysis of the party members elected to the dáil up to 1948 provides a fairly reliable guide to the sources of each party's strength. From the formation of their respective parties to 1948 there were 161 Cumann na nGaedheal or Fine Gael, 157 Fianna Fáil, and 52 labour deputies. These were distributed occupationally in the following way:

Occupation of Members in Three Main Parties

A. *Professional Occupations*

	Cumann na nGaedheal Fine Gael	Fianna Fáil	Labour
Barristers	14+5*	6	..
Solicitors	8	8	1
Medical doctors	7	9	..
Veterinary surgeon	1	..	..
Engineers	1	3	..
University teachers	6	..	..
Other teachers	5	15	2
Journalists	5	2	..
Accountants	2	..	..
Total number	49	43	3
Percentage of party membership	30	27	6

* Indicates members who qualify for inclusion under this heading although they were principally engaged in some other occupation.

B. Commercial, Finance, and Insurance occupations

Company directors	8	5	..
Shopkeepers	26	19	..
Chemist	..	1	..
Publicans	6	3	1
Agent	1	..	..
Commercial travellers	..	2	..
Shop assistant	..	1	..
Cattle dealer	..	1	..
Cattle salesmen	2	..	..
Auctioneers	2+1*	1	..
Insurance officials	0+1*	2	1
Total number	45	35	2
Percentage of party membership	28	22	4

C. Agricultural Occupations

Farmers	40+20*	48+6*	1+1*
Percentage of party membership	25	31	2

D. Miscellaneous Occupations

Secretaries of trade or other association	1	3	..
Trade Union officials	..	..	26
Clerks	1	1	5
Local government employees	2+1*	3+1*	..
Hospital official	..	1	..
Building contractors	7	3	..
Hotel proprietors	2	0+1*	..
Cinema proprietor	..	1	..
Bookmaker	..	1	..
Foundry owners or managers	1	1	..
Carpenter or cabinet maker	..	..	1
Coachbuilders	1	2	..
Upholsterer	1	..	..
Bricklayers	1	..	1
Tailors	..	1	1
Compositors	..	1	1
Bookbinder	..	..	1
Harness maker	..	..	1
Employee of Electricity Supply Board	..	..	1
Railway employees	..	..	2
Mill operatives	..	..	3
Labourers	..	..	3
Total number	17	18	46
Percentage of party membership	11	11	88

* Indicates members who qualify for inclusion under this heading although they were principally engaged in some other occupation.

E. Unclassified

Total number . . .	10	13	..
Percentage of party membership	6	8	..

It will be seen that there is no pronounced difference in the occupational composition of the two main parties. Cumann na nGaedheal–Fine Gael has a slight lead in the professional and commercial groups and Fianna Fáil in the agricultural group. But Cumann na nGaedheal–Fine Gael has had a larger number of members who carried on farming in addition to their principal occupation; it has had many more barristers among its members; and of its eleven teacher members six have been university teachers, a group unrepresented among the Fianna Fáil members. In the absence of statistics for the entire party membership any conclusion must perforce be tentative, but it is probably safe to say that Fine Gael is still, in the main, the party of wealth, property, and position and that Fianna Fáil draws its support from a wider circle. In a country where social divisions are neither sharp nor rigid a social cleavage is not to be expected, especially between parties which were originally aspects of a single party. One revealing contrast between the parties is the number of protestant members in each. There were nine protestants among the Fine Gael deputies as against two among the Fianna Fáil. Since the major part of the protestant population favoured the maintenance of the Commonwealth link it is natural to find a higher proportion of protestants in the party, which, until 1948, stood for co-operation with the Commonwealth. On the other hand it should be noted that Fianna Fáil has had continuously from 1927 the only Jew in the dáil; and that its national executive in 1954 included an ex-moderator of the presbyterian church, an anglican, and a methodist.

The other parties are more purely sectional. All the deputies in the old farmers' party and in Clann na Talmhan have been connected with agriculture, but neither party succeeded in attracting more than a small proportion of the total farming community. The treaty issue dominated Irish politics so completely in the early days of the state that many potential supporters of the farmers' party were lost to the two parties primarily concerned in the contest. Now that these parties have become firmly established on a basis, largely, of agricultural support it is doubtful if there is room for a separate farmers' party.

The Irish labour party has suffered from the same circumstances and from the preponderantly agricultural economy of the country. The urban industrial population which forms the backbone of labour parties elsewhere is comparatively small in Ireland and, as the election results for the city of Dublin reveal, the labour party has not succeeded in winning the full support of what industrial population there is. Moreover, unlike the British labour party, it has not secured the backing of any considerable section of the middle class, with the result that it has remained a relatively small party. The occupational analysis of the party members who have been elected to the dáil shows the extent to which it is the party of the organized workers.

There is more homogeneity in the labour party than in the two major parties. Fifty per cent. of the members have been trade union officials and most of the others have followed occupations which are organized in trade unions. The professions are meagrely represented. In the two larger parties farmers and shopkeepers figure prominently —41 per cent. in Fine Gael and 43 per cent. in Fianna Fáil; in the labour party they are significantly absent. When this occupational analysis is taken in conjunction with the geographical distribution it is clear that the main strength of the party lies in the support of the small farmers and agricultural labourers.

An examination of the geographical distribution of the parties is complicated by the existence of proportional representation, by the revisions of the constituencies, and by the fluctuations in party strengths. The maps[1] show the strength of the three principal parties measured by the number of first preference votes cast at the general elections following on the original demarcation and the two revisions of the constituencies. These maps, on the whole, confirm the impression gathered from the occupational analysis of party members in the dáil. It is clear from them that the two large parties have drawn support from widely scattered areas in the country. There are few constituencies that can be regarded as special strongholds of one party. In 1923 the republicans were stronger in the west than in the east or south but Cumann na nGaedheal also had strong support in the west and pockets of weakness in the east and south. Cumann na nGaedheal was stronger than its principal rival in the border counties, and in the county and city of Dublin it far outstripped the other parties. This geographical distribution is consonant with the social divisions in the state.[2] The maps for 1937 and 1948 show

---

[1] See Appendix. [2] By 1937 Fianna Fáil had become the largest party in the state.

that its support was no more drawn from one area than from one class in the country. The corresponding maps for Fine Gael reflect the declining fortunes of the party. In 1937 its main centres lay in the east and south where the large graziers, the strongest opponents of Fianna Fáil, were to be found. By 1948 when the party was at a low ebb the main areas of support had shrunk to the south-east and north-west, with two isolated districts on the east coast. In the course of this period a change had come over the distribution of parties in the city of Dublin. Fine Gael lost its preponderance to Fianna Fáil and its strength became concentrated in the southern half of the city. The maps showing the distribution of the labour party are equally revealing. Its failure to win the support of the urban working class is clearly illustrated by the maps of Dublin city, and the fact that its strength has always lain in the southern half of the country bears out the contention that it relies mainly on the rural working class.

IX

THE MECHANISM OF THE DÁIL

THE two houses of the oireachtas hold their meetings in Leinster House, Dublin, an eighteenth-century mansion that was once the town residence of the dukes of Leinster. When the independent state came into being it was the headquarters of the Royal Dublin Society. Just before the provisional parliament was due to meet in September 1922 the Royal Dublin Society offered to provide temporary accommodation at Leinster House. The Free State constitution contained a provision—which has been repeated in the new constitution—that the houses of the oireachtas should sit in or near the city of Dublin or in such other place as they might determine.[1] Once the constitution had been enacted the immediate problem was to find a temporary home for the oireachtas pending the erection of a parliament house. Four buildings were considered: the head office of the Bank of Ireland which had been the meeting place of the eighteenth-century Irish parliament; the Royal Hospital, Kilmainham; Dublin Castle; and Leinster House. In addition, a proposal to erect a temporary building on Leinster Lawn or Merrion Square was put forward. A joint committee set up to consider the matter reported in favour of Leinster House[2] which was accordingly taken over from the Royal Dublin Society on the payment of a sum of £68,000. Since then approximately £70,000 has been expended on structural alterations. The project of a new building has been shelved.[3]

The constitution of the Irish Free State provided that the oireachtas was to be summoned and dissolved by the representative of the crown. It was to hold at least one session each year and the date of the reassembly and the conclusion of each session was to be fixed by the dáil subject to the proviso that a session of the senate was not to be concluded without its consent. A week after the constitution came into operation the governor-general attended in state a joint meeting of the houses and outlined the government's legislative proposals in

---

[1] *Constitution of I.F.S.*, art. 13; *Constitution of Ireland*, art. 15. 1. 3.
[2] *Dáil Debates*, iv. 1550, 1560–70, 1993; vi. 564–99, 2139–55, 2899–2981; vii. 2941–50; viii. 911–35.
[3] Ibid. cii. 320.

his address. A similar ceremony was held when the dáil reassembled after the general election of 1923,[1] but that was the last occasion on which the governor-general appeared before the oireachtas. In view of the feeling in the country it is more surprising that this dominion practice was ever adopted than that it was abandoned so quickly. The cessation of formal openings had two practical effects on the working of the dáil: there was no longer any opportunity for a statement in the dáil of the government's programme; and there was no occasion for marking off sessions by prorogations. Since 1923 each new dáil has met without any formality other than the reading by the clerk of the proclamation relating to its summons and of his report on the issue of writs and the returns. What constitutes a session has never been clearly defined. The use of the term in standing orders implies that it is a period coterminous with the life of the dáil[2] but in the 1937 constitution the word is used to mean a single sitting[3]. Until 1933 members were required to subscribe to the parliamentary oath set forth in the constitution before taking their seats; since the abolition of the oath they have merely to sign the roll of members.

The first business of a newly-elected dáil is the selection of the ceann cómhairle or chairman. To begin with the current British practice was followed. When the dáil met after the enactment of the constitution Michael Hayes, a member of the pro-treaty party, was proposed by William T. Cosgrave and seconded by the leader of the opposition.[4] This procedure was repeated and Hayes was re-elected until after the general election of September 1927 when, although Hayes was elected unopposed, his nomination was not seconded by the leader of the new opposition party, Fianna Fáil. In the next dáil (1932) the Fianna Fáil party, now in a majority, nominated Frank Fahy, a member of the party. Hayes was also nominated by his party and Fahy was elected by a majority vote.[5] From this time until his retirement in 1951 Fahy was re-elected unopposed at the opening of each new dáil although his nomination was not seconded by the leader of the opposition until 1944. No attempt was made to oust him when his party lost its majority in 1948. This forbearance was not wholly altruistic; with his narrow majority the new taoiseach could ill afford a member from his own side of the house for the office. When Fahy had intimated his intention not to accept re-election in 1951 the taoiseach nominated a

[1] *Dáil Debates*, ii. 97–106; v. Appendix. [2] S.O. 20, 101.
[3] *Constitution of Ireland*, art. 15. 7.
[4] *Dáil Debates*, ii. 4. [5] Ibid. xli. 19.

labour deputy, Patrick Hogan, who had served as deputy chairman in five dáils. He was elected unopposed after his nomination had been seconded by the leader of Clann na Talmhan and endorsed by the leader of Fianna Fáil.[1] While the evidence is not extensive enough to justify sweeping generalizations it points to the fact that the chairmanship of the dáil has not become a party perquisite. In contrast to the practice at Westminster where since 1801 a retiring speaker has always withdrawn from politics both Hayes and Fahy continued to be active members of the dáil after their relinquishment of the chair. Until 1927 the speaker of an outgoing dáil had to contest a constituency in a general election. In that year a Constitution Amendment Act declared that a speaker who was willing to accept office again would be automatically re-elected to the dáil for the constituency he had represented before.

Although the ceann cómhairle was to begin with a party nominee he was required to act as an impartial chairman of the dáil. A standing order closes the office to any minister or parliamentary secretary.[2] He does not take part in debates and he has no deliberative vote. In the event of an equal division of the house he possesses a casting vote which is exercised on the principle of maintaining the *status quo* or providing an opportunity for a review by the house. Only when these principles did not apply would the ceann cómhairle vote according to his interpretation of the merits. On the two occasions on which the ceann cómhairle was called upon to give his casting vote he acted on these principles. The first was in 1923 when the dáil was equally divided on the question of paying compensation to the potato growers of north Louth for the loss of their crops. He gave his vote against the proposal on the ground that a motion calling for the expenditure of public funds ought to command a majority in the dáil independent of the chairman's vote.[3] The second occasion was in August 1927 when the labour vote of censure on the government resulted in an equal division. The ceann cómhairle held that his vote against the motion was justified because a vote of censure which would involve the fall of the government should be carried by a majority of members and not by the casting vote of the chairman.[4] On another occasion the leas-cheann cómhairle acted on the same principles. A tie occurred in 1934 on an amendment to the bill for the revision of the constituencies. The leas-cheann cómhairle voted for

[1] *Irish Times*, 14 June 1951. [2] S.O. 14.
[3] *Dáil Debates*, ii. 1331. [4] Ibid. xx. 1749.

the amendment in order to give the house a further opportunity of considering the matter.[1]

The ceann cómhairle thus bears a closer resemblance to the speaker of the House of Commons than to the speaker of a dominion parliament. In Canada the office is often a stepping-stone to a ministerial post, with the result that the Canadian speaker is unwilling to sever connexions with his party. In New Zealand the speaker refrains from political activity during his term of office, but there have been instances of a speaker voting as a private member in committee in support of the government that nominated him. The speakers in the Australian legislatures remain active politicians and are expected to serve the interests of their party.

The ceann cómhairle's function is to preside over the house, call members who wish to speak, enforce the rules of debate, and maintain order. He puts questions and announces the decision of the house. The closure can only be applied when he is in the chair and he has the right to refuse a motion of closure if he considers that the question has not been adequately discussed. It is his duty to certify a money bill as such. Unlike the speaker of the House of Commons the ceann cómhairle presides over committees of the whole house. There is no ceremonial of any kind attached to the office, and it was not until 1946 that the ceann cómhairle was provided with a gown.[2]

The vice-chairman or leas-cheann cómhairle is elected by the house and holds office for the whole term of the dáil. He acts as the ceann cómhairle's deputy and he also supervises the proceedings relating to private bills. When he is not in the chair he reverts to his ordinary duties as a member. Following on the recommendation of the committee on procedure and privileges in 1928[3] the convention has become established that the leas-cheann cómhairle, in his capacity as a private member, does not initiate debates on controversial topics. The office has been filled, in the main, by members drawn from the parties in opposition and it has usually been held for fairly long periods by the same individuals. The ceann cómhairle is empowered by standing orders to nominate a panel of members from which a temporary chairman may be drawn when necessary.[4]

---

[1] *Dáil Debates*, lii. 277–9, 361.
[2] *Report of Committee on Procedure and Privileges re Wearing of Gown by Ceann Cómhairle*, 25 June 1946.
[3] *Second Report of the Committee on Procedure and Privileges. Office of Leas-cheann Cómhairle*, 20 Apr. 1928.
[4] S.O. 15.

The Mechanism of the Dáil

The other officers of the house are the clerk and the assistant clerk who are appointed by the taoiseach on the nomination of the ceann cómhairle and the minister for finance. The superintendent, the captain of the guard, and the librarian, who are officers common to both houses, are appointed by the taoiseach on the recommendation of a committee consisting of the chairman of each house and the minister for finance. The functions of the clerks are to attend in the house and to compile official minutes of proceedings. They also advise the chairman on any matter of procedure which may arise. The superintendent and the captain of the guard are responsible for the maintenance of order in the houses and their precincts and for the general supervision of matters relating to the upkeep of the parliamentary buildings. The librarian controls the library and reading rooms and discharges all duties connected with papers laid on the tables of the houses.

Regulations of the house are based on provisions of the constitution and on standing orders, supplemented by rulings from the chair and by minutes of the committee on procedure and privileges. When the dáil is in session it normally meets on Tuesday, Wednesday, and Thursday at 3 p.m. and on Friday at 10.30 a.m. On the first three days it adjourns not later than 11 p.m. and on Friday not later than 2.30 p.m. The last half-hour on each day is set aside for the adjournment debate in which a member can bring up for discussion, with the approval of the chair, any matter of which he has given notice.[1] The quorum necessary to constitute a meeting of the dáil is twenty members.[2] If attention is drawn by any member to the fact that a quorum is not present, or if on the result of a division the absence of a quorum is revealed, the bells are rung and if, after an interval of three minutes, a quorum is still not present the chairman must suspend the meeting to a later hour or adjourn the house until the next sitting day.[3] There is no period, as in the House of Commons, when a count cannot be demanded. Since 1932 the proceedings have been opened by prayer.[4] Every sitting of the house is governed by a printed order paper which is prepared under the direction of the ceann cómhairle. The taoiseach determines the order in which government business appears and the order in which it will be taken is announced by a minister at the beginning of business each day.[5] Business is normally taken in the following order: questions, private business, public business, and private members' business. On three days a week an hour is set aside

---

[1] S.O. 20.   [2] S.O. 18.   [3] S.O. 19.   [4] S.O. 23.
[5] Malone, *Notes on Procedure in the Oireachtas*, p. 35.

for questions to ministers. They must relate to public affairs connected with the minister's department or to matters of administration for which he is officially responsible.[1] The minister's reply is not open to debate but should the questioner be dissatisfied he may raise the matter for further discussion on the motion for the adjournment of the house.[2] The extent to which members avail themselves of this procedure for eliciting information is revealed by the following table.

Year	Total number of questions asked	Year	Total number of questions asked
1923	394	1936	1,093
1924	2,106	1937	1,358
1925	1,113	1938	934
1926	1,089	1939	1,045
1927	784	1940	710
1928	1,778	1941	1,420
1929	1,184	1942	1,422
1930	826	1943	1,240
1931	1,169	1944	1,291
1932	701	1945	1,332
1933	926	1946	1,748
1934	1,030	1947	2,117
1935	1,406	1948	2,653

Private business is concerned with private bills which are bills promoted by outside bodies for the particular interest or benefit of any person or locality. They are governed by joint standing orders of both houses which provide that they must originate in the senate where the first and second stages are taken. After the second stage a resolution referring the bill to a joint committee of both houses is passed and the concurrence of the dáil to the resolution is asked. If the dáil agrees the passage of a similar resolution is regarded as signifying the dáil's approval of the bill in principle. It is next considered by the joint committee which is empowered to take evidence, to hear counsel on behalf of the promoters and objectors, and to make amendments. The fourth and fifth stages are then taken in the senate and the bill is sent to the dáil where it comes up for fourth stage, the other stages being waived. The passage of the bill by the dáil leads to its enactment.[3]

An hour-and-a-half on Wednesdays and two hours on Fridays are available for bills and motions by private members but the government may appropriate a part or whole of this time for its own business.[4] Normally from Easter until the summer recess the government

[1] S.O. 31.
[2] Malone, op. cit., p. 87.
[3] Ibid., pp. 40, 49.
[4] S.O. 80.

requires the whole of private members' time for financial business. The time allowed for debate on a motion proposed by a private member, other than a motion relating to any stage of a bill, is three hours.[1] Public bills promoted by private members are known as private members' bills. Standing orders prescribe that they should be referred to a select or special committee after passing the second stage.[2]

The remainder of the dáil's time is at the disposal of the government for the conduct of public business. The procedure on public bills is similar to the practice of the House of Commons. On the first stage leave is sought to introduce the bill. No debate is permitted but if the bill is opposed an opposition member may state the objections to it. If the dáil accepts the bill on its first stage the date for the second stage is fixed, sufficient time being allowed for deputies to study the measure. On the second stage the debate is confined to the general principle of the bill. Members may speak once only but the minister responsible for the bill is allowed to conclude the debate. The third stage is the committee stage. Practically all bills are referred to a committee of the whole house; bills are rarely referred to special committees. In committee the bill is considered in detail section by section, and amendments are debated. Discussions in committee are less formal than debates in the house; motions need not be seconded and members may speak more than once. When the committee stage is completed the measure is reported to the dáil. Unless a bill is recommitted to a committee the report or fourth stage follows, usually after an interval in which, if it is a government bill, the minister in charge has an opportunity of considering suggestions made in committee and of having the amendments he has accepted in principle put into proper form. It is open to any member to put down amendments on the fourth stage but no amendment previously rejected in committee of the whole house is in order. The fourth stage is, in fact, a revision of the work of the third stage but sections are not considered separately—discussion takes place only on definite amendments arising out of the committee procedure—and members may not speak more than once on each amendment. On the fifth stage, which corresponds to the British third reading, only amendments of a purely verbal nature may be offered. When the bill has passed the fifth stage it is transmitted to the senate where the procedure on the stages—other than the first which is omitted—is similar. Amendments made by the senate are considered by the dáil in committee.[3] After being

[1] S.O. 83.   [2] S.O. 81.   [3] S.O. 130.

passed by the two houses the bill is presented by the taoiseach to the president for his signature and for promulgation by him as law.[1]

A different procedure is laid down in standing orders for the treatment of hybrid and consolidation bills. A hybrid bill is a public bill affecting private interests.[2] As in the case of a private bill preliminary notice by advertisement is required before introduction. Otherwise the bill follows public bill procedure except that the committee stage in the house where it originates is replaced by a joint committee before which counsel on behalf of petitioners may appear and evidence is taken.[3] The procedure on consolidation bills was adopted by both houses on the report of a joint committee in 1946. A consolidation bill is a bill to consolidate existing statute law on a particular subject-matter and it must be certified by the attorney-general not to contain substantive amendment of the law. Amendments on the second stage are restricted to forms in challenge of the attorney-general's certificate. When the bill has been read a second time it is normally referred for committee stage to a standing joint committee of both houses on consolidation bills which can take evidence, but which cannot make amendments except of a consolidating nature. Amendments on the remaining stages are similarly restricted. When the bill has passed in the originating house all stages preceding the fourth stage are waived in the other house and amendments are restricted as in the joint committee.[4]

The form in which a bill is presented is governed by the general requirements as to the form of the resulting statute prescribed in the Interpretation Act, 1927. This act provides that all acts of parliament shall be divided into sections numbered consecutively; that these sections may be subdivided as is convenient; that the sections may be grouped into parts or chapters; and that the acts shall be capable of being cited by their short titles. Standing orders relating to the detailed consideration of bills presume that bills follow a standard pattern: a long title, a preamble (if desired), consecutively numbered sections, and schedules as requisite. The form of bills is thus the same as in the British parliament except that in the Irish parliament the enacting formula is, 'Be it enacted by the oireachtas as follows'. There is a parliamentary draftsman and drafting staff in the office of the attorney-general but they are concerned only with government bills.[5]

[1] S.O. 85–100; Malone, op. cit., pp. 40–47; Bryan R. Cooper, 'Procedure of Dáil', in *The Freeman*, 31 Mar. 1928.   [2] S.O. 103.
[3] Malone, op. cit., p. 50.   [4] S.O. 104–14; Malone, op. cit., pp. 52–53.
[5] Ibid., pp. 41–42, 52.

Since there is nothing in the Irish parliament corresponding to the British and dominion system of prorogation the concluding sitting in any calendar year does not terminate proceedings. Bills may be taken up in the following year at the stage they had reached. A dissolution of the dáil, however, has in practice been treated as putting an end to all current proceedings in the house.[1]

The procedure by which the dáil exercises its financial control is also modelled on the British, though it differs at certain points. Its work falls into two compartments: the control of taxation and the control of expenditure. A motion to impose a charge on the people can only be made by a member of the government in a committee of the whole house called a committee on finance. The financial year runs from 1 April to 31 March. Early in the financial year, usually in May, the minister for finance makes the budgetary statement when presenting his taxation proposals for the year. He first gives an exhaustive review of the financial position as a whole, including an account of savings effected in the year's expenditure and of new expenditure about to be incurred as a result of changes of policy outlined in the statement. He then submits a number of financial resolutions for imposing new taxes or altering existing ones. Under the provisions of the Provisional Collection of Taxes Act, 1927, these resolutions have immediate statutory effect when passed by the committee on finance and, provided certain conditions are fulfilled, they may remain operative for a period of four months. Owing to the urgency of the situation the bulk of the motions are passed with little or no discussion though, when the first has been moved, leaders of all opposition parties may, and generally do, make short statements on the budget. It is customary for the last motion to be of a general character and on it the general debate on the budget takes place. When the resolutions have been carried in committee they are considered on report. At this stage members may put down amendments to resolutions in order to reduce, but not to increase, any of the proposed new taxes. Taxes which are already in force cannot be dealt with at this stage except those which require renewal annually. When the report stage has been completed the Finance Bill is introduced. Its purpose is to give continuing effect to the provisions of the financial resolutions, and the opportunity is usually taken to settle other outstanding financial matters not requiring financial resolutions. The second stage of the Finance Bill furnishes another opportunity for

[1] S.O. 102; Malone, op. cit., pp. 32–33.

debating the whole scheme of government finance. On the committee stage it is possible to deal with existing taxation. After the committee stage the Finance Bill passes through the usual report and final stages and is submitted to the senate which has powers of recommendation only.[1]

All grants of money for supply must be considered by the dáil before they can be paid. There are, however, certain annually recurring payments such as the salaries of judges and interest on national loans which are paid out of the central fund. This fund corresponds to the consolidated fund in Great Britain. Into it all receipts of the state from taxation and other sources are paid and from it all state expenditure is met. But only in the case of a limited number of services can payment be made from it without annual voting. The proposals of the government for the outlay necessary for carrying on the work of the state come before the dáil in the form of estimates for public services which are prepared in great detail by the departments concerned in the autumn and presented some time before the opening of the financial year. In addition, before the budget is introduced, a comparative table is presented showing on the expenditure side the bulk sums represented by the estimates plus expenditure not subject to annual review which is charged directly on the central fund by statute; and showing on the revenue side the estimated yield in the current year of each category of permanent or semi-permanent taxes. Finally, in conjunction with the budgetary statement, a table is presented showing the effects on the previous position of any proposed increases or reductions of taxation and of any new schemes involving expenditure. Each estimate is discussed in committee on finance. Amendments of two kinds may be moved. If exception is taken to the whole character of the expenditure or to the general policy of the department concerned a deputy may move that the vote be referred back for further consideration. If the objection is to one particular item a deputy may move that the vote be reduced by a certain sum in respect of that sub-heading. When all the estimates have been considered and passed the Appropriation Bill is brought in authorizing the issue of the amounts voted from the central fund. This bill passes through all the stages of an ordinary bill and on its second stage the whole expenditure policy of the government can be discussed again.[2]

[1] S.O. 115–16; Malone, op. cit., pp. 74–79; Cooper, 'Procedure of Dáil', in *The Freeman*, 7 Apr. 1928.
[2] S.O. 117–21; Malone, op. cit., pp. 75–83; Cooper, 'Procedure of Dáil', in *The Freeman*, 14 Apr. 1928.

A further check on expenditure is provided in the reports of the comptroller and auditor-general, a constitutional officer appointed by the president on the nomination of the dáil. His function is to control all disbursements and to audit all moneys administered by or under the authority of the oireachtas. The audited accounts, together with the reports of the comptroller and auditor-general, are referred for examination to a committee of the dáil known as the committee of public accounts. It presents to the dáil periodical reports on the results of its examination which are printed and published.[1] To enable the supply services to be carried on while the individual estimates are being discussed in detail by the dáil a vote on account granting supply for four months is passed before the conclusion of the preceding financial year and given legislative effect in the Central Fund Act.[2] To provide for additional expenditure not included in the budget but rendered necessary by new legislation passed during the year or by administrative exigencies, additional or supplementary estimates may be submitted. They are given legal sanction by the next ensuing Central Fund or Appropriation Act.

The bulk of the committee work in the dáil is performed by committees of the whole dáil—the house itself acting as a committee. In this respect the dáil resembles the New Zealand House of Representatives where all bills are dealt with in committee of the whole house and the Australian legislatures where standing or select committees are sparingly employed. The third stage of practically all bills is taken in committee of the whole dáil, the body which also considers amendments made to bills by the senate and bills returned from such select and joint committees as have been authorized to take evidence. Resolutions dealing with taxation and supply are introduced in a committee of the whole dáil, known on such an occasion as a committee on finance. Other committees, called select and special committees, are set up when the need for them arises. Select committees are established to consider and report on some particular bill or problem. They may be authorized to examine witnesses and records, and they may be linked with similar committees from the senate to form joint committees. Select and joint committees are designed to furnish the dáil with information. Special committees correspond to the British standing committees; they discuss and examine bills on the third stage in the manner normally done by the dáil itself in committee. The dáil possesses, and has on one occasion

---

[1] Malone, op. cit., p. 82.   [2] Ibid., p. 79.

used, the power to order that part of a bill be taken in committee by the whole dáil and the remainder in a special committee. Standing orders lay down that every private member's bill which has passed its second stage must be referred to a select or special committee. In addition to these *ad hoc* committees there are sessional and annual committees. At the beginning of each session the dáil appoints a committee of selection chosen so as to be impartially representative of the house. The function of this body is to nominate the members of select, special, and other committees. The committee on procedure and privileges is also appointed at the beginning of each parliament. It consists of the ceann cómhairle and a varying number of members nominated by the committee of selection. The committee of public accounts is a select committee appointed at the beginning of each financial year to examine and report to the dáil on the accounts showing the appropriation of the money granted by the dáil to meet the public expenditure. The members must not include a member of the government or a parliamentary secretary, and the chairman is always a leading member of the opposition. Joint committees, containing representatives of the dáil and the senate, are constituted to deal with private, hybrid, and consolidation bills and to supervise the oireachtas library and restaurant.[1]

Unlike the House of Commons the dáil does not receive petitions presented either by outside bodies or by members. This was not the practice prior to the coming into operation of the Free State constitution. On 10 January 1922 a delegation from the labour party was permitted to make a statement before the dáil on the economic situation.[2] Since the labour party had refrained from contesting the 1921 general election in order, in part at any rate, to assist Sinn Féin their request could not well be refused. In the following month three deputations sought a hearing before the house. The acting speaker asked for the direction of the dáil. The pro-treaty members were opposed to the admission of any deputations; the other members were in favour of receiving the deputations. Eventually it was decided to receive one—a total abstinence delegation—provided it was the last.[3] The question of petitions was raised again in November 1923 when the corporation of Dublin asked permission for the lord mayor and council to appear before the dáil and present a petition concerning

[1] S.O. 64, 67, 72, 87–93, 115–23; Malone, op. cit., pp. 36–37, 49–50, 52, 57, 99–100, 103.
[2] *Treaty Debate*, p. 391.
[3] *Dáil Official Report, 1921–2*, pp. 103–6.

political prisoners on hunger strike.[1] Dublin had shared with London the privilege of presenting petitions to the House of Commons at the bar of the house. The ceann cómhairle pointed out that this did not necessarily give the corporation the right to appear before the dáil. The matter of petitions was referred to the committee on procedure and privileges which reported that the guarantees contained in the constitution provided ample opportunity for the expression of every point of view held by citizens without the expedient of petitions.[2] No further attempt was made to present ordinary petitions to the dáil.

The rules of debate in the dáil are modelled on those of the House of Commons. Any matter for discussion by the dáil must be brought before it by motion for a resolution or order, or by the introduction of a bill. Such matters as adjournments of the dáil, the appointment of a chairman, and expressions of condolence, censure, thanks, and opinion are dealt with by resolution. The suspension of members, the appointment of committees, the printing of bills and documents, and questions of procedure generally are effected by order. All proposals for legislation are submitted as bills. Except where standing orders prescribe that a question shall be proposed from the chair no debate can take place until a motion has been moved by a member. In the house, but not in committees (including committees of the whole house), motions must be seconded. A motion may be withdrawn by the proposer with the unanimous assent of the dáil. In December 1949 a new precedent was established when the question of withdrawal was pressed to a division. A motion cannot be disposed of by moving the adjournment of the house since all business unfinished at the adjournment stands postponed to the next day. Provision exists in the standing orders for disposing of a motion by means of a motion to proceed to the next business, but this device has not been employed for over twenty years. Amendments to a motion, which must be relevant to the motion and not equivalent to a direct negation, may be submitted two days previous to the debate, and the chairman may accept amendments moved at shorter notice. When a motion has been moved and seconded any amendments which have been offered are moved immediately and the subsequent debate covers both the motion and the amendments. At the conclusion of the debate a decision is taken first on the amendments and then, without further debate, on the original or amended motion. When the question is

---

[1] *Dáil Debates*, v. 998–1003.   [2] Ibid. vi. 1438.

put by the chairman members signify their assent or disapproval by saying ta or nil, the Irish equivalent of yes and no. If the chairman's statement of the result is challenged by at least five members a division is taken, those in favour of the motion passing into the ta lobby on the left of the chair and those against into the nil lobby on the right. As the members pass through the turnstiles their names are recorded by the clerks and they are counted by the tellers who are members of the house nominated by the chair for the purpose of the division. Members must address their speeches to the chairman from their places in the house, standing and, in the case of male members, with heads uncovered. Reading from a prepared text is not permitted though a member of the government may be allowed to read an important statement. There is no time limit to speeches. The selection of speakers is at the discretion of the chairman who favours, first, front bench members on both sides of the house and thereafter members likely to express different points of view. Ordinary members are referred to by name, prefaced by the title deputy; ministers and parliamentary secretaries by the title of the office they hold. A member is described as teachtar dáil and the letters T.D. are used in the same way as M.P. in Great Britain. Questions of relevancy and order are decided by the chairman who may require a member to discontinue his speech, demand the withdrawal of unparliamentary language, order a deputy to leave the house or secure his suspension for a period. In the event of grave disorder the chairman may adjourn the house or suspend the sitting for a time. A debate can be brought to an end by means of a motion for the closure. The form of closure operated in the dáil is the simple closure. Provided that the ceann cómhairle is in the chair any member may move 'That the question be now put'. The ceann cómhairle has power to refuse such a motion if he considers that it is an infringement of the rights of a minority or that the question before the house has not been adequately discussed. If he accepts the closure motion it must be decided without amendment or debate. The dáil standing orders contain provision for what is known as the contingent closure which is designed to dispose of any other question before the house when the simple closure is moved. This provision has never been employed. When it is considered necessary to have the proceedings on a bill restricted other than by simple closure resort is had to closure by compartment, that is the guillotine. The purpose of a guillotine motion is to ensure the completion of the debate on a bill within a certain number of days, and to allocate the time that is to be devoted to the various stages of the bill. The chairman of the dáil has not the power, known as the kangaroo, of selecting amendments to be debated. The closure has been applied infrequently in recent years but it was used in periods of political stress, as the following table shows.[1]

Number of Times Closure Applied

Year	In dáil	In committee
1928	15	1
1929	3	1
1930	1	0
1931	1	1
1932	6	1
1933	6	12
1934	1	5
1935	5	1
1936	1	0
1937	4	0
1938	0	0

The oireachtas is not a bilingual body in the sense that the parliaments of Canada and South Africa are bilingual. The proceedings of the dáil may be conducted either in Irish or in English,[2] but although Irish is described in the constitution as the national and first official language[3] it is little used in the dáil. A very small number of members are competent Irish speakers; of the remainder some understand but do not speak the language and the rest are exclusively English speaking. The result is that even those members who are able to speak in Irish are forced to use English if they wish to be understood by the majority of the members. It is not uncommon to find a member or minister beginning his speech in Irish and then changing to English with some such remark as, 'As I have been saying'. The infrequency with which Irish is spoken in the house has often been deplored by bilingual members, but any attempt to conduct a major debate in Irish is apt to arouse the resentment of the non-Irish speakers. On the other hand the fact that the revival of the national language was one of the most cherished aims of the founders of the state has induced some members to pay lip service to an ideal which they themselves do nothing to promote and has led others to adopt a policy of discreet silence. In an attempt to gauge the amount of Irish

---

[1] S.O. 38–60; Malone, op. cit., pp. 1–26.   [2] S.O. 11.
[3] *Constitution of Ireland*, art. 8. 1.

used in the dáil an analysis has been made of the *Dáil Debates* covering three complete years separated by ten-yearly intervals. In 1926 when the dáil was well established but was still without its complete membership, 0·38 per cent. of the column space in the *Debates* is in Irish; by 1936 the percentage has increased to 0·97 per cent.; and by 1946 to 1·13 per cent. It might be added that the percentage in 1946 would have been much lower but for the fact that one minister introduced the estimates for his department in Irish. In the first year seven members and in each of the other two years eleven members spoke in Irish.[1]

Parliamentary privilege is guaranteed by the constitution. Each house is empowered to make its own rules and standing orders, to ensure freedom of debate, to protect its official documents and the private papers of its members, and to take action against any person molesting or attempting to corrupt its members in the exercise of their duties.[2] Deputies are answerable to the dáil for their conduct in the house, and the dáil has the power to suspend a deputy. Members of the public and representatives of the press are admitted to sittings of the dáil. In a special emergence, however, both may be excluded on the motion of a minister assented to by two-thirds of the members present.[3] Members are guaranteed freedom of speech in the house and are privileged from arrest, except in cases of treason, felony, and breach of the peace.[4] A member may resign by signifying his intention in writing to the ceann cómhairle.[5] An allowance towards expenses of £52 a month free of income tax is paid to members. Though it is styled an allowance this payment is, in the case of some members, the sole source of income.[6] The allowance was originally fixed at £30 a month. In 1938 it was increased to £40 a month and at the same time provision was made for the payment of salaries of £800 and £500 a year to the leader of the largest and second largest opposition parties. Pensions were also provided for ex-ministers who have held office for more than three years. The amount varied from £300 to £500 a year according to the length of service. Like the members' allowances the salaries of the opposition leaders were increased by

---

[1] In 1955, in an effort to encourage the use of Irish in the dáil, the committee on procedure and privileges provided deputies with a list of 150 phrases in English and Irish. It contained such observations as 'Talk sense'; 'That is not the answer to my question'; 'The deputy should withdraw that statement'; and 'What about the election speeches?'

[2] *Constitution of Ireland*, art. 15. 10.   [3] S.O. 73–74.
[4] *Constitution of Ireland*, art. 15. 12.   [5] S.O. 133.
[6] *Dáil Debates*, cvii. 212–14, 359.

30 per cent. in 1947. The ministerial salaries fixed soon after the state came into being remained unaltered until 1947 when they were increased by from 20 to 30 per cent. In addition, members are allowed vouchers entitling them to free first-class rail travel or a mileage allowance if they use their own cars when travelling on business connected with their duties as members between their homes, their constituencies, and the capital.

Attendance of members at meetings of the dáil is not compulsory. It was only after the assassination of the vice-president in 1927 that steps were taken to force the republican abstentionists into the house. Both before and after that date frequent complaints of irregular attendance are found.[1] The suggestion that some sort of attendance register should be kept has been turned down on the ground that the mere signing of a register would not guarantee the presence of a member in the house.[2] Apart from attendance, it is clear that a relatively small proportion of the members participate in debates. In the Free State constitution debate in 1922, for example, there were 34 speakers; on the second stage of the bill to abolish the oath in 1932 there were 54; and on the second stage of the Republic of Ireland Bill in 1948 there were 43. The extent to which private members are active in the house can be measured roughly by analysing the column space devoted to such members in the three volumes of the general index to the *Dáil Debates* covering, respectively, the years 1922–7, 1927–37, and 1937–40. The following table suggests that a high proportion of the private members are seldom heard in the house.

Number of Private Members whose Entries Occupy the Following Number of Columns in the Volumes of the General Index

Volume	Under 1	1–2	2–10	10–20	Over 20
1922–7	51	24	37	10	3
1927–37	69	50	77	14	7
1937–40	59	23	38	3	2

It is well, however, to bear in mind a warning given by Michael Hayes in the senate: 'You can indicate the number of times that a man or woman intervened in formal debate, but there is no method of finding whether he talked sense or nonsense or the extent of his irrelevancy.'[3]

[1] *Dáil Debates*, iv. 579, 838–9; viii. 2288; xi. 2455; xx. 480; xxxiii. 824, 2281; xliv. 1774–5; lxvii. 249, 1336; xciii. 1224; civ. 1862; cviii. 950.
[2] Ibid. cvi. 901.
[3] *Senate Debates*, xxxi. 424.

Irish parliamentary papers, like their British counterpart, may be divided into those connected with its own proceedings issued by the dáil itself, and those presented from outside. To regulate the business of each sitting the dáil issues an order paper which corresponds to the British blue paper and white paper. When the house is in session it is compiled on the conclusion of each sitting in preparation for the next meeting. The dáil order paper is printed on green paper to distinguish it from the senate order paper which is printed on yellow paper. In addition to the business to be taken on the date indicated at the head of the order paper other information of use to members is included. The order paper lists bills in select, special, and joint committees, bills in progress and business ordered and dáil bills with the senate; it gives notice of the place and time of committee meetings; and it records papers which have been laid on the table of the dáil and motions of which notice has been given. Items which are too numerous to be conveniently included in the order paper, such as private members' motions and amendments to bills, may be printed on separate sheets.

The dáil is also responsible for the printing of bills, committee reports, and records of its proceedings. When leave has been given for the introduction of a bill it is printed before being read a second time. The reports of committees are printed on presentation. Minutes of proceedings are kept by the clerk of the dáil and after being read and signed by the ceann cómhairle are printed as the *Journal of the Proceedings of the Dáil*. An official report of each day's debates is also issued under the supervision of the ceann cómhairle. A revised edition of the official report with an index is published in bound volumes. A general index to the debates, covering a period of years, has been published on three occasions.

The great mass of official papers which are laid before the oireachtas falls into two categories, statutory and non-statutory returns. The first comprises all those papers whose submission to the oireachtas is prescribed by statute; the second is made up of papers presented by government departments on their own initiative or by outside bodies.

X

THE DÁIL AND THE SECOND CHAMBER

TWICE in the course of its history the dáil has functioned as a unicameral legislature: during its revolutionary period (1919–21) and for the interval between the abolition of the first senate in 1936 and the creation of the second under the new constitution of 1937. The problem of evolving a satisfactory second chamber was not of course peculiar to Ireland, but the difficulty was accentuated in Ireland by circumstances which aroused considerable prejudice against an upper house. Only when the bitterness engendered by revolution and civil war had begun to subside and when the first senate had been swept away did a more normal relationship develop between the two houses.

The initial mistrust can be attributed in part to general factors militating against the popularity of any second chamber that might have been created, and in part to the origin and nature of the body that was actually constituted. A certain stigma was attached to the senate by reason of the fact that provision had been made for the setting up of conservative, semi-nominated second houses by the Home Rule Act of 1914 and by the Government of Ireland Act, 1920, both of which were obnoxious in all their parts to the men who had successfully carried through the revolution. Moreover, the senate was inevitably regarded by the dáil as something of an interloper. When it came into being the dáil had been in existence for four years; the senate could lay no claim to popular origin or to the glamour of a revolutionary past. The events leading to the establishment of Seanad Éireann did little to commend it to many of the dáil members for it was largely the outcome of an agreement with a group which, rightly or wrongly, was regarded as inimical to the national cause. When the treaty negotiations were going forward in London Griffith discussed the question of safeguards for the unionist minority in the new state with three prominent unionists from the twenty-six counties. These three, Dr. Bernard, provost of Trinity College, Dublin, Andrew Jameson, and the earl of Midleton, argued strongly for a senate. Griffith informed them that he and his colleagues were in favour of a bicameral parliament and promised to consult them about the constitution and powers of the second house when the time came for setting it up.[1] This undertaking was implemented in June 1922 when representatives of the British Government, the Irish provisional government, and the Southern unionists reached an agreement on the nature of the senate which was to be constituted.[2] In thus attempting to reconcile the minority to the new order the architects of the treaty exposed the senate to the hostility of the extreme section of their party. Finally, the composition of the first senate made it suspect in the eyes of the more nationalist-minded members of the dáil. Unlike the dáil which was a democratically elected body the senate was, at the beginning, partially nominated. The great majority of the nominated senators were drawn from the wealthy, privileged class, the old ascendancy, which had been hostile to the revolutionary movement. Eight of them were peers, four baronets, and one a knight; eleven had served in the British army; thirteen had been educated at English public schools or at Oxford, Cambridge, or Trinity College, Dublin. The majority of those senators who had been associated with the nationalist movement in the past had belonged to the constitutional rather than the revolutionary side of it whereas a high proportion of the dáil members had been active participants in the Anglo-Irish war. There was a marked contrast, too, in the religious composition of the two houses: the dáil was a preponderantly catholic body but twenty-four of the sixty original senators were non-catholic. Facts like these, often exaggerated by propagandists, did not make for harmony in an atmosphere charged with resentment and distrust.

The dáil's suspicion of the senate was not the outcome of rivalry for power; there was never any doubt about which was the repository of the sovereign rights of the people. Indeed the unionist signatories of the agreement on the senate expressed dissatisfaction with the result of their efforts,[3] a fact which should have redounded to the advantage of the senate. The committee which was set up to draft the constitution aimed at devising a second chamber with no control over the executive or over administration, with no power to thwart the will of the electorate, and yet with legislative functions sufficiently real to attract capable members.[4] The result was a constitution in which the powers of the senate were severely restricted. All money bills were to originate in the dáil. They were to be sent to the senate which had

---
[1] O'Sullivan, *Irish Free State and its Senate*, p. 75.
[2] Ibid., p. 76.   [3] *Irish Times*, 16 June 1922.
[4] J. G. Douglas, *President de Valera and the Senate*, pp. 18–19.

to return them within twenty-one days with its recommendations. Any or all of these recommendations could be accepted or rejected by the dáil. The senate had no further power over money bills. Bills other than money bills could be introduced in the senate and the senate was able to amend such bills originating in the dáil. Prior to 1928 it could suspend a bill for 270 days but if it rejected a bill, or amended it in a way unacceptable to the dáil, the bill went to the governor-general for the royal assent at the end of the suspensory period, at first without any further action and after 1928 on a resolution of the dáil. A constitutional amendment of 1928 increased the period for which the senate might hold up a non-money bill to eighteen months, with a further sixty days if the bill was presented a second time. But this enlargement of the senate's powers was to some extent counterbalanced by its loss of the right to invoke a referendum. The senate was empowered to request a joint sitting with the dáil to discuss any non-money bill, but as the power of joint voting was not conceded the provision represented no real accession of strength for the senate. A potentially greater power was the senate's right to force a referendum on any bill other than a money bill or a bill declared by both houses to be urgently necessary for the public safety. A majority of the members of the senate could secure the suspension of a bill for ninety days after it had been passed by both houses by presenting a written demand to the president of the executive council within seven days. At any time before the expiration of the suspensory period a referendum on the suspended bill might be demanded by three-fifths of the members of the senate. Indirectly this provision enlarged the senate's power of suspension, for even if a referendum was not demanded the senate, at the end of the 270 days for which it could suspend a bill, could demand the further suspension of ninety days. In the outcome neither the joint sitting nor the referendum was invoked by the senate and both were deleted from the constitution in 1928.

Meantime a more effective means of resolving deadlocks between the houses had been found in conferences which could be requested by either house. The subsidiary role designated for the senate was further revealed in the provisions of the constitution governing the relations of the executive to the legislature. The executive council was to be responsible to the dáil alone and until 1932 senators were excluded from membership of it. Even over the composition of the senate the dáil exercised an effective influence. Half the members of the first senate of the Irish Free State were nominated by the president of the executive council who was himself responsible to the dáil. The remaining thirty were elected by the dáil, voting on principles of proportional representation. Over further senate elections, as originally planned in the constitution, the dail's influence was to be less direct. One-quarter of the original members of the senate were to retire at the end of three years. For the election to fill their places the whole country was to be treated as a single constituency, voting was to be by proportional representation and all citizens over thirty were to be entitled to vote. The fifteen new senators were to be elected from a panel containing three times as many names as there were vacancies to fill (45), plus the names of any former senators who wished to stand again. The forty-five panel candidates were to be nominated, two-thirds by the dáil and one-third by the senate, voting by proportional representation. But this method proved to be so cumbersome when it was employed in 1925 that the constitution was amended on the recommendation of a joint committee. Under the new arrangement senators were elected by the members of the two houses, voting together on the principles of proportional representation, from a panel of names compiled by the two houses. Each house, before a senate election, compiled a list of as many candidates as there were vacancies to fill and these two lists were combined to form the panel.

Apart from the first election in December 1922, when the dáil directly selected half the upper house, there were four elections, at triennial intervals, for the Free State senate: one according to the procedure originally laid down in the constitution and three under the amended system. On each occasion a number of outgoing senators were re-elected, but of the new members the great majority were drawn from the dáil's panels and many of them were former members of the dáil.

The relations between the dáil and the senate of the Irish Free State deteriorated rapidly after the accession of the Fianna Fáil party to power in 1932, but right from the beginning the ministry and the dáil made it clear that they were not prepared to interpret the provisions of the constitution in a generous spirit. The senate was treated as a cooling chamber in which the executive council did not feel the necessity of maintaining a permanent spokesman. Ministers had the right of audience in the senate but they did not always find it convenient to attend, with the result that the business of the house was often held up. It was not until 1930 that the senate adopted a standing order requiring the minister or parliamentary secretary in charge of a bill to open the debate on the second reading in the senate. The absence of ministers also prevented the senate from instituting parliamentary questions as part of its proceedings.[1] Until 1929 senators were excluded from membership of the executive council under the terms of the constitution, but it was quite within the competence of the president to appoint an extern minister or a parliamentary secretary from the upper house. No such appointment was made; and even after the constitutional amendment of 1929 no senator was admitted to the executive council until 1932. In minor ways, too, the inferior status of the senate was emphasized. On the two occasions on which the governor-general addressed the oireachtas the ceremony was held in the chamber of the dáil and the chairman of the dáil presided.[2]

Any attempt on the senate's part to enlarge the scope of its activity was unfavourably received. When it advocated the appointment of a joint standing committee on foreign affairs its message to the dáil was neither discussed nor acknowledged.[3] Its request for the setting up of a joint committee to consider the question of admitting senators to membership of the executive council was rejected by the dáil without a division.[4] Nor did it succeed in persuading the president of the executive council to initiate any of the government's more involved but largely uncontroversial bills in the senate. Cosgrave once announced his intention of adopting this policy but he never carried it out. Instead, the government continued, in spite of the senate's protests, to send up batches of bills which often had to be considered in a very short time. In an effort to check the practice the senate amended its standing orders to provide that three days should elapse between the receipt of a bill from the dáil and its appearance on the order paper and to prevent more than one stage of a bill being taken on the same day. But by having the standing orders suspended the government was still able to rush legislation through the senate.

Prominent ministers made no secret of their belief in the senate's inferiority. Cosgrave himself, when introducing the bill to admit senators to the executive council, showed little enthusiasm for the measure—a fact that did not escape the notice of opposition speakers[5] —and later he proposed an amendment to confine the privilege to

[1] *Senate Debates*, i. 502, 507; ii. 210–14.　　[2] O'Sullivan, op. cit., p. 561.
[3] Ibid., pp. 122–3; *Senate Debates*, iii. 29–44.
[4] O'Sullivan, op. cit., p. 207; *Dáil Debates*, xviii. 1147–70.
[5] Ibid. xxviii. 1291–2.

one senator.[1] When the same topic was under discussion earlier O'Higgins argued that the nature of the senate made its members unsuitable for ministerial office.[2] J. A. Burke sharply criticized the senate for inserting an amendment of a contentious nature in the Local Government Electors Registration Bill in 1923;[3] and Blythe threatened to boycott a special committee which the senate was proposing to set up on the financial agreement with Great Britain in 1926.[4] Some members of the government party went even further. Costello declared that his party held no brief for the senate as it was constituted at the time;[5] McGilligan admitted that the desirability of changing the senate was recognized from the start;[6] and Davis was reported to have said that he would be glad to see the senate abolished.[7]

While the Cosgrave administration remained in office no major conflict developed between the houses. Both were content to accept the position created by the treaty and both were essentially conservative in outlook. The senate exercised its power of suspension on three occasions but the bills concerned did not involve any fundamental question of policy. The numerous amendments inserted in bills were either accepted by the dáil or not insisted upon by the senate. With a change of government in 1932 a clash became inevitable. For one thing, the senate was becoming increasingly a reflection of the dáil. Yet the method of election to it was such that its political complexion did not change as quickly as the dáil's; there was bound to be a hangover from the previous political régime. Even if the political atmosphere had been less highly charged the possibility of a storm might have been forecast. For another, the parties which now controlled the dáil had been consistently hostile to the senate. The labour party had always been opposed to a second chamber of any kind,[8] and the Fianna Fáil party was still far from wholehearted in its acceptance of the dáil let alone the senate. The leaders of the party had lost no opportunity of denouncing the senate; they branded it as an institution designed 'to give political power to a certain class that could not get that power if they had to go before the people at a free election'; as a 'bulwark of imperialism'; as 'a place or state of rest where discredited politicians repose for a time before they go—

[1] *Dáil Debates*, xxviii. 1808.
[2] Ibid. xviii. 1167.
[3] Ibid. vi. 132–3.
[4] *Senate Debates*, viii. 12–62.
[5] *Dáil Debates*, li. 1886.
[6] Ibid. lxvii. 1444.
[7] Ibid. li. 2048.
[8] Ibid. i. 768, 1139–40; ii. 997; li. 1875.

I would not like to say where they go to'; as 'a tame dog, prepared to do anything the executive council orders them to do'.[1] Finally, the new government's policy of loosening the constitutional and economic ties with Great Britain and the Commonwealth and the political unrest into which the country was plunged by the activities of extra-parliamentary political organizations created the circumstances in which the conflict was able to develop. The government's first step towards the carrying out of its policy brought the two houses into collision. A bill to abolish the parliamentary oath was introduced into the dáil and passed unamended, but the senate inserted a clause to the effect that it should not come into force until an agreement had been reached with the British government on the question of the oath. The dáil rejected the amendment, and the bill eventually became law without the senate's assent. This initial disagreement was followed by a period of relative harmony, although political feeling was running high in the country. The senate discharged its functions as a revisionary chamber; accepted measures which were vigorously opposed by the opposition party in the dáil; and worked amicably with the ministers who came in contact with it.[2] That there had been no fundamental change in the outlook of either house was shown, however, by the senate's rejection of two bills designed to democratize the local government franchise[3] and by the introduction of a bill to curtail the senate's power of delay from eighteen months to three months. In the course of the debate on the third of these measures de Valera declared that in his opinion the senate served no really useful purpose and that in certain circumstances he would be prepared to abolish it altogether.[4] The senate rejected the bill, proposing instead a joint committee to consider the expediency of changing its constitution and powers. The resolution was ignored by the dáil: it appeared on the order paper for almost two years but was not debated. The bill itself never became law, for by the time the suspensory period had elapsed the abolition of the senate was impending.

The immediate precursor of the final conflict was a dispute over the extra-parliamentary associations. The senate revealed its sympathies for the Blue Shirt movement by securing from the committee on procedure and privileges a condemnation of the minister for defence for

[1] Ibid. xxii. 140–1; xxiv. 598.
[2] O'Sullivan, op. cit., p. 347.
[3] Local Government (Dublin) Bill and Local Government (Extension of Franchise) Bill.
[4] *Dáil Debates*, xlviii. 783–4.

having ordered the exclusion of two uniformed members of the organization from the visitor's gallery in the senate chamber after they had obtained the chairman's permission to attend.[1] It followed up its success by attacking the government's policy of granting commissions in a new volunteer force to ex-members of the I.R.A. As an expression of its disapproval it inserted an amendment to the annual Army Bill limiting its operation to four months. Since the bill had to be passed before a certain date the government was obliged to accept the amendment, but its resentment was forcibly expressed by the minister for defence: 'This action on the part of the senate is part of the obstructive tactics which have been used by elements here and in England to obstruct and sabotage the efforts of this government to maintain and defend the rights of the people.'[2] No sooner was this episode over than the senate became embroiled with the dáil once again on the question of the Blue Shirts. When the government introduced the Wearing of Uniform (Restriction) Bill as a means of breaking up the organization the majority in the senate opposed the bill strongly and eventually rejected it.[3] On the following day, 22 March 1934, a bill to abolish the senate was introduced in the dáil.

The abolition bill—the Constitution (Amendment No. 24) Bill, 1935—was passed by the dáil after a debate which was conducted on party lines. On the one side it was contended that the existence of a second chamber was an essential guarantee against party dictatorship; that the senate had done its work efficiently; and that the attack on it was a violation of Griffith's agreement with the Southern unionists. On the other side it was argued that the problem of evolving a satisfactory second chamber was well-nigh insoluble; that a senate was not an indispensable part of a democratic system of government; and that the existing senate was a partisan body.[4] In this last charge lies the key to the whole situation. The senate contained, and was likely to contain for some time, a majority of members antagonistic to the government party. They had already opposed the first stages in the implementation of the government's policy; to its completion they were certain to be equally hostile. A restriction of the senate's powers of delay might have enabled the government to complete its programme within the lifetime of the existing dáil, but the circumstances surrounding the establishment of the senate tipped the scales in favour

---

[1] O'Sullivan, op. cit., pp. 355–8.   [2] *Dáil Debates*, li. 1337–42.
[3] *Senate Debates*, xviii. 749–876.
[4] *Dáil Debates*, l. 1977–2122, 2127–48; li. 1828–1972.

The Dáil and the Second Chamber

of abolition. This is what lay behind the statement of de Valera, who declared: 'The second chamber, as at present constituted, appears to me to be an absolute menace to this country';[1] and of Lemass, who said: 'It is not the seanad that constitutes the barrier to action by the government, it is the majority that happen to have power in the seanad at the present moment through the accident of circumstances.'[2]

As was only to be expected the senate rejected the bill for its own abolition.[3] More than that, it attempted to stave off or at least postpone its destruction by introducing a bill to bring into immediate operation the referendum on constitutional amendments which had been suspended for a further eight years in 1929.[4] When the dáil took the course of ignoring the bill the senate's expectancy of life was reduced to the suspensory period fixed by the constitution. In this interval the strained relations between the houses persisted. The senate defeated an attempt by the government to carry through its proposed revision of the local government franchise by means of a new bill introduced in the senate;[5] it once again limited the period for which the Defence Forces Act should remain in operation;[6] it rejected a bill for the abolition of university representation in the dáil;[7] and it came near to rejecting a bill for the revision of the dáil constituencies.[8] The government, for its part, treated the senate with scant regard. Mention has been made of the fate accorded to the senate bill for restoring the referendum. When the chairman of the senate accepted for discussion a motion condemning the action of the new armed police in shooting a youth during an affray at a Cork cattle sale yard the minister for lands protested and withdrew from the house with his supporters.[9] And in the final stages of the abolition bill the same disregard for the senate was revealed. At the end of the eighteen months suspensory period the bill was again sent to the senate in accordance with the terms of the constitution. This time, instead of rejecting the bill outright, the senate offered to pass it provided it was not put into operation until a bill for the establishment of a new senate had been passed by the dáil. To consider an amendment of this nature and other amendments providing for the period of transition the senate proposed a conference between members representing the two houses.[10] During the two days on which this

[1] *Dáil Debates*, li. 1461.
[2] Ibid. li. 1871.
[3] *Senate Debates*, xviii. 1525–6.
[4] Ibid. xviii. 1162–94.
[5] Ibid. xviii. 1037–46.
[6] Ibid. xviii. 1641–63.
[7] Ibid. xviii. 2003–6.
[8] Ibid. xix. 1294–1301.
[9] O'Sullivan, op. cit., p. 419.
[10] *Senate Debates*, xx. 1813.

motion was debated no member of the government attended the senate;[1] nor was any reply to the proposal vouchsafed by the dáil. The additional suspensory period of two months was allowed to run its course. It terminated on 11 February 1936, but the final step—the motion of enactment by the dáil—was not taken until 28 May,[2] and in the meantime no intimation of the government's intention was conveyed to the senate. The bill terminating the existence of the senate was signed by the governor-general on the following day, 29 May 1936.

On many occasions in the course of the debates on the abolition bill the opposition expressed fears about the dangers of an unrestricted single chamber legislature. In reply de Valera suggested a number of ways in which safeguards might be provided: the articles in the constitution guaranteeing fundamental rights might be made unalterable except by a specified majority in the dáil or by a referendum;[3] the standing orders of the dáil might be amended to ensure a further revision of bills after the report stage and before the final reading;[4] or the dáil might adopt the Norwegian system of selecting a proportion of its members to form a revising chamber.[5] On the general question of the desirability of a second house de Valera declared himself unconvinced, yet 'if anyone can indicate to us how to set up a second chamber which will serve us and will not be a definite barrier to progress or be simply a reproduction of the conditions in this house, I shall still keep simply an open mind'.[6] While the Free State senate remained in existence, however, no steps were taken either to embody the suggested safeguards in the constitution or to investigate the possibility of evolving a new senate which would meet with general approval.

The reason for the delay was due partly, as de Valera subsequently admitted,[7] to the desire to be rid of a senate while the proposed new constitution was being enacted and partly to the obvious fact that the whole question of a second chamber or alternative safeguards could most conveniently be considered when the new constitution was under discussion. Once the old senate was gone no time was lost. On the final stage of its abolition, the motion for the enactment of the abolition bill, de Valera announced his intention of introducing a new constitution and accepted a suggestion by MacDermot that a

[1] *Senate Debates*, xx. 1813–1936, 1939–2008.   [2] *Dáil Debates*, lii. 1195–1348.
[3] Ibid. lii. 1877–8; *Senate Debates*, xviii. 1217.
[4] *Dáil Debates*, li. 2285, 2320; lii. 1812; lix. 2553, 2554.
[5] Ibid. li. 2143.   [6] Ibid. lix. 2664.   [7] Ibid. lxix. 1608.

The Dáil and the Second Chamber

commission should be set up to weigh the merits of a senate.[1] Eleven days after the abolition of the senate the executive council appointed a commission of 23 members to make recommendations on the constitution, functions, and powers of a second chamber if it should be decided to include one in the new constitution. The commission consisted of the chief justice who was chairman, the attorney-general who was vice-chairman, 7 members of the dáil, 5 ex-senators, 4 university professors, 2 civil servants, and 3 others.[2] The principal opposition party refused to co-operate in the work of the commission on the grounds that its participation would be tantamount to condoning the abolition of the previous senate and that there was no guarantee of a new senate being established as a result of the commission's recommendations.[3] The outcome of the commission bore out de Valera's forebodings about the complexity of the problems involved in devising a satisfactory second chamber and illustrated the wide divergence of views held on the subject. Although the commission was not as fully representative as it might have been it produced no fewer than ten separate reports or reservations: one majority report, three minority reports, and six notes by individual members. No one of these was adopted in its entirety, but the suggestions contained in them were drawn upon when the new constitution was being framed.

The draft constitution, published on 30 April 1937, contained provisions for a senate. In the subsequent debate de Valera maintained that his own views about a senate had not changed; he still believed that such a thing as an ideal senate was not possible. But, he recalled, when the previous senate was being abolished there had been members of the opposition who argued that even a bad senate was better than no senate at all. If a large section of people in the country felt that there was something important in having a senate he was prepared to give way even though he was indifferent to it himself.[4] A more positive reason for reviving the senate was his desire to prevent the fundamental provisions of the new constitution being lost sight of in disputes over details.[5] The senate which he devised, however, was not intended to be a check upon the dáil; it was designed, rather, as a house in which questions might be approached from a slightly different angle.[6] This aim is reflected in the restricted powers conferred upon

---

[1] *Dáil Debates*, lix. 2657–66.
[2] *Report of the Second House of the Oireachtas Commission* (1936).
[3] *Dáil Debates*, lxvii. 1412.
[4] Ibid. lxii. 55–56.
[5] Ibid. xcviii. 273.
[6] Ibid. lxix. 356; xcviii. 284.

the new senate, in the limit fixed for its duration, and in the provisions laid down for its constitution.

The powers of the senate as defined by the constitution rendered the senate incapable of challenging the dáil. Permission was given for the inclusion of two senators in the government, but the government remained responsible to the dáil alone. Like its predecessor the new senate is incapable of initiating money bills or of holding them up for longer than twenty-one days, but it has the right to appeal to a committee of privileges, through the president, against the ceann cómhairle's certification of a particular bill as a money bill. Its suspensory power over ordinary bills is cut down to ninety days, after which, on a resolution of the dáil, a bill is deemed to have passed after 180 days. Moreover, the period of ninety days may be abridged if a bill is declared urgent by the government, but in that case the act remains in force for ninety days only unless, before the expiration of that time, both houses agree to keep it in force for a longer period. The most that the senate can do, in the event of disagreement with the dáil, is to petition the president not to sign the bill in dispute, and even that it cannot do alone. A majority of the senate and one-third of the dáil may present a joint petition to the president requesting him not to sign a bill, other than a constitutional amendment, on the ground that the bill contains a proposal of such national importance that the will of the people ought to be ascertained. If the president accedes to the petition either a referendum or a general election must be held.[1] A further safeguard against the type of conflict which had developed between the houses under the Free State constitution is provided by making the lifetime of the senate roughly coterminous with that of the dáil: the constitution specifies that a general election for Seanad Éireann shall take place not later than ninety days after a dissolution of the dáil.[2] Since the dáil is able to influence the composition of the senate this provision is a guarantee against a recurrence of the 1932 situation when the party in control of the dáil found itself opposed by a hostile majority in the senate.

The manner in which the senate is constituted reveals the twofold desire to prevent a clash between the houses and to avoid the creation of a senate which will be a mere replica of the dáil. The constitution provides for the establishment of a senate partly nominated and partly elected on a basis of vocational representation. Of the 60 members

[1] *Constitution of Ireland*, arts. 20, 21 22, 23, 24, 27.
[2] Ibid., art. 18.

The Dáil and the Second Chamber

11 are nominated by the taoiseach, 6 elected by the two universities—3 from each—and 43 elected from five panels of candidates made up of persons having knowledge and practical experience of: (1) the national language and culture, literature, art, education, and such professional interests as may be defined by law; (2) agriculture and allied industries and fisheries; (3) labour, whether organized or unorganized; (4) industry and commerce, including banking, finance, accounting, engineering, and architecture; (5) public administration and social services, including voluntary social activities. Not more than 11 or less than 5 senators may be elected from any one panel.[1]

These provisions represent the attempt to supplement a chamber based on geographical democracy with a second house formed on a functional basis. Since the economic life of the country is not organized on a functional basis the method of forming the senate has got to be indirect, but, should conditions change, the constitution authorized the introduction of legislation to permit any functional or vocational group or council to elect directly a number of senators in substitution for an equal number from the corresponding panel.[2]

The detailed arrangements for senate elections were left to ordinary legislation. A bill on the subject was referred to a select committee consisting of 15 deputies representative of all parties in the dáil. The opposition members of this committee put forward a scheme by which the senate would be elected from candidates nominated by the dáil by an electoral college consisting of 10 representatives of Fianna Fáil, 7 of Fine Gael, 4 of labour, and 1 independent. The government refused to accept this but abandoned their own scheme for an electoral college made up of all candidates for the dáil at the previous general election who had received over 500 first preference votes, voting in proportion to the support they had received. The plan decided upon provided that 5 of the members to be elected should represent cultural and educational interests, 11 agriculture, 11 labour, 9 commerce and industry, and 7 administration. The panels were to be formed in the following way: the taoiseach and leader of the opposition were each to nominate 2 candidates to the administrative panel. The dáil was to nominate 69 candidates to all panels combined, each candidate being nominated by two members of the dáil and each member of the dáil having only one nomination. The remaining candidates, who were not to exceed 75, were to be nominated by vocational bodies

[1] Ibid., art. 18.   [2] Ibid., art. 19.

such as chambers of commerce, trade unions, and professional organizations, employing the method of proportional representation. From these panels the new senate was to be chosen by an electoral college consisting of the members of the dáil and seven members, elected by proportional representation, from each of the county councils and borough councils in the country. This made an electoral college of 355 members. Each elector was to receive a ballot paper containing the names of all the candidates in alphabetical order and was to vote, according to the principles of proportional representation, irrespective of the panel on which the candidate had been nominated.

From the beginning the opposition contended that this complicated system of election would produce only a pale reflection of the dáil, a chamber in no sense vocational.[1] Even de Valera admitted that at the start roughly half the members of the senate would be elected by the dáil.[2] It soon became apparent not only that the vocational element was going to figure inconspicuously but also that the system of election lent itself to corrupt practices. In the first election the political candidates carried the day. Such non-political bodies as the Royal Irish Academy, the Royal Dublin Society, the College of Surgeons, and the primary and secondary teachers' associations failed to return any members. More than this, rumours were current that candidates had purchased the votes of senate electors. These rumours increased in number and substance until they received confirmation in the prosecution and conviction of an offender after the 1944 senate election.[3] Long before this the opposition had put down a motion expressing disapproval of the method of electing the senate, but it was not until October 1945 that the motion came up for discussion.[4] The government accepted the motion and in the following month a joint committee was set up to consider the problem of senate elections.[5] On the basis of the committee's report a bill was introduced in 1947 altering the method of nominating and electing the panel members.[6] The most significant change was the increase in the size of the senate electorate which was now to consist of the members of the newly-elected dáil, the outgoing senate, and the county and borough councils, making a total of approximately nine hundred. In this way the government hoped not only to make corruption difficult or impossible

[1] *Dáil Debates*, lxix. 309, 314, 319, 328.
[2] Ibid. lxix. 363.
[3] Ibid. lxxiii. 1.
[4] Ibid. xcviii. 124–96.
[5] Ibid. xcviii. 1076.
[6] Seanad Electoral (Panel Members) Bill, 1947.

but also to augment the authority of the senate by giving it an indirect mandate from the people.[1]

Number of Former Deputies Elected to the Senate

Year	Number elected	Percentage
1938 (1)	17	35
1938 (2)	19	39
1943	16	33
1944	14	29
1948	14	29
1951	15	31

As the foregoing table shows the number of former deputies elected to the senate has remained fairly constant at approximately one-third of the house. But this takes no account of the nominated members, many of whom were former deputies, nor of the defeated candidates at dáil elections who figure prominently among both the elected and the nominated senators. If these are added to the senators who sat in the first senate the percentage of members with previous political experience is considerably increased. For example, in the second senate of 1938 twenty-one members were former deputies and sixteen former senators, making a total of 62 per cent.; and in the senate of 1948 sixteen members were former deputies and six had been members of the first senate, making a total of 37 per cent. The tendency for senators to be re-elected is also marked. To take just one example: in the senate of 1944 sixteen members were former deputies, eleven had been members of the first senate, and fifteen had been members of the 1938 senate, making a total of 70 per cent. of the whole.

If the scheme for the new senate has not resulted in a house markedly different in composition from the dáil it has eliminated the former friction between the houses. The taoiseach's power of nominating eleven senators is in itself a guarantee that the government will enjoy a majority in the second house. Between its inception and 1949 the senate did not suspend a bill. As the following tables (p. 152) show the dáil accepted the great majority of such bills as had been amended by the senate and only once did it reject outright a senate recommendation on a money bill.

As a working arrangement for resolving differences over amendments resort has been had to a conference between representatives of both houses. In 1943 the dáil requested a conference to consider two

[1] *Senate Debates*, xxxiv. 1640.

senate amendments to the Intoxicating Liquor Bill, 1942, which had been altered by the dáil and insisted upon by the senate. As a result

Bills Amended by the Senate

Year	Bills passed without amendment	Bills amended	Bills accepted by dáil as amended	Amendments rejected in dáil	Amended bills accepted with alteration
1938	15	2	2	..	..
1939	20	8	8	..	..
1940	23	6	5	..	1
1941	16	7	6	..	1
1942	12	9	8	..	1
1943	13	5	4	..	1
1944	10	6	6	..	..
1945	21	11	10	..	1
1946	14	13	11	..	2
1947	30	7	7	..	..
1948	18	..	..	..	..
1949	19	3	3	..	..

Money Bills on which the Senate made Recommendations

Year	Money bills passed without recommendation	With recommendation	Accepted by dáil	Rejected by dáil	Amended by dáil
1938	11	..	..	..	..
1939	8	..	..	..	..
1940	6	..	..	..	..
1941	5	1	..	..	1
1942	6	..	..	..	..
1943	6	..	..	..	..
1944	6	..	..	..	..
1945	6	..	..	..	..
1946	9	1	1	..	..
1947	12	1	..	1	..
1948	6	..	..	..	..
1949	9	..	..	..	..

of the conference agreement was reached.[1] The senate has shown itself ready to defend its privileges but it has neither the inclination nor the power to challenge the supremacy of the dáil.

[1] *Dáil Proceedings*, xxii. 48, 64; *Senate Proceedings*, xx. 75, 79.

XI

THE DÁIL AND THE EXECUTIVE

I. THE NOMINAL EXECUTIVE

THE status accorded to Ireland in the Anglo-Irish treaty of December 1921 determined the general pattern of the executive; the Irish negotiators were obliged to abandon the republic and accept the monarchical structure of a British dominion. Since the crown symbolized the link with Great Britain and the Commonwealth and the less than independent status of the country, it was strongly assailed from the first by the republicans and accepted without enthusiasm by the pro-treaty party. In the original draft of the constitution the monarchical element had been whittled down to an extent which the British regarded as inconsistent with the terms of the treaty.[1] When the amended draft was before the dáil O'Higgins, the minister responsible for the bill, admitted that he felt himself in an unpleasant position having to stand over the clauses relating to the crown.[2] He assured the house that there was no need to take at its face value any clause which appeared to vest power in the king or his representative[3] for all real power lay in Ireland. Any statement to the contrary was merely the keeping up of certain symbols,[4] symbols which, as another minister declared, were of much importance to the British but of little or none to the Irish.[5] The power of the crown, O'Higgins claimed, had been reduced to the irreducible minimum.[6] Yet these ministerial assurances did not prevent an attempt being made to insert an amendment providing that no act of state should be done, and no executive action should be taken, otherwise than upon the initiative and with the authority of the executive council.[7] It is indicative of the dáil's sentiments that when one deputy declared that they were all republicans[8] and another that the vast majority of Irishmen would have had the crown excluded from the constitution if it had been possible, their statements went uncontradicted.[9]

As in the other dominions the crown was represented in the Irish

---

[1] *Dáil Debates*, i. 1008.   [2] Ibid. i. 760.   [3] Ibid. i. 1168.
[4] Ibid. i. 1242.   [5] Ibid. i. 1260.   [6] Ibid. i. 1082.
[7] Ibid. i. 1253.   [8] Ibid. i. 1074.
[9] Ibid. i. 776.

Free State by a governor-general whose powers and functions were modelled on those of his Canadian counterpart. Parliament was to be summoned and dissolved by the governor-general but the date of the reassembly and the conclusion of each session was to be fixed by the dáil, with the proviso that sessions of the senate were not to be concluded without its own consent. No scope was left the governor-general for the exercise of discretionary power either in selecting a president of the executive council or in granting a dissolution. The constitution provided that the president should be nominated by the dáil and that a dissolution could only be advised by a president who retained the support of a majority in the dáil. The power to recommend the appropriation of money could only be exercised on the advice of the executive council; the signifying of the royal assent to bills was merely a matter of form; and the right to reserve bills for consideration in Britain was in desuetude throughout the Commonwealth by the time the Free State came into existence.

Not only was the Irish Free State foremost among the dominions in restricting the powers of the governor-general but it also took the lead in asserting its influence on his appointment. Although it was not until the Imperial Conference of 1930 that a dominion's right to nominate its own governor-general was acknowledged as a general principle the Free State clearly enjoyed the privilege from the beginning. During the treaty debate Griffith read a letter from Lloyd George undertaking to consult the Irish government before filling the office.[1] O'Higgins referred to this undertaking when an amendment was moved to the constitution on the advice of the executive council, but he warned the house that the matter was 'one of the most touchy and thorny points with the British'.[2] The British government is said to have contemplated the appointment of a prominent peer as the first governor-general[3] but the person eventually selected was T. M. Healy, K.C., a catholic Irishman and former nationalist member of parliament. The negotiations leading to his appointment have not been made public but it was stated in the dáil later that he was appointed by agreement between the two governments and that the second governor-general was chosen solely upon the advice of the Irish government.[4]

Of more real significance to the dáil than the formal powers vested

---

[1] *Treaty Debate*, p. 21. [2] *Dáil Debates*, i. 1775, 1778.
[3] D. Gwynn, *The Irish Free State, 1922–7*, p. 66.
[4] *Dáil Debates*, xxvii. 443; xxxiii. 2160.

in the crown was the parliamentary oath which was specified in the treaty and incorporated in the constitution. Some concession was made to Irish susceptibilities in the wording of the oath. Instead of being, as in the other dominions, a straightforward oath of allegiance to the king, the Irish oath prescribed allegiance first to the constitution of the Irish Free State, secondly to the crown in virtue of the common citizenship between the two countries and the association of Ireland with the Commonwealth of Nations. Even so, it was unpalatable to many of the deputies who were prepared to stand by the treaty. When it was administered for the first time in the dáil the leader of the labour party stated that he and his colleagues in the party took the oath as 'a formality, a condition of membership of the legislature, implying no obligation other than the ordinary obligation of every person who accepts the privileges of citizenship'.[1] The government party itself was not enamoured of the oath; according to Blythe[2] they regarded it as of no importance, an empty formula. As for the republicans, the whole force of their resentment against the treaty settlement tended to be focused on the parliamentary oath. Their attitude to it provoked one of the principal political controversies in the history of the Irish Free State and left the dáil for four years without an effective opposition.

As the civil war was petering out in the spring of 1923 de Valera, through the medium of two senators, made an unsuccessful attempt to secure from the Free State government a peace settlement acceptable to the republicans. One of the conditions he put forward was that no citizen should be debarred from parliament by any political oath. The government refused to violate the treaty by agreeing to the proposal.[3] The republicans, under the name Sinn Féin, contested the general election of August 1923, making it clear that they intended to pursue the abstentionist policy which had been the inevitable concomitant of the civil war, and presenting the parliamentary oath as an additional justification for their decision. Early in 1926 a section of the republicans, under the leadership of de Valera, became convinced of the futility of the abstentionist policy. This led to a split in the republican ranks, and to the formation of a new political party, Fianna Fáil, which fought the next general election mainly on the issue of the oath. The first move to surmount the barrier of the oath had already been made before the election. In January one member

---

[1] *Dáil Debates*, ii. 3. [2] Ibid. xli. 2132.
[3] O'Sullivan, *Irish Free State and its Senate*, pp. 228–9.

of the party, Dan Breen, resigned, took the oath, and entered the house. Shortly afterwards he introduced a bill for the abolition of the oath, but it was rejected on the first stage, the view of the majority party being, as before, that any tampering with the oath constituted a violation of the Anglo-Irish treaty.[1] An attempt at direct repeal having failed, the party next resorted to a legal opinion. On the day that the new parliament was to assemble it was announced that the views of three members of the Irish bar had been sought. They had held that there was no authority in anyone under the treaty, or the constitution, or the standing orders of the dáil to exclude any member from the house before the house had been duly constituted and the chairman duly elected. Any member might be proposed and elected as chairman without taking any oath; and if any member was excluded the chairman would not have been validly elected.[2] Acting on this advice the members of the party presented themselves for the first meeting of the new dáil, but when they refused to take the oath they were denied admission to the chamber.[3] It was the action of the Cumann na nGaedheal government which at length brought the Fianna Fáil party into the dáil. One of the bills introduced as a result of the assassination of Kevin O'Higgins was designed to prevent abstentionists from being elected to the oireachtas by providing that every candidate at the time of his nomination should undertake to swear the oath if he was elected. Rather than accept political extinction the Fianna Fáil deputies complied with the provisions of the constitution relating to the oath, but they maintained at the time and subsequently that they succeeded in doing so without swearing an oath.[4] Entry into the dáil did not affect the party's determination to abolish the oath, but so long as it remained in the minority there was no hope of achieving its object by means of ordinary legislation. A new line of attack was found in the article of the constitution providing for the initiation of legislative proposals by the people. A petition was completed in the manner prescribed in the constitution and brought before the dáil by de Valera on 3 May 1928.[5] The government raised objections to the reception of the petition. While the question was still under discussion it forestalled any further action by introducing a bill to abolish both the initiative and the referendum. As a further precaution the bill was declared urgently necessary for

[1] *Dáil Debates*, xix. 990–1.
[2] *Irish Independent*, 23 June 1927.
[3] Ibid., 24 June 1927.
[4] *Dáil Debates*, xli. 1101–2.
[5] Ibid. xxiii. 806–8.

The Dáil and the Executive

the preservation of the public peace so that no appeal could be made to a referendum.[1] The oath continued to figure prominently in the Fianna Fáil party programme, and when the party was returned to power after the general election of 1932 one of its first actions was to introduce a bill to remove the oath from the constitution. The effect of this bill on the relations between the two houses of the oireachtas has been examined elsewhere.

The governor-general was never permitted to figure more prominently than was necessary even within the narrow sphere fixed for him by the constitution. Only on two occasions did he formally attend the opening of parliament and each time the ceremony was boycotted by the labour party.[2] Strong exception was taken to his action in paying an official visit to the colonial secretary because it appeared to confirm the dual nature of his office—as representative of the king and the imperial government,[3] an interpretation which the Irish Free State rejected even before it was abandoned by the Imperial Conference of 1926. The phrase 'governor-general in council' was avoided in Irish statutes and in the few instances where statutory powers were conferred on him the fact that they were exercisable on the advice of the executive council was specifically stated. When the governor-general expressed his views on the abstentionist policy of the opposition the leader of the labour party secured a disclaimer of responsibility from the president of the executive council.[4] From the time that the Fianna Fáil party entered the dáil attacks on the governor-general were redoubled, one deputy going so far as to declare that he had not attempted to assassinate the lord lieutenant in 1919 in order to put another man in his place.[5] When the party came to power in 1932 the members of the government refused to attend public functions at which the governor-general was present. After some months of recrimination James McNeill was dismissed and Donal O Buachalla was appointed in his place. That this was a preliminary to the abolition of the office was clear from the beginning. The new governor-general was not a prominent member of the party; unlike his predecessors he did not reside in the Viceregal Lodge; he received a salary of £2,000 a year, not the £10,000 laid down in the constitution; and he seems to have performed no function other than to affix his signature to bills. The next stage in the abolition of the office

---

[1] *Dáil Debates*, xxiv. 1758–1850.
[2] *Irish Times*, 13 Dec. 1922; 4 Oct. 1923; *Dáil Debates*, ii. 98–102.
[3] Ibid. xvii. 32.   [4] Ibid. xvii. 24–29.   [5] Ibid. xli. 768.

was the enactment of two amendments to the constitution in 1933: the Constitution (Amendment No. 20) Act which transferred from the governor-general to the executive council the power of recommending the appropriation of money; and the Constitution (Amendment No 21) Act which abolished the governor-general's right of reserving legislation for consideration in Great Britain. Both bills passed the dáil without opposition.[1] The abdication of King Edward VIII provided the occasion for the final step: one of the two bills presented to the hastily summoned dáil, and passed under a guillotine motion, abolished the office of governor-general and removed from the constitution all references to the king exercising functions in internal affairs.[2] Bills were no longer to require the royal assent; instead they were to become law on the signature of the chairman of the dáil who was also to summon and dissolve parliament on the direction of the executive council. A later act distributed the remaining functions of the governor-general, repealed the act providing for his salary and establishment, and made provision for the last holder of the office.[3]

The only function left to the crown was in the sphere of external affairs. The second act[4] passed at the time of the abdication crisis elaborated a clause in the first which embodied the idea of external association proposed by de Valera during the treaty negotiations in 1921. It was provided that, so long as Ireland remained associated with the countries of the British Commonwealth, the king recognized by them 'as the symbol of their co-operation' might be employed by the executive council for the appointment of diplomatic and consular agents and the conclusion of international agreements.

For the remainder of its existence the Irish Free State presented something of a constitutional anomaly. The form of its constitution implied the existence of a permanent symbol of authority in which executive power was nominally vested. With the elimination of the crown this formal embodiment of executive authority was removed and, according to the attorney-general, executive authority was vested in the people.[5]

A more normal position was restored under the constitution of 1937. It instituted an elective presidency which, in certain specified

[1] *Dáil Debates*, xlix. 1427, 1428, 2113–15.
[2] Ibid. lxiv. 1281; Constitution (Amendment No. 27) Bill, 1936.
[3] Executive Powers (Consequential Provisions) Bill, 1937.
[4] Executive Authority (External Relations) Act, 1937.
[5] *Dáil Debates*, lxiv. 1378.

The Dáil and the Executive

matters, was to act as the constitutional organ through which executive power was to be exercised. It was also to form a constituent part of the oireachtas. Some peculiarities in the nature of the presidency would seem to arise from the aims of de Valera, the author of the constitution. The form and wording of the constitution suggests that, on the one hand, he was anxious to emphasize the democratic ethos of the state, and, on the other, to disguise its republican character until such time as the unification of the country had been effected. It is probably for these reasons that the president was not designated as the head of the state and that executive power was not formally vested in him. The constitution merely declares that executive power should be exercised by or on the authority of the government. De Valera later contended that the real head of the state was the government; that authority lay with it and did not devolve down from a nominal head. He also denied that the king, whose functions in the external sphere were reaffirmed in the new constitution, was in any sense the head of the state.[1] Nevertheless, the continued employment of the king created an element of ambiguity which was seized upon by the opposition. It was only with the repeal of the Executive Authority (External Relations) Act in 1948 that the president was formally recognized as what he had been in effect from the beginning, the nominal head of an independent republic.

The president is elected by direct vote of the people, on the same register as the dáil, by secret ballot on the system of proportional representation. He holds office for seven years and may be re-elected once. Candidates for the office may be nominated either by twenty members of the oireachtas or by four county or county borough councils, but each group of members and each group of councils may nominate only one candidate. Former or retiring presidents may nominate themselves. The president cannot be a member of either house of the oireachtas; he is forbidden to hold any other office of profit; he is required to take an oath of allegiance to the constitution; and he may be impeached for misbehaviour. In the absence or incapacity of the president a commission consisting of the chief justice, the chairman of Dáil Éireann, and the chairman of Seanad Éireann is empowered to act in his stead. The president is assisted by a council of state composed of (*a*) the taoiseach, the tánaiste, the chief justice, the president of the High Court, the chairman of Dáil Éireann, the chairman of Seanad Éireann, and the attorney-general; (*b*) persons

---
[1] *Dáil Debates*, cxiii. 422–3.

who have held the office of president, taoiseach, chief justice, or president of the executive council of the Irish Free State; (c) seven others nominated by the president.

Many of the president's functions are merely formal. He appoints the ministers selected by the dáil; he nominally commands the defence forces; and he signs and promulgates acts of the oireachtas. But in addition the president enjoys certain powers which were denied to the governor-general of the Irish Free State. He may, after consultation with the council of state, convene a meeting of either or both houses of the oireachtas, or address a message to the oireachtas on a matter of national importance. While he normally summons and dissolves the dáil on the advice of the taoiseach he may, at his discretion, refuse a dissolution to a taoiseach who has lost the support of a majority in the dáil. This is the only circumstance in which he is authorized to act in his absolute discretion; but while other of his powers are exercised after consultation with the council of state he is not bound to accept its advice. He is empowered to intervene in disputes between the two houses of the oireachtas. If the senate appeals to him against the decision of the ceann cómhairle that a particular bill is a money bill he may appoint a committee of privileges, consisting of an equal number of members from each house with a judge of the Supreme Court as chairman, to decide the question. Or he may withhold his signature from a bill, other than a money bill or a constitutional amendment, on the joint petition of a majority of the senate and one-third of the dáil. The bill must then be submitted for decision to the people, either as a referendum or at a general election. His concurrence is necessary, also, to enable the dáil, on the plea of national emergency, to abridge the time permitted for the consideration of a bill by the senate. Finally, the president has the power to submit any bill, other than a money bill or constitutional amendment, to the Supreme Court for a decision on its constitutional validity.

Though the discretionary powers entrusted to the president in the legislative sphere are real enough, they are not of a nature likely to precipitate a dispute with the dáil. The president is protected by the fact that the responsibility for the ultimate decision on matters referred to him rests elsewhere. Hitherto the president has not incurred the serious displeasure of the dáil. The first president, Dr. Douglas Hyde, was unanimously selected. He had never been an active politician, and his advanced age made it unlikely that he would be officious in the discharge of his duties. Three opportunities for the exercise of his discretionary powers occurred during his tenure of office. The government was defeated in the dáil on 9 May 1944[1] and the taoiseach advised a dissolution which he granted. The other occasions arose in respect of two bills which he referred to the Supreme Court for a ruling on their constitutionality.[2] This action had repercussions when the next presidential election fell due. The tánaiste, Sean T. O'Kelly, had been considered for the post by the government when the presidency was created. At the expiration of Hyde's term of office he was nominated by the government party and the selection of a party president was urged so that 'there would be no friction, no time lost in settling difficulties that should not have arisen'.[3] He was elected after a contest conducted on party lines, but he succeeded, during his tenure of the presidency, in working harmoniously with a government composed of the parties which opposed his election. In 1952 he was re-elected unopposed for a second term.

II. THE REAL EXECUTIVE

Within the monarchical framework prescribed by the Anglo-Irish treaty there was room for ingenuity and experiment in devising the form of the effective executive. For a variety of reasons the authors of the draft constitution were not attracted to the British cabinet system. It depends for its effective working on two great parties. They expected the introduction of proportional representation to lead to a multiplicity of parties, to unstable governments, and to a lack of continuity of policy. Accordingly they set themselves to forestall the party system. They realized that they were launching a new state, that they had no traditions of government to rely on, that it would take a long time to build up an efficient civil service. In these circumstances it would be an advantage to have at least a proportion of the ministers chosen solely on the basis of their fitness for office, and not of their political services, and to make it possible for these ministers to bring forward proposals in the dáil without feeling that their rejection would endanger the whole ministry. Moreover, as was only to be expected in a country where the executive had for so long been regarded with hostility, they had no sympathy with the contemporary

---

[1] *Dáil Debates*, xciii. 2466–7.
[2] *Dáil Proceedings*, xix. 18–19; xxiii. 24, 88–89; [1940] I.R., p. 470; [1943] I.R., p. 334.
[3] *Round Table*, xxv. 311.

tendency to strengthen the executive at the expense of the legislature. It is significant that in the revolutionary period Dáil Éireann was loosely referred to as the government of the republic. Their aim was to make the dáil a genuinely deliberative assembly in which each measure would be analysed on its merits and in which there would be the maximum of individual liberty for the deputies. That could not be achieved by adhering to collective responsibility. It is possible, too, that some members of the constitution committee saw in the scheme of non-parliamentary ministers a means of evading the parliamentary oath and so of admitting the anti-treaty party to a share in the administration.[1]

The executive proposed by the constitution committee represented a blending of the Swiss and British systems. It was to consist of twelve members, at least four of whom should be members of the dáil. The remaining eight were to be chosen from citizens eligible for membership, but not actually members while they held office. If they were members at the time of their appointment they would have to resign their seats. The dáil might, however, on the motion of the president of the executive council, permit a maximum of three of the non-parliamentary or extern ministers to become members of one or other house of parliament. The four parliamentary members were to occupy roughly the position of a cabinet. The president was to be appointed on the nomination of the dáil; his colleagues by the dáil on the nomination of the president. In effect, the dáil was to elect the president and he was to nominate his colleagues. They were to be collectively responsible and were to resign when they lost the support of a majority in the dáil. The most important political offices were to be filled by them; it was suggested that they might hold the portfolios of defence, home affairs, foreign affairs, and finance. One of them should be president and another vice-president. The extern ministers were to be nominated individually by a special committee of the dáil which was to be fairly representative of the house. The committee, in making its nominations, was to have special regard to the suitability of each candidate for a particular ministry and was to submit each nomination separately to the dáil. If functional or vocational councils were established ministers might be members of them and might be nominated on their advice. These ministers, though not members of the dáil, were to have all the rights and privileges of members except the right to vote. They might be required to attend the dáil and answer

[1] *Dáil Debates*, i. 487–8, 1243, 1307, 1558.

questions, and each was to be individually responsible to the dáil for his own ministry. Though they were to act collectively with the parliamentary ministers as an executive they were not to resign if the president was defeated; they were to hold office for the whole term of the dáil. They could only be removed on the report of a committee of the dáil for malfeasance in office, incompetence, or failure to carry out the expressed will of parliament. It was suggested that extern ministers should be appointed to the departments of education, justice, the post office, trade and commerce, local government, public health, agriculture, labour, and fine arts.[1]

The decision on this draft scheme for the executive was left to a free vote of the house. After a lengthy debate the dáil approved of the scheme in principle and appointed a committee to consider the details. The recommendations of the committee provoked a renewed debate which ended in the rejection of the scheme in favour of the compromise proposed by the committee. In the executive which emerged the extern ministers were cast for a far less prominent role than in the original draft. They were made completely subservient to the parliamentary ministers. Their appointment was no longer mandatory, it was permissive; the number that might be appointed was not fixed; they were debarred from membership of the executive council and they were permitted to hold seats in the dáil. The measure of control which they could exercise over their departments was severely restricted by the fact that the executive council, from which they were excluded, was to prepare the financial estimates. Otherwise the conditions governing the extern ministers were much the same as in the draft constitution: they were to be chosen by a committee of the dáil; they were to be individually responsible to the dáil; and they were to hold office for the full term of the dáil.

The ascendancy of the executive council was assured even if the provisions for extern ministers had been utilized to the full. But in fact the scheme was never given a fair trial. In the first dáil under the constitution three extern ministers were appointed to the portfolios of agriculture, the post office, and fisheries. In the following dáil a fourth was added—local government. All three ministers were appointed on a party vote without regard to any special technical knowledge possessed by them; all were active politicians, members of the dáil and the nominees of the executive council.[2] They were,

---

[1] *Dáil Debates*, i. 1243–5.
[2] Ibid. v. 193–4.

for all practical purposes, indistinguishable from the other ministers and, as the leader of the opposition declared, they 'preferred to be responsible to the executive council rather than to the dáil'.[1] The executive council was, accordingly, doing no more than bringing the constitution into line with the realities of the position when, on the recommendation of a special committee,[2] it introduced a constitution amendment bill which virtually abolished the extern ministers. This act,[3] which authorized the increase of the executive council up to the maximum number of twelve ministers allowed by the constitution, left the president free to decide whether to nominate extern ministers or not. No appointments were made after the passing of this act in 1927.

The constitution fixed the maximum number of ministers at twelve. Of these not fewer than five or more than seven were to form a cabinet, styled the executive council, which was to be collectively responsible to the dáil. It was to include the prime minister, who, as a concession to republican sentiments, was named the president of the executive council, the vice-president, and the minister for finance, and all the ministers were to be members of the dáil with the right to attend the senate. A constitutional amendment of 1929 authorized the appointment of one senator to the executive council.[4] The constitution of 1937 affected only minor alterations in the nature of the executive. The official title is changed to the government and the principal minister is styled the taoiseach and his deputy the tánaiste. The upper and lower limits of the government are fixed at fifteen and seven respectively and there is no provision for extern ministers. Permission is given for the appointment of two senators to the government. The taoiseach's position is very similar to that of the president of the executive council. The only notable differences are that he is required to keep the president generally informed on matters of domestic and foreign policy—an approximation to the duty of the British prime minister; that the granting of a dissolution of the dáil after he has been defeated is not absolutely forbidden, as in the Free State constitution; it is left to the discretion of the president; and that he is empowered to dismiss a minister with whom he cannot work harmoniously. The only means by which the president

---

[1] *Dáil Debates*, xvii. 421; xxi. 75.
[2] *Report of Special Committee on Certain Proposals for Legislation to Amend the Constitution*, 30 Nov. 1926, iv.
[3] Constitution (Amendment No. 5) Act, 1927.
[4] Constitution (Amendment No. 15) Act, 1929.

of the executive council could rid himself of an unacceptable colleague was by resigning and remodelling his government. Apart from these changes the powers and duties of the government and its relations with the oireachtas remain the same as under the previous constitution.

The desire of the constitution committee to elevate the status of the legislature, and especially of the dáil, is reflected in the provisions of the Free State constitution governing its relations with the executive. Most of these provisions were unaffected by the constitution of 1937. The executive possesses no veto over legislation. The head of the state is deprived of any discretionary power in the selection of a prime minister by the provision, common to both constitutions, that the prime minister shall be nominated by the dáil. His colleagues have to be approved by the dáil before they are formally appointed. The government is made responsible to the dáil alone, and the three most important ministers are required to sit in the dáil. Originally all the members of the government had to be drawn from the dáil; subsequently the Free State constitution was amended to permit of the appointment of one senator, and under the constitution of 1937 two senators may be admitted to the government. The control of the armed forces of the state is vested in the oireachtas, and the right to declare war is reserved, in the first constitution for the oireachtas and in the second for the dáil. In the Irish Free State the dáil was empowered to fix the date for the re-assembly and conclusion of each session of the oireachtas, and a president of the executive council who had lost the confidence of the dáil was unable to secure a dissolution. The first of these provisions meant little in practice, and the second was never put to the test. In the new constitution both are altered. The dáil is to be summoned and dissolved by the president on the advice of the taoiseach, and the granting of a dissolution to a defeated taoiseach is left to the discretion of the president.

In spite of their institution of extern ministers, their transformation of the conventions of cabinet government into positive law, and their reservation of significant powers for the legislature, the framers of the Free State constitution failed to prevent the establishment of a powerful cabinet system. In part the reason lay in the rejection of the most vital feature in the original draft constitution and, in part, in the political circumstances of the new state. With the extern ministers subordinated to their parliamentary colleagues there was little to distinguish the Irish executive council from the British cabinet. Its development on British lines was assured by political events. The issue of the treaty split the country into two camps so effectively as to counteract the tendency of proportional representation to produce a wealth of parties. The small parties which did emerge and the independents were obliged to take their stand in the constitutional controversy. The consequence was that what was virtually a two-party system of the kind favourable to the British form of cabinet government took firm root. Furthermore, this problem of the country's constitutional status created the demand for strong government, first to meet the republican challenge to the state, then to direct the politico-economic struggle with Britain, and then to preserve neutrality during the World War. It emphasized, too, a propensity already evident in Irish political life to see in a prominent individual the symbol of a particular policy. Cosgrave was the political heir of Griffith and Collins, the champion of the treaty settlement. De Valera was the one surviving leader of the 1916 rising, the link with the revolutionary republic. Each in turn occupied a position analogous to that of a British prime minister and each was marked out for that position by the popular will as expressed at a general election. Only when the constitutional conflict was within sight of settlement can the dáil be said to have exercised a decisive influence on the selection of a prime minister. When, after the general election of 1948, the smaller parties and the independents agreed to form an inter-party government which would declare the state an independent republic, the deputy selected as taoiseach was not Mulcahy, the leader of the largest party in the coalition, but Costello, who had been less actively involved in the events which had given rise to the constitutional split. It was the first occasion on which the occupant of the premiership was not accurately predictable immediately the results of the general election became known. With the constitutional issue finally settled, and with the smaller parties prepared to act together, a new situation has been created. The outcome of the election of 1951 was in doubt until five independents gave their vote in favour of de Valera. Unless the electoral system is changed, and a change has been advocated at various times, it seems reasonable to expect a recurrence of the group form of government usually associated with proportional representation.

The cabinet system brought with it what the framers of the Free State constitution would have regarded as its attendant evils. The dáil did not become a deliberative assembly. Deputy Thrift summed up the position admirably when he said: 'It is more or less inevitable

The Dáil and the Executive

that this house should become, and gradually will more and more become, the instrument for registering and recording the decision of the executive council.'[1] The government controls the time-table of the dáil. Under standing orders one and a half hours on Wednesdays and two hours on Fridays are set aside for private members' motions and bills, but the government has the power to appropriate part, or the whole, of this time for government business, and in practice it takes the whole of it from Easter to the summer recess for financial business. The taoiseach determines the arrangement of government business on the order paper, and a minister announces at the beginning of each meeting the order in which the items will be taken. Instances have occurred of urgent and important matters being discussed although they had not appeared on the order paper.[2] The government takes the initiative, almost exclusively, in introducing legislative proposals. In the fifteen years, 1923-37, 694 government bills were introduced in the dáil, as against fifty private members' bills of which only twelve became law. The introduction of financial measures is reserved absolutely to the government. No charge upon the public revenue or upon the people whether by way of motion or amendment can be proposed by any member other than a minister. A bill incidentally involving expenditure may be introduced by a private member, but before it proceeds to the committee stage a message must be received from the government recommending the monetary proposals, and an enabling money resolution must be proposed by a minister.[3] The practice of retaining practically all bills in committees of the whole house strengthens the government by enabling it to use its majority more effectively than it might be able to do in a standing committee. Its majority also arms it with the weapon of the closure. Finally, in the authority delegated to ministers to make statutory rules, orders, and regulations the executive possesses a power which is held by some to encroach on the legislative supremacy of the oireachtas itself. Thus a minister may be empowered to amend an act, to dispense with certain requirements of an act in particular cases, or to extend the application of an act. Executive rules and orders have even encroached on the dáil's control of finance. Under the Emergency Imposition of Duties Act, 1942, the government can impose taxation by executive order without first obtaining parlia-

---

[1] *Dáil Debates*, li. 2011.
[2] Malone, *Notes on Procedure in the Houses of the Oireachtas*, pp. 34-35.
[3] Ibid., pp. 80-81.

mentary sanction, and under the Supply and Services (Temporary Provisions) Acts it can suspend duties.[1]

The influence of the government has been enhanced by the experience and prestige which come with long periods of office. In spite of the frequency of general elections Irish governments have been remarkable for their stability. Between 1922 and 1948 there were only two prime ministers. The Cumann na nGaedheal party was in power for ten years, the Fianna Fáil party for fifteen. In this time the government was defeated in the dáil and resigned or appealed to the country on only three occasions: in 1930, when the second stage of a private member's bill to amend the law relating to old age pensions was carried against the wishes of the government;[2] in 1938, when the government failed to prevent the carrying of a private member's motion to establish compulsory arbitration in disputes concerning civil service pay and conditions;[3] and in 1944 when the government was defeated on the second stage of a Transport Bill.[4] On the first occasion the president of the executive council was re-elected after the leaders of the two main opposition parties had been unsuccessfully nominated; on the second and third occasions the government was restored after a general election. With the will of the electorate unequivocally expressed and with party discipline strictly enforced there is neither occasion nor need for conflict between the executive and the legislature, especially since there exist certain safety valves for the release of the dáil's curbing energies. The legislative policy of the government can be criticized in debates on the various stages of bills, and the dáil is not so large and the pressure of business so great as to preclude a large number of deputies from speaking. The administrative action of the ministry can be criticized and controlled by means of questions addressed to ministers. If a deputy is dissatisfied with an answer he can raise the matter for further discussion on the motion for the adjournment of the house at the conclusion of business for the day, or a motion to adjourn the house on a definite matter of urgent public importance may be submitted. The dáil can also express its attitude to the government through motions of censure or of confidence. Finally, the dáil has means of criticizing and, to some extent, of controlling the financial policy of the government. The estimates for public services are submitted for scrutiny and debate to a

[1] On this subject see F. C. King, *The Drift to Absolutism*, a paper read before the Statistical and Social Inquiry Society of Ireland on 30 Oct. 1952.
[2] *Dáil Debates*, xxxiv. 239–42.
[3] Ibid. lxxi. 1866–8.
[4] Ibid. xciii. 2466–7.

committee of the whole dáil known as a committee on finance, and there is a further opportunity for debate on the different stages of the consequential bills, and on the votes for the various departments. In the comptroller and auditor-general there exists an officer whose duty is to control all disbursement and to audit accounts. His reports and audited accounts are referred for examination to a committee of the dáil known as the committee of public accounts which is representative of all parties in the dáil and has as its chairman a prominent member of the opposition. Though it is not by such methods that governments are changed under present conditions, they offer occasions for ventilating views which may influence the electorate to which ultimately both the government and the dáil are responsible.

XII

THE DÁIL AND THE EXECUTIVE

LEGISLATION

As we have seen the executive is primarily responsible for the nature and scope of the legislation passed by the dáil. Not only does the private member take little part in the initiation of legislation, but the dáil is precluded by the rigidity of the party system from making any substantial alterations to legislative proposals laid before it. A bill is rarely amended to meet the views of the government's critics; it is either passed or rejected outright. Nevertheless, the ultimate control over the legislative programme rests with the dáil. The government is created and sustained by the dáil, and the senate is powerless to defeat any measure which has won the approval of the dáil.

The volume of legislation has been considerable. In the twenty-six years between the establishment of the Irish Free State in December 1922 and the end of 1948 a total of 1,057 acts were placed on the statute book. The greatest number passed in any one year was 62 in 1924 when the oireachtas was endeavouring to cope with the problems involved in founding a new state and in protecting it from internal attack; the smallest number was 22 in 1944 when the World War had reduced legislation to a minimum. The average number of statutes for the years 1923–48 is 40 a year. The average number for the British parliament in the same period is 57 a year.

Taken as a whole this body of legislation bears a close resemblance to the legislation of any other modern state. It is designed, for the most part, to deal with problems which are not peculiar to any one country. The fact that legislation is concerned mainly with new developments and leaves largely untouched the basic social structures makes for uniformity. The founders of the independent Irish state adopted both the social and legal framework of the previous régime. Attention has been drawn to the promptness with which the republican dáil stamped out the flames of incipient social revolution during the struggle for independence. It has been pointed out that the legal code administered by the republican courts was the law as it existed prior to the establishment of the dáil. The Free State constitution provided that the laws hitherto in force in the twenty-six counties should continue to be of full force and effect, in so far as they were not inconsistent with the constitution, until they were repealed or amended by the oireachtas.[1] As a consequence of this provision the Adaptation of Enactments Act, 1922, was passed immediately after the constitution became operative so that British laws might be interpreted and adapted to meet the circumstances of the new state.

It is true, however, that Irish legislation has certain distinctive and significant features which reflect the peculiar circumstances of the country. To illustrate this point the acts of the oireachtas have been grouped according to subject-matter under five main headings.

Analysis of Legislation 1922–48

A. *Constitutional and public administration* (345)
    Constitutional 51+3.[2]
    Electoral 25.
    Local government 57.
    Electoral (local government) 17.
    Administration of justice 46.
    Administrative and legal amendment 20.
    Emergency and public safety 48.
    Appointment and remuneration of ministers and officials 15.
    Police and prisons 22.
    Defence forces 44.

B. *Financial* (143)
    Taxation and expenditure 92.
    Miscellaneous financial measures 28.
    Pensions, superannuation, and compensation 23.

C. *Social welfare* (189)
    Social services 61.
    Public health, welfare, and amenities 19.
    Hospitals 13
    Housing and rents 32.
    Town planning 3.
    Regulation of professions 9.
    Educational and cultural 21.
    Gambling 13.
    Licensing laws 13.
    Censorship 5.

[1] *Constitution of I.F.S.*, art. 73.
[2] The constitution of 1937 and the two amendments to it.

D. *Economic* (335)
    Land and agriculture 79.
    Marketing of agricultural produce 47.
    Regulation of trade, including customs 69.
    Organization and encouragement of industry 38.
    Fisheries 17.
    Electric, gas, and water supplies 18.
    Transport and communications 46.
    Conditions of labour 15.
    Industrial relations and trade unions 6.
E. *Miscellaneous* (45)
    Expiring laws acts 27.
    External affairs 6.
    Others 12.
  Total number of acts 1,057.

From this analysis certain facts emerge. In the first place it is clear that a great deal of attention has been devoted to constitutional legislation. The dáil enacted one constitution and approved a second for submission to a plebiscite. Twenty-seven amendments were made to the Free State constitution and two to the 1937 constitution. Legislation relating to Anglo-Irish agreements of a constitutional nature was enacted; provision was made for the payment of members of the oireachtas; citizenship laws were passed; various changes consequent upon the adoption of the new constitution were effected and the scheme of external association was established and ended by statute. In addition, a considerable number of electoral acts were passed. The most important of these were the Electoral Act, 1923, and the Prevention of Electoral Abuses Act, 1923, which form the basis of electoral law. Of the remainder three relate to the election of the president, seven to senate elections, and two to the revision of constituencies.

A second distinctive feature of the Irish legislative programme has been the number of acts concerned with the creation and functioning of the machinery of government. Many of the constitutional and electoral acts fall under this classification but there are others as well. The Free State government set about revising the whole system for the administration of justice. Acts were passed to effect the winding up of the dáil courts which had functioned during the Anglo-Irish war. By the Courts of Justice Act, 1924, the British system of courts was abolished and striking changes were introduced both in establishment and administration. The adoption of a new system in a new state necessitated other alterations which were also effected by statute. It is indicative of the formative work undertaken in the early years of the state that of the forty-six statutes included under the heading 'Administration of justice' thirty-three were passed before 1932. Another sphere in which the Free State government made a break with the past was in the system of local government. The revolutionary dáil had virtually destroyed the hated poor law system. Under the Free State constitution the position was regularized and the law relating to local government was revised. The Ministers and Secretaries Act, 1923, created eleven departments of state and fixed the salaries of ministers and parliamentary secretaries. Regulations governing the recruitment and control of the civil service were prescribed by statute. Other acts dealt with the establishment of the army and police force. The Defence Forces Act, 1923, which was re-enacted annually, laid down regulations for the organization, training, and discipline of the army, and the Gárda Síochána Act, 1924, established on a permanent footing the police force which had been created by an act of the previous year. All this legislation was supplemented, amended, or repealed by other acts as the need arose.

Abnormal conditions before and after the establishment of the state were responsible for another distinctive group of statutes. Indemnity acts were passed to protect from legal proceedings those who had served either the British or the Irish government during the Anglo-Irish struggle or the Free State government during the civil war; statutory provision was made for the payment of compensation for damage to property; and a whole crop of public safety legislation grew up to prevent the overthrow of the state by its domestic foes. To the early years of the Free State also belong the emergency acts necessitated by the 1926 general strike in Great Britain. Twenty-five of the forty-eight statutes under this heading were enacted before 1932. For some years after the change of government in 1932 there was a lull in emergency legislation due in part to the absence of external danger and in part to the different outlook and methods of the new government in tackling the constitutional problem which was the root cause of the internal strife. But from 1939 onwards public safety measures once again began to appear on the statute book. There were two reasons for this: the renewed offensive of the I.R.A. forced the government to seek additional powers for the protection of the state, and the outbreak of the World War necessitated special measures to tide the country over the crisis.

A further notable feature of Irish legislation revealed by the above analysis is the preoccupation with the land and agriculture. This is the natural outcome of the country's economic structure. The policy of land purchase, begun under the British administration, was carried on by a series of land acts extending over the period under consideration. In addition there were acts relating to drainage, livestock, noxious weeds and pest control, seed supply, and relief from rates for agricultural land. Schemes for re-afforestation were put on foot. An act of 1931 replaced the department of agriculture and technical instruction by a department of agriculture and set up county committees of agriculture which were to prepare annual schemes for agriculture and other rural industries. An agricultural credit corporation was set up to provide loans for agricultural developments. By means of bounties, subsidies, and guaranteed prices the growing of flax, sugar beet, oats, and wheat was encouraged. Other statutes were concerned with the marketing of agricultural produce. The purpose of most of these was to increase the output, improve the quality, and promote the sale of the country's more important products.

The large number of statutes under the heading 'Regulation of trade' is indicative of another significant sphere of the legislature's activity. While some of the statutes in this group relate to matters in no way peculiar to Ireland—such as trade marks and hire-purchase —the great majority are tariff measures inspired by special political and economic circumstances. The Cumann na nGaedheal government's policy of cautious protection is reflected in a number of statutes imposing duties on specific articles and in its establishment of a tariff commission to examine and report on applications for customs changes. After 1932 the volume of protective legislation increased as a result of the economic war with Britain and of the new government's policy of self-sufficiency. By the Emergency Imposition of Duties Act, 1932, the government secured practically unlimited powers to impose, vary, or limit, by order, customs duties on any goods imported into the country. From this time on there were numerous acts confirming orders made under the 1932 statute. Fifty of the sixty-nine acts grouped under this heading belong to the post-1932 period.

Finally, some comment is necessary on the group of statutes relating to industrial development. The counterpart of the protectionist policy was the attempt to foster native industries and to exploit native resources. Prior to 1932 the pace was slow. Acts were passed to promote the manufacture of sugar, to authorize the leasing of state mines, and to encourage the tourist industry. By the Trade Loans (Guarantee) Act, 1924, and the annual acts continuing it, the minister for industry and commerce was empowered to guarantee on behalf of the state certain classes of loans the application of which was calculated to promote employment or to effect a reduction in the retail price of essential commodities. Under the provisions of these acts industrial concerns were able to secure loans necessary for their development. After 1932 the interest of the new government in industrial expansion was reflected in a number of statutes. In order to extend the scope of the Trade Loans Acts—under which no loans had been guaranteed between 1929 and 1932—a new Trade Loans Act was passed in 1933 removing limitations in the earlier acts. Loans were no longer to be confined to corporate bodies but might be guaranteed to individuals, and a loan had not to be expended only upon the acquisition or erection of fixed assets but might be used for working capital. The purpose of this act and its predecessors was to provide industrialists with loans repayable in fixed sums over a fixed period of years. To facilitate the provision of invested capital the Industrial Credit Act, 1933, was passed. It set up a company which was to underwrite share and bond issues of public companies and to advance money to persons engaging in trade or industry. The government realized that the industries which it was striving to establish might be destroyed if powerful external concerns enjoyed unrestricted means of engaging in manufactures in the state. The Control of Manufactures Acts of 1932 and 1934 sought to obviate this danger by prescribing that new industries must be owned or controlled by nationals. In addition to these acts others were passed in the post-1932 period to promote the production of cement, sugar, and industrial alcohol, to encourage the utilization of turf for fuel and power, to provide for the exploitation and development of the country's mineral deposits, and to stimulate the tourist industry.

In view of the political, social, and economic ties between the two countries it is not surprising to find that Irish legislation has tended to follow the British pattern when it has not been concerned with problems and conditions peculiar to Ireland. There have been at least two notable instances of Irish legislation preceding British legislation on the same matter: the Unemployment Assistance Act, 1933, provided for the relief of unemployed persons who did not come within the scope of the Unemployment Insurance Acts—the corresponding legislative provision in Britain was not made until June 1934[1]—and the Children's Allowances Act, 1944, instituted the payment of children's allowances in Ireland a year before they were introduced in Britain.[2] But in many instances the oireachtas has adopted in whole or in part enactments which the British parliament had already passed. In some cases the Irish acts followed quickly on the British, in others only after an interval of years. Examples of this legislative plagiarism occur all through the period 1922–48. The Increase of Rent and Mortgage Interest (Restrictions) Act, 1923, corresponded in substance to the British act of the same title passed in 1920. The Gaming Act, 1923, followed a British act of 1922. The Railways Act, 1924, contained provisions similar to those in the British statute, the Railways Act, 1921. The Trade Loans (Guarantee) Act, 1924, was the equivalent of British Trade Facilities Acts. The Summer Time Act, 1925, was for the same purpose as the corresponding British acts. The School Attendance Act, 1926, was similar in character to British acts on the same subject. The Industrial and Commercial Property (Protection) Act, 1927, established a statutory code relating to patents, trade marks, and copyright on similar lines to British acts. The Legitimacy Act, 1931, brought the law of the Free State into line with British law on this matter. The Road Traffic Act, 1933, followed to a large extent similar legislation in Britain. The Workmen's Compensation Act, 1934, was much on the lines of a British act of 1925. The Town and Regional Planning Act, 1934, followed the British Town Planning Act, 1932. The Hire-Purchase Act, 1946, was modelled on the British act of 1938.

Nevertheless, the oireachtas has not followed the legislative lead of the British parliament with the same consistency as the Northern Ireland and dominion parliaments have done. There have been significant divergences apart from the groups of statutes already discussed. This may have been due in part to the claims which those statutes made on the attention of the oireachtas. Certainly up to 1948 time was not found, for example, to satisfy the desire of professional groups like architects, engineers, and accountants for statutory registration such as exists in Great Britain. Nor did the oireachtas undertake any legal revision or codification of laws of the kind that has been carried out by the British parliament.[3] Again, the parliament of a small agricultural country like Ireland has less varied and complex problems

[1] In the Unemployment Act, 1934.
[2] By the Family Allowance Act, 1945.
[3] Since 1948 some progress has been made in these fields.

to cope with than the parliament of a highly industrialized world power; many British statutes relate to problems which have no counterpart in Ireland. Other differences may be attributed to the more limited resources of Ireland. The oireachtas has not been able to keep pace with the British parliament in such matters as educational reform and health services nor in the scale of benefits available under pension, unemployment, and health insurance schemes. Finally, Irish legislation differs from British in that it has been influenced positively and negatively by Roman catholic teaching and outlook. A censorship of publications was established by an act of 1929; statutes were passed legalizing betting and sweepstakes; the sale, advertisement, and importation of contraceptives was forbidden; the constitution of 1937 prohibited the enactment of any statute providing for divorce; in thirty years of independence no measure legalizing the adoption of children was passed; and a so-called 'mother and child' scheme was abandoned in face of clerical opposition. Even in statutes relating to matters which fall less directly within the scope of catholic social and moral teaching, evidence may be found of concessions to catholic sentiments. For example, the Conditions of Employment Act, 1936, and the Holidays (Employees) Act, 1939, provide that employers may substitute church holidays for state public holidays.

As in Great Britain and elsewhere a certain amount of legislation in Ireland has been inspired by the desire to negative or modify inconvenient judicial decisions. Two such acts were passed in quick succession in 1923. When the Court of Appeal ordered the release of an interned republican by writ of *habeas corpus* the oireachtas next day rushed through the Public Safety (Emergency Powers) Act, 1923, to enable the executive to continue the internments. On the issue of the writ of *habeas corpus* the state claimed the right to make a return, relying for cause on the provisions of the new act which had enabled the minister to make an order that the public safety would be endangered by the release of the prisoner. The Court of Appeal held that the return was bad because the Public Safety Act had contravened article 47 of the constitution by not containing a declaration of both houses of the oireachtas that it was necessary for the immediate preservation of the public health and safety.[1] To meet this situation a new act, containing the necessary declaration, was passed

---

[1] *R. (O'Brien)* v. *The Governor of Military Internment Camp and Minister for Defence*, 1924] I.R. 32, 37.

on the following day. Another example of this type of legislation was the Copyright (Preservation) Act, 1929, which was passed to protect the holders of copyright after the Supreme Court had held that the Copyright Act, 1911, ceased to apply to the Free State when it became a dominion.[1] The Courts of Justice (No. 2) Act, 1931, was passed as the result of a decision of the Supreme Court dealing with circuit court costs, pending the issue of the Rules of Court.[2] The act enabled the Taxing Master to tax such costs on any scale which he thought proper, and it validated costs already taxed. A decision of the Supreme Court in reference to the tidal waters of the River Erne[3] made necessary the Fisheries (Tidal Waters) Act, 1934. The Offences against the State (Amendment) Act, 1940, followed on the decision of the High Court in a case arising out of the Offences against the State Act, 1939.[4] The Accidental Fires Act, 1943, was passed to alter the existing law under an act of 1715 as interpreted by the Supreme Court.[5] The act provided that no legal proceedings could be instituted by a person suffering damage by reason of an accidental fire occurring in or on the buildings or land of another person. A decision of the Supreme Court arising out of a claim for a military pension[6] led to the passing of the Military Service Pensions (Amendment) Act, 1945.

Legislation has also been passed for the purpose of forestalling judicial decisions. This was the method employed on two occasions to render nugatory the right of appeal to the judicial committee of the privy council which existed under the Free State constitution. The Land Act, 1926, declared that the interpretation placed upon the Land Act, 1923, by the Irish courts in the case of *Lynham* v. *Butler*[7] was and always had been the law; and the Copyright (Preservation) Act, 1929, forestalled the findings of the judicial committee in the case of the *Performing Right Society* v. *Bray Urban District Council*[8] by providing that no remedy should be recoverable in respect of any infringement, before the passing of the act, of a copyright declared by the act to have subsisted in the Free State. An attempt to forestall a decision of the Irish courts was made by the Sinn Féin Funds Act, 1947, which

---

[1] *Performing Right Society* v. *Bray Urban District Council*, [1930] I.R. 509.
[2] *Quinn and White* v. *Stokes and Quirke*, [1931] I.R. 358, 558.
[3] *Moore and Others* v. *the Attorney-General*, [1934] I.R. 44.
[4] *The State (Burke)* v. *Lennon and the Attorney-General*, [1940] I.R. 136.
[5] *Richardson and Webster* v. *Athlone Woollen Mills Co. Ltd.*, [1942] I.R. 581.
[6] *The State (McCarthy)* v. *O'Donnell and Minister for Defence*, [1945] I.R. 126.
[7] [1925] I.R. 231.
[8] [1930] I.R. 509.

provided that all further proceedings in the pending action *Buckley and Others* v. *the Attorney-General and Another* should be stayed and that the High Court should on application *exparte* on behalf of the attorney-general dismiss the action and direct the Sinn Féin funds lodged in the Court to be paid out to a board set up by the act. This board was empowered, after payment of the costs already incurred by the parties to the action, to make payments out of the balance to persons in needy circumstances as a result of their services to the national cause during the revolutionary period. The act was subsequently held by the Supreme Court to be repugnant to the constitution.[1]

The legislative competence of the oireachtas was limited by the provisions in both the Free State and the 1937 constitutions which vested in the judiciary the power to pronounce on the constitutional validity of any law. In addition, until 1933, the courts were in a position to declare legislation invalid because it contravened the Anglo-Irish treaty. No occasion arose for the exercise of the latter power. Nor was any act declared invalid while the Free State constitution remained in force. The first Public Safety Act on which, as we have seen, the Court of Appeal made a ruling was held to be not invalid but only incapable of immediate application because it had not complied with the formal requirements prescribed by the constitution. For the whole period of the Free State's existence amendments could be made to the constitution by ordinary legislation. Consequently it was possible to guard against any measure being challenged as unconstitutional either by inserting a saving clause, as was done in the Public Safety Act, 1927, or by enacting the measure as a constitutional amendment, as was done in 1931 when the government required new public safety legislation. After the first two years the 1937 constitution became unalterable by ordinary legislation. The establishment of a rigid constitution created the conditions in which the judicial review of legislation could function. It can be evoked in two ways: the constitutional validity of any law may be challenged in the High Court from which an appeal lies to the Supreme Court; or the president, after consultation with the council of state, may refer a bill[2] to the Supreme Court for a decision on its constitutionality. Measures passed by the oireachtas were considered by the courts under both procedures in this period. In 1940 the High Court held that a

---

[1] *Buckley and Others* v. *Attorney-General and Another*, [1950] I.R. 67.
[2] Money bills, constitution amendment bills, and bills declared urgent by the government are excepted.

minister of state in signing a warrant under section 55 of the Offences against the State Act, 1939, was administering justice which was contrary to the constitution.[1] This decision was not reviewed in the Supreme Court because of a technical bar to appeal in the case of an order of *habeas corpus*. The provisions of part iii of the Trade Union Act, 1941, by purporting to deprive citizens of the choice of persons with whom they might associate, were declared by the Supreme Court to be at variance with the emphatic assertion in article 40 of the constitution of the citizens' right to form associations and unions.[2] The Sinn Féin Funds Act, 1947, offended against the declarations contained in article 43 of the constitution as to rights of private property and was also repugnant to the constitution as being an unwarrantable interference by the oireachtas with the operation of the courts in a purely judicial domain.[3] The Supreme Court, affirming the High Court, held in 1950 that the provisions of section 165 of the Mental Treatment Act, 1945, were not repugnant to the constitution as infringing the personal rights of the citizens.[4]

An instance of the Courts pronouncing on the constitutionality of a bill arose out of the Offences against the State (Amendment) Bill, 1940, which was designed to remedy the constitutional defects which the High Court had found in the Offences against the State Act, 1939. The bill was referred by the president to the Supreme Court which held that it was not repugnant to the constitution.[5] The School Attendance Bill, 1942, was also referred to the Supreme Court by the president. On this occasion the court ruled that section 4 of the bill was repugnant to the constitution.[6] In view of this decision the president declined to sign the bill.

It remains to note that the legislative output of the oireachtas has been dwarfed by the mass of statutory rules, orders, and regulations made by the government or by individual ministers in accordance with powers conferred by statutes. The growth of this delegated legislation is a phenomenon common to many states and particularly striking in Great Britain. In Ireland the volume of delegated legislation has increased steadily since 1922. In the twelve years from

[1] *The State (Burke)* v. *Lennon and the Attorney-General*, [1940] I.R. 136.
[2] *National Union of Railwaymen and Others* v. *Sullivan and Others*, [1947] I.R. 77.
[3] *Buckley and Others* v. *Attorney-General and Another*, [1950] I.R. 67.
[4] *In re Philip Clarke*, [1950] I.R. 235.
[5] *In the Matter of Article 26 of the Constitution and in the Matter of the Offences Against the State (Amendment) Bill*, [1940] I.R. 470.
[6] *In the Matter of Article 26 of the Constitution and in the Matter of the School Attendance Bill, 1942*, [1943] I.R. 334.

6 December 1921 to 31 December 1933 over 3,000 orders were made.[1] In the period 1939–45, not counting the emergency powers orders occasioned by the war, 2,420 orders were promulgated.

Over this extensive range of subsidiary law the oireachtas, in theory, exercised a measure of control. Normally the act which delegated the power of making rules, orders, or regulations reserved to the oireachtas the power of annulment by providing that every regulation made should be laid before each house of the oireachtas and that within a specified period—usually twenty-one sitting days—the regulation could be annulled by resolution of either house. Occasionally a resolution of both houses was necessary for an annulment. In a few cases a resolution of approval from both houses was required before the regulation became operative. Other acts empowered the government or a minister to make orders but laid down that such orders had to be confirmed by statute. In some cases the orders were valid when made but lapsed if not confirmed within a stated period.

By no means all rules, orders, and regulations were brought to the notice of the oireachtas in one or other of these ways; many of them were never 'laid on the table', others received little publicity and were not made easily accessible to members. On the other hand members showed no disposition to examine systematically those regulations which were submitted to the oireachtas. The problems inherent in legislation by order were debated at length on a private member's motion in 1946.[2] Government spokesmen contended that such legislation was necessary and inevitable however undesirable it might be in theory. They stressed the fact that the powers of legislation enjoyed by ministers were conferred and could be revoked by the oireachtas. Opposition members expressed concern about the ever-growing numbers of orders and about the lack of real control exercised by the oireachtas, but they propounded no solution to the problem and the motion was not pressed to a division. In the following year the government introduced a bill which provided for the printing and publishing of statutory rules and orders. When such statutory instruments were made notice was to be given in the official gazette—*Iris Oifigiúil*—and the instruments themselves were to be printed and published in an official numbered series.[3] In accordance with this act the task of collecting and publishing past orders was undertaken.

---

[1] G. Gavan Duffy and Art O'Connor (ed.), *A Register of Administrative Law in Saorstat Éireann*, p. iii.
[2] *Dáil Debates*, xcix. 1651 et seq.   [3] *Senate Debates*, xxxiv. 1345–64.

Orders made in the period 1922–38 were collected and bound in twenty-three volumes. They included orders which had already been printed, orders which had appeared only in *Iris Oifigiúil*, and orders which, being for departmental use, had not hitherto been published. Orders of an executive, local, or temporary character, or having a limited application, were shown in italicized form in the index to the printed volumes but were not included in them. Orders of merely personal application or otherwise having little or no public interest were omitted both from the volumes and the index. A further set of eleven volumes was prepared covering the period 1939–45. Since then an annual volume has been published.

XIII

THE DÁIL AND THE EXECUTIVE

EXTERNAL AFFAIRS

THE avowed aim of all governments and parties since the formation of the state has been to assert the independence and to secure the unification of the country. For this reason problems of external relations have attracted more attention than they would otherwise have done in a state which could hope to play only a minor role in international affairs. In fact the interest in external relations has been merely another facet of the preoccupation with the problem of the country's constitutional position. To an even greater extent than in domestic legislation the formulation and direction of an external policy has been the work of the executive. Yet the dáil enjoys certain constitutional powers in this field and it has usually displayed a lively interest, admittedly on party lines, in any question of external relations which came before it.

The constitution of the Irish Free State vested the control of the armed forces in the oireachtas and provided that the state should not be committed to active participation in any war without the assent of the oireachtas, save in the case of actual invasion.[1] The constitution of 1937 repeated the first of these provisions but reserved to the dáil alone the right to declare war.[2] It also provided that every international agreement to which the state became a party should be laid before the dáil, that with the exception of agreements or conventions of a technical and administrative character no international agreement involving a charge upon public funds should be binding unless it was approved by the dáil, and that no international agreement should be part of the domestic law of the state except as might be determined by the oireachtas.[3] The new provisions were probably inspired by Fianna Fáil's resentment of the position under the Free State constitution when the Anglo-Irish treaty was part of the municipal law of the state and when the executive council had concluded agreements with the British government which were not laid before

[1] *Constitution of I.F.S.*, arts. 46, 49.
[2] *Constitution of Ireland*, arts. 15. 6. 1°, 28. 3. 1°.
[3] Ibid., art. 29. 5–6.

the dáil. Obviously these constitutional rights in themselves would not have afforded frequent opportunities to the dáil of considering external relations. But the responsibility of the government to the dáil ensured that each major move in the country's foreign policy would fall within the dáil's purview. Members of the dáil have been able to express their views on external relations in the debates on the annual estimate for the department of external affairs, on the numerous constitutional amendments affecting relations with the British Commonwealth, and on motions or bills relating to special problems or developments. Nevertheless, complaints were made in 1926 that the dáil was not being kept fully informed about international affairs. The leader of the opposition, Thomas Johnson, submitted a motion calling upon the minister for external affairs to make more frequent statements in the dáil and to publish relevant documents relating to matters in which the state was concerned, either through its membership of the League of Nations or of the Commonwealth. In the course of the debate one deputy suggested the setting up of a committee representative of all parties in the house analogous to the foreign affairs committee of the French chamber of deputies or of the American senate. The minister denied that the dáil had been kept in the dark though he admitted that his statements had been made 'not very often, relatively seldom'. He gave an assurance that the government would not commit the dáil to anything without its consent. The motion was agreed to without a division.[1]

Attention naturally tended to be focused on the crucial problem of relations with Great Britain and the Commonwealth, but even on other questions of external policy the desire to emphasize the independent status of the country was always an important consideration. While the Irish Free State constitution was still in process of enactment the dáil passed a resolution directing the government to apply for membership of the League of Nations as soon as they found it advantageous to do so. It was pointed out in the discussion that admission would be of great value as a 'pre-eminent test of sovereignty'.[2] The Irish Free State was admitted to the League in September 1923. Just over a year later the executive council registered the Anglo-Irish treaty under the League covenant as an international document, a step which evoked a protest from the British government.[3] The first treaty to be submitted to the Free State dáil was the

[1] *Dáil Debates*, xiv. 539–74.   [2] Ibid. i. 391; iii. 365.
[3] Ibid. ix. 2740–3.

Anglo-American liquor treaty which was signed on 23 January 1924. The motion for approval provided the occasion for a general discussion on the constitutional relationship with Britain. The minister for external affairs pointed out that while citizens of the other dominions were issued with passports on which they were described as British subjects, Irish nationals were described on their passports as citizens of the Irish Free State and of the British Commonwealth of Nations. He also asserted the right of the Free State to have direct diplomatic relations with foreign states as well as with the Commonwealth countries and announced the government's intention of exercising the right by appointing a fully accredited representative at Washington.[1]

By taking this step in October 1924[2] the Irish Free State anticipated by more than two years the appointment of a diplomatic representative by any of the older dominions, for though Canada had received the consent of the British government to the appointment of a Canadian minister at Washington as early as 1920 it was not until 1926 that the appointment was made. The treaty for the renunciation of war (the Briand–Kellogg pact) was approved by the dáil in February 1929 after a debate in which the Fianna Fáil party showed more concern about relations with Britain than about the wider international situation.[3] The Irish Free State diverged from the Commonwealth policy in 1929 on the question of accepting as compulsory the jurisdiction of the Permanent Court of International Justice in disputes between signatory states. Great Britain and the other members of the Commonwealth signed the so-called optional clause with a reservation as to intra-commonwealth disputes; the Irish Free State signed without reservation. In seeking the approval of the dáil the minister for external affairs acknowledged the particular relationship between members of the Commonwealth, but he declared that while the government would try the ordinary method of negotiation in disputes with Great Britain it could in no event rule out the possibility of appeal to the International Court.[4] Through its membership of the League of Nations the Irish Free State was able to play an independent role in international affairs. In 1926 the government made an unsuccessful attempt to secure election to the Council of the League.[5] Four years later the Irish Free State was elected in succession to Canada with the

---

[1] *Dáil Debates*, vi. 2925–9, 3030–6.
[3] *Dáil Debates*, xxviii. 277–320, 334–74.
[4] Ibid. xxxiii. 886.
[2] *Iris Oifigiúil*, 17 Oct. 1924.
[5] *Round Table*, xvii. 138–9.

support of Great Britain and the other dominions, though the Irish representative had asserted in submitting his country as a candidate that he did so on its own merits, and not as a member of any group or combination of states.[1]

The change of government in 1932 did not affect Ireland's participation in the work of the League. De Valera was elected president of the League Assembly in 1932. At the opening meeting he caused something of a sensation by setting aside the speech prepared for him by the secretariat and delivering instead a solemn warning and challenge to the assembled delegates. His speech had a cold reception from the Assembly but was enthusiastically welcomed by the press of many countries. In spite of the religious tie with Italy the Fianna Fáil government stood by the League policy of sanctions against Italy during the Abyssinian war. Its decision won general approval in the dáil, though the opposition contended that the occasion should have been utilized to end the economic war with Britain.[2] The complication of religious affinities with one of the belligerents arose again during the Spanish civil war. Despite strong opposition pressure for the recognition of the insurgents the government adopted a policy of non-intervention and joined the International Non-Intervention Committee. In February 1937 the committee extended the non-intervention agreement to cover the recruitment of volunteers for service in Spain. The bill to give effect to this decision in the Irish Free State was vigorously assailed by the opposition who fought it on the issue of communism versus christianity.[3] Though its policy in both these international crises coincided with that of Great Britain the Irish government acted on its own initiative. De Valera vehemently denied an allegation that he had acted at the dictation of Britain.[4]

The growing tension in Europe threw into relief the problem of the defence facilities which the British retained in the Irish Free State under the terms of the Anglo-Irish treaty. In June 1936 de Valera stated in the dáil that the aim of his government was to secure the withdrawal of the British forces so that the country might remain neutral if a European war broke out. So long as Britain retained bases in the country it would be liable to attack by any enemy of Great Britain. He contended that the British fear of foreign attack through Ireland was groundless; his government was prepared to guarantee

[1] O'Sullivan, *The Irish Free State and its Senate*, p. 251.
[2] *Dáil Debates*, lix. 499–500.
[3] Ibid. lxiv. 1197–1226; lxv. 597–640, 642–864, 895–1024.
[4] Ibid. lxxii. 641, 686–7.

The Dáil and the Executive: External Affairs

that the full strength of the nation would be used to resist any attempt by a foreign power to abuse Irish neutrality.[1] The steady deterioration in the European situation was probably responsible for the British government's decision to placate Ireland. Early in January 1938 de Valera announced in the dáil that a meeting was to take place between representatives of the two governments.[2] At a series of meetings in the next few months three matters came under discussion: partition, the defence facilities, and the economic war. No solution of the first problem was found, but on 25 April 1938 three agreements were signed in London by representatives of the two governments which declared themselves 'desirous of promoting relations of friendship and good understanding between the two countries, of reaching a final settlement on all outstanding financial claims of either of the two governments against the other, and of facilitating trade and commerce between the two countries.[3] The first of these agreements annulled the provisions of the Anglo-Irish treaty relating to British defence facilities in Éire. The British bases at Cobh, Berehaven, and Lough Swilly were to be transferred to the Irish government by 31 December 1938, and the British government renounced its right to extended facilities in time of war or strained relations with a foreign power. The agreements were confirmed by a resolution of the dáil which was passed without a division after a three days' debate.[4] During the debate de Valera repeated the assurance that his government would not allow Irish territory to be used as a base of attack against Great Britain, but his determination to preserve Ireland's neutrality was unaffected by the agreement.[5] The threat of a European war reacted on Anglo-Irish relations again when it moved the British government to introduce compulsory military service in the spring of 1939. The possibility of conscription being extended to Northern Ireland aroused the resentment of the nationalist minority there and drew a protest from de Valera. His action was unanimously endorsed by the dáil.[6] Although the British government decided not to apply conscription in Northern Ireland the further question remained of the position of Irishmen living in England. De Valera unsuccessfully

---

[1] *Dáil Debates*, lxii. 2659–60.
[2] Ibid. lxix. 2888.
[3] *Agreement between the Government of the United Kingdom and the Government of Eire, signed in London, 25 April 1938*, [Cmd. 5728], H.C. 1937–8, xxx. 1001.
[4] *Dáil Debates*, lxxi. 32–60, 163–304, 306–456.
[5] Ibid. lxxii. 694–715.
[6] Ibid. lxxv. 1415, 1429–60.

protested against the British government's treatment of them as British subjects.[1]

When war became inevitable the dáil was summoned to consider two bills necessitated by the decision to remain neutral. The first proposed to amend the article of the constitution which provided that emergency legislation might be passed for the purpose of securing the public safety in time of war. Time of war was now extended to mean a time when there was taking place an armed conflict in which the state was not a participant. Apart from some doubts about the effects of neutrality on the partition issue there was no opposition to the government's policy and the bills were passed without a division.[2]

Throughout the war the energies and resourcefulness of the Irish government and people were taxed to the utmost in avoiding the dangers which beset a small neutral state strategically placed in the midst of a warring world. All political parties were convinced that the policy of neutrality was both justifiable and expedient. The government was therefore assured of well-nigh unanimous support in the dáil on the basic aspect of its policy, however much it might be criticized for the means it employed to sustain that policy. James Dillon, vice-chairman of the Fine Gael party, spoke for a small minority when he advocated a policy of co-operation with Britain and America. But his colleagues in the party were quick to dissociate themselves from such a proposal and to reaffirm their support for neutrality.[3] At the other extreme the militant republicans of the I.R.A. saw in the war an opportunity for renewing their campaign of violence, but they too had little popular support and no champions in the dáil.[4] De Valera was probably fully justified in maintaining that a proportion as high at least as 90 per cent. of the people of the country supported the policy of neutrality.[5] But if there was no significant internal demand for an abandonment of neutrality the pressure from abroad was at times considerable, and the possibility of invasion could never be entirely discounted. In view of the past relations between the two countries approaches by Great Britain were relatively easy to resist, but when America entered the war the Irish government was placed in an acutely embarrassing position. De Valera immediately announced that the policy of the state remained unchanged, that they could only be a friendly neutral.[6] The stationing of

[1] *Dáil Debates*, lxxvi. 311–12, 972–5.   [2] Ibid. lxxvii. 1–190.
[3] Ibid. lxxxiv. 1864–5, 1882, 1884.
[4] Ibid. lxxviii. 1309–1524, 1527–1648.
[5] Ibid. lxxxiv. 1908.   [6] *Irish Times*, 15 Dec. 1941.

American troops in Northern Ireland created a further delicate situation, for de Valera felt obliged to protest against what he regarded as a violation of the national territory. A more serious crisis was precipitated by the presentation of an American note on 21 February 1944 requesting the closing of the German and Japanese embassies in Dublin. Having failed to enlist the aid of Canada and Australia in attempting to secure the withdrawal of the American note the Irish government replied that it was unable to comply with the demand since the closing of the embassies would be tantamount to an abandonment of neutrality.[1] De Valera himself admitted subsequently that Ireland owed her immunity to the concurrence of wills of two men, the British prime minister and the American president.[2] Their decision to allow considerations of international morality to outweigh an immediate military advantage ensured the success of the Irish policy of neutrality, though the propriety with which the Irish government observed its obligations as a neutral would have made any other course difficult for them as the declared champions of international right and justice.

Since the conclusion of the war the isolation which came in the wake of neutrality has not been entirely broken down. Though Ireland participated in the economic work of the United Nations Organization it had for long no share in its political activities. As early as November 1943 de Valera declared that Ireland was ready to join any international organization which aimed at collective security and the maintenance of peace on the basis of the equality of sovereign right between nations, large and small.[3] A motion recommending the government to seek admission to the United Nations Organization was passed by the dáil without a division in July 1946,[4] but the Irish application for membership was vetoed by the Soviet Union in September 1947 and Ireland was not admitted until 1956. On the other hand the Irish government refused to join the Atlantic Pact ostensibly as a protest against the partition of the country.[5] Ireland has, however, become a member of the Council of Europe. The minister for external affairs took part in the preliminary discussions which led to the drafting of the statute setting up the Council, and on 13 July 1949 the dáil unanimously adopted a motion approving of the statute.[6]

[1] *Irish Times*, 11 Mar. 1944.
[2] *Dáil Debates*, cii. 1465-6.
[3] Ibid. xci. 2016.
[4] Ibid. cii. 1481.
[5] Ibid. cxiv. 323-6.
[6] Ibid. cxvi. 694-716, 741-8.

On the major external problem of relations with Great Britain and the Commonwealth the fiercest party contests were fought. The Irish governments before and after 1932 were at one in their desire for unity and independence, but they interpreted the meaning of independence in different ways and consequently employed different methods to attain their ends. The Cumann na nGaedheal government aspired to the fullest measure of independence for a united Ireland within the framework of the Commonwealth. The Fianna Fáil government was convinced that independence could only be realized under a republican polity, but it was prepared to enter into a form of external association with the Commonwealth, partly in the hope of inducing the Ulster unionists to accept a united Ireland and partly in the belief that association was desirable in itself. Each policy in its turn contributed significantly to the developing conception of the nature and form of the Commonwealth.

The protracted debate in the dáil on the Anglo-Irish treaty revealed the reluctance with which Ireland entered the Commonwealth. Speaker after speaker on the pro-treaty side qualified or excused his acceptance of the proposed settlement. Even such prominent supporters of the treaty as Collins, Griffith, and O'Higgins looked forward to an enlarged freedom. Collins said of the treaty: 'I do not recommend it for more than it is. Equally I do not recommend it for less than it is. In my opinion, it gives us freedom, not the ultimate freedom that all nations desire and develop to, but the freedom to achieve it.' Griffith declared: 'It is not an ideal thing; it could be better. It has no more finality than that we are the final generation on the face of the earth.' O'Higgins expressed similar sentiments. 'I hardly hope that within the terms of the treaty there lies the fulfilment of Ireland's destiny but I hope and believe that what remains may be won by agreement and by peaceful political evolution.'[1] From the beginning, then, the pro-treaty party was committed to the policy of extracting as much as possible from the dominion status which it had won for the country.

For this reason the Free State government was ready to co-operate with like-minded states in the Commonwealth to secure the removal of anomalies in inter-imperial relations and the acceptance of a more precise definition of dominion status. From the institution of the state it carefully noted any constitutional practices within the Commonwealth that appeared incompatible with the conception of complete

[1] *Treaty Debate*, pp. 32, 47, 337.

co-equality of status.[1] Desmond Fitzgerald, minister for external affairs, held that: 'The advent of Ireland, from the fact that the Irish nation was known historically and culturally, made known to people abroad, even to a greater extent than did the event of the signature of the treaty of Versailles, that these nations known as dominions were full sovereign states in the world.' Yet he admitted at the same time that dominion status was 'adolescent but not entirely adult', and he indicated a number of matters that he intended to raise at the next Imperial Conference.[2]

The Imperial Conference of 1926 began the task of readjustment. A committee on inter-imperial relations was appointed under the chairmanship of Lord Balfour. This committee produced a definition of the dominions[3] which, though expressed in non-legal and ambiguous terms, was open to an interpretation consonant with the Free State's view. On some of the inequalities of status which were recognized as existing the committee put forward recommendations. It pointed out that the reference to 'the United Kingdom of Great Britain and Ireland' in the royal title was not in accordance with the new status of the twenty-six counties and it proposed an alteration. It recommended that the governor-general of a dominion should cease to have any of the functions or attributes of a representative of the British government. It declared that questions affecting appeals to the judicial committee of the privy council should not be determined otherwise than in accordance with the wishes of the part of the Empire primarily affected. In order to safeguard the position of the United Kingdom in relation to the Irish Free State, however, the qualifying statement was added that where changes in the existing system were proposed which, while primarily affecting one part, raised issues in which other parts were also concerned, such changes ought only to be carried out after consultation and discussion. The committee also formulated rules which should regulate the conduct of foreign relations. Other anomalies, the committee suggested, should be referred to committees of experts with a view to their removal.[4] Fitzgerald subsequently asserted that the report of the Imperial Con-

---
[1] *Dáil Debates*, xvii. 879.   [2] Ibid. xvi. 259, 264.
[3] They are autonomous communities within the British Empire, equal in status, in no way subordinate one to another in any aspect of their domestic or external affairs, though united by a common allegiance to the crown, and freely associated as members of the British Commonwealth of Nations.
[4] K. C. Wheare, *The Statute of Westminster and Dominion Status*, pp. 24–39; *Dáil Debates*, xvii. 711–28.

ference, which embodied the recommendations of the Balfour committee, was based largely upon the memoranda compiled by the Irish ministry for external affairs.[1]

Opposition members in the dáil attacked the report not so much on the details of its proposals as on the general ground that it failed to satisfy the national aspirations of Ireland.[2] Ministers were able to reply that they had not gone to London to negotiate a new treaty with the British government; they had gone to bring practice into form with the constitutional position. They made no claim to having arrived at perfection but they maintained that the report was satisfactory inasmuch as it improved the position and made it clearer than before that there was a root principle which was co-equality.[3]

It now became the aim of the Free State government to consolidate this co-equality by securing the removal of the last remnants of the old order of imperial control.[4] For this it looked to the further conferences foreshadowed in the 1926 report. Meantime it was on the alert to detect anything that might savour of external interference: when a council of regency was established in Great Britain during the king's illness it pointed out how improper it would be for political persons like the prime minister of Great Britain to sign Irish documents in the name of the king.[5] Free State ministers attended the conference on the operation of dominion legislation and merchant shipping legislation in 1929 and the Imperial Conference in 1930. At the opening of the 1930 conference Patrick McGilligan, the minister for external affairs, stated the Irish attitude in unequivocal terms:

For us the recognition of our position as a free and sovereign state comes before all other considerations.... While certain elements in the old system of imperial control were maintained, even though it was only in form, the will to co-operate was correspondingly weakened. We most earnestly urge upon the present conference the need for removing finally those last obstacles to harmonious and easy intercourse. So long as any form of control remained co-operation had to be tinged with some colouring of compulsion. That made it less wholehearted and less effective. I should not be frank with you if at this juncture I did not definitely place before you in what seems to our government to be the proper perspective the considerations which should govern the proceedings of this conference.[6]

The process of removing legal and conventional inequalities was carried a stage further by the conferences of 1929 and 1930. It was

[1] *Dáil Debates*, xxxiii. 2199. [2] Ibid. xvii. 728–55, 756–70, 876–95.
[3] Ibid. xvii. 895–7, 903, 920. [4] Ibid. xxvii. 432; xxx. 792. [5] Ibid. xxx. 875.
[6] *Imperial Conference, 1930. Appendices to the Summary of Proceedings*, [Cmd. 3718], H.C. 1930–1, xiv. 701.

The Dáil and the Executive: External Affairs

decided that a governor-general should be appointed by the king on the advice of the ministers in the dominion concerned. The power of disallowance was no longer to be exercised in relation to dominion legislation and the dominions were authorized to delete disallowance from their constitutions. The power of reservation was also dealt with. The governor-general's discretionary right to reserve bills for the consideration of the British government was henceforth to be exercised in accordance with the advice of the dominion ministers and the British government was no longer to instruct a governor-general to reserve bills presented to him for assent. Furthermore, it was recognized that it would not be in accordance with constitutional practice for the British government to advise the king on reserved bills contrary to the views of the government of the dominion. Other restrictions were removed by the Statute of Westminster in 1931. By its terms no act of the British parliament was to extend to a dominion except at the request and with the consent of the dominion's government, no dominion act was to be rendered void on the ground of repugnancy to an act of the British parliament, and the dominion parliaments were given full power to make laws having extra-territorial operation.[1]

Not all the restrictions thus removed had applied with equal force to the Irish Free State—some had not applied at all—but the Irish government was none the less interested in the decisions on them. The status of the Free State was largely defined by analogy; consequently the Irish government was as eager to see the other dominions moving towards independence as it was to assert Irish sovereignty.[2] But it was independence and sovereignty within the Commonwealth at which the Free State ministers aimed. They believed that the state could enjoy greater freedom and greater security as a member of the Commonwealth than as an independent republic.[3] When the Statute of Westminster was being enacted amendments were moved both in the House of Commons and in the House of Lords designed to ensure that the Statute should confer on the oireachtas no greater power of amending the Free State constitution than it had before.[4] When it appeared that the British government was considering the inclusion of some such amendment Cosgrave wrote a letter of protest to the prime minister, but he also gave an assurance that the

---

[1] Wheare, op. cit., pp. 139–75.
[2] *Dáil Debates*, xxxiii. 2202.
[3] Ibid. xxii. 1645–6.
[4] 260 *H.C. Deb.*, 5s., 303; 83 *H.L. Deb.*, 5s., 231.

Statute would not be used to alter the treaty position, that he and his colleagues regarded the treaty as an international agreement which could not be altered except with the consent of the British government.[1] By 1931 they were able to contend that their goal was wellnigh reached,[2] and much of the credit for this achievement they claimed for themselves. McGilligan believed that the Anglo-Irish treaty and the constitution of the Irish Free State had given a new direction to constitutional thought, and had set going new forces and new processes in constitutional speculation within the Commonwealth.[3] Every advance in the dominions' position since 1922 had been primarily due, he declared, to the activities of the Free State government.[4] In making this assertion he was doing less than justice to the part played by Canada and South Africa at the Imperial Conferences but he was not distorting the facts unduly.

The government's record of achievement at the Imperial Conferences failed to reconcile the opposition to the treaty settlement. To the members of the Fianna Fáil party anything that suggested the removal of external control was welcome, but they accused the government of failing to carry out the promise made by the founders of the Free State to use the treaty settlement as a stepping-stone to independence which to them meant a break with the Commonwealth. The policy of the government was calculated, they feared, to make the people satisfied with dominion status; it was designed to 'nail us, to copper-fasten us, for ever to the British Empire and its king'. Their aim was the restoration of the republic. There might be value in the association of near neighbours, but that association, if it was to exist in the future, must be based on the free will of the Irish nation; the existing association was not based on this free will.[5] The difference in outlook between the government and the principal opposition party was summed up by one Fianna Fáil member when he said that whereas the government regarded the difference between Ireland being inside and outside the British Empire merely as a matter of degree of independence, they regarded it as a matter of essence.[6]

The Fianna Fáil victory in 1932 was responsible for two important developments. For one thing the dáil became more directly concerned with Commonwealth relations than it had been hitherto. The pre-

[1] 260 *H.C. Deb.*, 5s., 311; *Dáil Debates*, cxiii. 481.
[2] Ibid. xxxix. 2354.   [3] Ibid. xxx. 793.
[4] Ibid. xxvii. 447.
[5] Ibid. xxvii. 437; xxx. 851-2; xxxiii. 2077-83; xxxix. 2309-13.
[6] Ibid. xxxiv. 161-2.

vious government had relied mainly on the Imperial Conferences and on negotiation with British ministers for the furtherance of its policy. The results of its labours were discussed sometimes on the motion for the adjournment, sometimes on special motions of approval. One important agreement—the Financial Agreement of 12 February 1923 concerning the payment of the land annuities—was never submitted to the dáil at all, and another—the Ultimate Financial Settlement of 19 March 1926—did not come up for discussion until eight months after it had been signed. The new government's policy of weakening the imperial tie involved successive legislative steps which provided the opportunity for more frequent and protracted debates than had been customary under the previous régime. Moreover, the complete change of attitude to Great Britain and the Commonwealth aroused strong political passions which were ventilated in the dáil on all possible occasions.

A second result of Fianna Fáil's accession to power was the termination, for the time at least, of the harmonious relations with Great Britain which had been maintained since the establishment of the state. While in opposition the party had made no secret of its determination to undo the treaty settlement, but its immediate aim, as set out in its election manifesto, was to abolish the parliamentary oath and to retain the land annuities and other annual payments in the state treasury. The land annuities were annual payments of about £3,000,000 made by Irish farmers in repayment of money lent to them for the purchase of their farms under the Land Purchase Acts of 1891–1909. Since 1923 the annuities had been transmitted each half-year by the Irish government to the British National Debt Commissioners pursuant to the Financial Agreement of 1923 and the Ultimate Financial Settlement of 1926. The other payments, amounting to £2,000,000 annually, were made up of various items including a sum of £600,000 for twenty years to the Local Loans Fund and 75 per cent. of the pensions payable to former members of the Royal Irish Constabulary.

No sooner was the new government installed in office than it revealed its intention not only of fulfilling its election promises but also of following an uncompromising and unconciliatory course. No formal notification of its plans was conveyed to the British government. When British ministers protested against the policy outlined by de Valera in the press and on the radio they were answered by an attack on the whole treaty position. At meetings with British ministers in Dublin and London in June 1932 de Valera stated openly that his ultimate aim was the abolition of partition and the establishment of an independent republic loosely associated with the British Commonwealth. Since his government had no mandate for this full programme he would be content, for the moment, to abolish the parliamentary oath which had been forced upon Ireland under duress and to retain the land annuities which had been paid without the approval of the dáil. He held that the removal of the oath did not run across the Anglo-Irish treaty; that it was a domestic matter. As for the annuities dispute, he was willing to accept arbitration provided the arbitration court was not confined, as the British insisted, to citizens of the Commonwealth.[1]

When the Irish government defaulted over payment of the half-yearly instalment of the land annuities in July 1932, the House of Commons passed a financial resolution enabling the government to collect the amount involved by means of customs duties levied on Irish imports. It followed up this action by passing the Irish Free State (Special Duties) Act. The Irish government retaliated with the Emergency Imposition of Duties Act which imposed penal duties on British imports. An Irish delegation attended the Commonwealth Economic Conference at Ottawa but no agreement was reached with Great Britain. A further conference with British ministers in London in October was equally unproductive, for the Irish ministers put forward a counter-claim of three or four hundred million pounds in respect to over-taxation since the Union of 1801 and to an unspecified amount representing damage caused by Britain's abandonment of the gold standard.[2] On the failure of these conferences the 'economic war' was left to take its course.

These events were not allowed to pass without challenge in the dáil. On 15 November 1932 the leader of the opposition moved a vote of censure on the government for its failure to conclude an agreement with the British government. He and other opposition spokesmen accused the government of having exposed the country to unnecessary dangers by its incompetence and recklessness, and they demanded the settlement of the disputes with Great Britain by negotiation.[3]

In the early months of the new government's life all the parties to the dispute—the Irish government, the British government, and the

---

[1] O'Sullivan, op. cit., pp. 286–7.
[2] Ibid., p. 290.
[3] *Dáil Debates*, xliv. 1594–1742.

Irish opposition—had thus taken a definite stand. The Fianna Fáil government proceeded during the next four years to work steadily towards the attainment of its goal. The parliamentary oath was abrogated. The right of appeal to the judicial committee of the privy council—which had been rendered nugatory by the previous government—was abolished. Under the Irish Nationality and Citizenship Act, 1935, Irish citizens ceased to be regarded in Irish law as British subjects. The crown was eliminated from the constitution in the manner described elsewhere.[1] External association was substituted for membership of the Commonwealth. Finally, the mutilated Free State constitution was replaced by a new constitution which was republican in all but name. On the financial dispute a decisive step was taken in March 1933 when the withheld payments were transferred to the exchequer from the suspense accounts in which they had been retained.[2] The economic war provided the justification and the opportunity for pursuing a policy of economic self-sufficiency. A drive for increased tillage was inaugurated and plans were evolved for the industrialization of the country.

The parliamentary opposition was bitterly hostile to the government's policy at almost every point, and since so much of that policy involved legislation it was given ample opportunity for the expression of its views. The vocal opposition of the British government died down after the first year of Fianna Fáil government, but it was not until the spring of 1938 that amicable relations between the two countries were restored. There were two stages in this development. The first was marked by the decision of the British government to treat the new constitution as not effecting a fundamental alteration in the relationship of Éire to the Commonwealth;[3] the second by the conclusion of three agreements in London on 25 April 1938. The first of these was the agreement, already referred to, relating to the treaty ports. By the second the Irish government agreed to pay the sum of £10,000,000 in final settlement of the financial claims and both governments undertook to abolish the penal duties which had been in force since 1932. The third was a comprehensive trade agreement designed to facilitate trade between the two countries. It was to remain in force for three years. The agreements were ratified by a resolution of the dáil which was passed without a division on 29 April 1938 after a three days' debate.[4]

[1] See pp. 157-8.   [2] *Dáil Debates*, xlvi. 676.
[3] *Irish Times*, 30 Dec. 1937.   [4] *Dáil Debates*, lxxi. 32–60; 163–304, 306–456.

The settlement of 1938 left unresolved two major problems concerning Anglo-Irish relations—the exact constitutional status of Éire, and partition. The constitution of 1937 was an ingenious instrument for securing the substance of an independent republican status while retaining whatever advantages might accrue from continued association with the Commonwealth, including possibly the reunification of the country. But such a solution was unacceptable to the republican diehards and it was sufficiently ambiguous to provide the opposition with a handle for embarrassing the government. When the crown was deleted from the Free State constitution in 1936 J. A. Costello declared that the bill created 'a political monstrosity, the like of which is unknown to political legal theory, such a monstrosity as exists nowhere in any polity in the world'.[1]

From that time it was the aim of the opposition members to elicit from de Valera a precise definition of the country's status. But for long de Valera walked warily. Only after the war was he prepared to state openly that the country was a republic. On the question of whether it was a republic within or outside the Commonwealth he was less specific. The most he would say was that if membership of the Commonwealth implied allegiance to the king or acceptance of the king as king in Ireland they were not in the Commonwealth.[2] This equivocal position was ended by the inter-party government which came into office in 1948. Although the Fine Gael Party, the largest component of the coalition, had always stood for the Commonwealth connexion, although the leader of the party, Richard Mulcahy, as recently as 1944 had advocated full membership of the Commonwealth, it now adopted the republicanism of its new Clann na Poblachta allies. On 7 September 1948 the taoiseach, J. A. Costello, announced in Ottawa his government's intention of repealing the Executive Authority (External Relations) Act. In October and November consultations were held with representatives of Great Britain, Canada, Australia, and New Zealand on the consequences which would follow on the Irish government's proposed action. The Republic of Ireland Bill received a unanimous second reading in the dáil on 26 November. On the previous day the prime minister stated in the House of Commons that the British government would not regard the enactment of this bill as placing Éire in the category of a foreign country, or citizens of Éire in the category of foreigners. The Republic of Ireland Act, 1948, which became law on 21 December,

[1] *Dáil Debates*, lxiv. 1293.   [2] Ibid. xcvii. 2573; cvii. 86.

came into force on 18 April 1949. From midnight on that date Éire ceased to be a member of the Commonwealth.

There remains the problem of partition. Since the formation of the state it has been a stock theme at parliamentary elections, a perennial topic of discussion in the oireachtas, and a recurring item on the agenda of Anglo-Irish conferences. Political groups and parties have vied with one another in expressing devotion to the idea of a united Ireland, but they have differed sharply on the means by which they proposed to bring it into existence. The republican extremists have sought to restore unity by force. They have been responsible for periodic outbursts of violence in Northern Ireland and in the rest of the country and for a time in 1939 they extended their activities to England.

The signatories of the Anglo-Irish treaty pinned great hopes on the clause which provided for a commission to determine 'in accordance with the wishes of the inhabitants, so far as may be compatible with economic and geographical conditions' the boundary between Northern Ireland and the Irish Free State in the event of Northern Ireland electing to retain the position it had secured under the Government of Ireland Act, 1920.[1] It was confidently expected that the commission would adjust the boundary in such a way as to leave Northern Ireland an uneconomic unit which would be compelled to seek union with the rest of the country. In December 1922 the Northern parliament exercised its right to opt out of the Irish Free State and the boundary provision came into operation. The Free State government's preoccupation with the civil war occasioned some delay, but in July 1923 it appointed Eóin MacNeill as the Free State representative on the boundary commission.[2] On 22 September 1923 the British government invited representatives of the two Irish governments to attend a conference to discuss matters arising out of the boundary clause in the treaty. The Free State government accepted 'in the hope that a basis might be found for their common end, the harmonious co-operation of the whole Irish people for their common weal'. The Northern government also agreed to attend, so that it only remained to fix the date of the conference. The colonial secretary, the duke of Devonshire, who was to preside, was too fully occupied with an Imperial Conference to hold the Irish conference in October. A tentative arrangement that it might meet on 15 November was upset by a political crisis in Great Britain which resulted in a general election.

---
[1] *Articles of Agreement for a Treaty between Great Britain and Ireland*, art. 12.
[2] *Dáil Debates*, iv. 1223.

Immediately on the formation of the new British government the matter was re-opened and the conference took place on 1 February 1924. After an adjournment to consider proposals for a settlement it re-assembled on 24 April but it was unable to reach an agreement. Two days later the Free State government asked the British government to complete the formation of the boundary commission without further delay. At this point the whole scheme was upset by the refusal of the Northern government to appoint a representative on the commission. The British government thereupon consulted the judicial committee of the privy council which reported that there was no constitutional means under existing British statutes of bringing the commission into existence.[1] To meet the situation an agreement was signed on 4 August 1924 by the British and Free State prime ministers amending the treaty to permit of the British government appointing a representative for Northern Ireland. This agreement was ratified by the two parliaments and the boundary commission was completed by the British government's appointment of Mr. Justice Feetham of the Supreme Court of South Africa as chairman and of J. R. Fisher, a former editor of the *Northern Whig*, as representative of Northern Ireland.

In the dáil the long delay had evoked questions and criticism from the government side of the house as well as from the opposition. When the bill to ratify the new agreement was introduced the labour party put forward the view that the Anglo-Irish treaty was no longer binding, that it had been broken by the cumulative delays on the part of the British government.[2] It was thus particularly desirable from the government's point of view that the findings of the commission should be favourable to the Free State. For the greater part of 1925 the commission carried on its deliberations without giving any indication of its intentions. But on 7 November 1925 the *Morning Post*, in a detailed forecast of the commission's award, predicted that the existing boundary would be left substantially unaltered except that a strip of Free State territory in co. Donegal would be added to Northern Ireland. This report, which was evidently well founded, precipitated a major crisis. The Free State representative on the commission resigned,[3] and feelings on both sides of the border ran high. As Cosgrave said, there was every likelihood that the old hatreds which were dying would revive.[4] Since the award of the commission would

[1] *Dáil Debates*, vii. 2609–10; viii. 2363.
[3] Ibid. xiii. 795–818.
[2] Ibid. viii. 2407–50.
[4] Ibid. xiii. 1301.

have been binding on all parties in spite of the resignation of the Free State representative it was decided, in the interests of peace, to anticipate the publication of its report by a conference. On 3 December 1925 an agreement was signed by representatives of the three governments providing that the existing boundary was to remain unaltered, that the Irish Free State was to be released from its liability under article 5 of the Anglo-Irish treaty for a share of the public debt of the United Kingdom and for the payment of war pensions, and that the powers of the council of Ireland in relation to Northern Ireland under the Government of Ireland Act, 1920, were to be transferred to the government of Northern Ireland though the two Irish governments were to meet when necessary to consider matters of common interest arising out of the exercise of those powers.

The boundary agreement was confirmed by acts of the British and Free State parliaments. In the dáil the Treaty (Confirmation of Amending Agreement) Bill was hotly debated for four days[1] on its second stage. Vigorous opposition was offered not only from the labour benches but also from other quarters of the house and an attempt was made by the opponents of the bill to induce the republican abstentionists to take their seats. Professor William Magennis broke with the Cumann na nGaedheal party on the issue and subsequently headed a short-lived splinter party. Captain W. A. Redmond contended that the government had been brought to accept a less satisfactory settlement than the old parliamentary party could have achieved had the country not abandoned the policy of conciliation and constitutionalism. D. J. Gorey, leader of the farmers' party, supported the agreement as the best that could have been extracted from a bad situation, a situation, however, which he described as being very largely of the government's own creation. While recommending the bill 'with full conviction that its endorsement would be the best step the dáil could take for the future of all Ireland and for the unity of all Ireland' the vice-president admitted that the agreement was no *summum bonum*, no ideal solution; it was only the best solution which they could get out of a very grave and a very difficult position.

The boundary agreement had a sequel in the Ultimate Financial Settlement which was concluded in March 1926. Agreement was reached on all outstanding financial claims and counter-claims not covered by the boundary settlement. When the terms of the settlement were made public in November 1926 they were strongly attacked

[1] *Dáil Debates*, xiii. 1299–1394, 1419–1513, 1547–1648, 1653–1769.

by Magennis who alleged that all the concessions had been on the Irish side, that the government had 'sold our nationals in Ulster into bondage and did not get the price'.[1] A similar attitude was adopted outside the dáil by the newly formed Fianna Fáil party. The falsification of the Cumann na nGaedheal government's expectations from the boundary commission left it with the alternative of working for unity within the Commonwealth framework. By scrupulously observing the obligations of dominion status and by governing prudently and efficiently it hoped to create the conditions in which unification would become possible. Cosgrave once declared that if he got the offer of a free and independent republic for the twenty-six counties, or even less power than they had with the unity of the country, he would plank for unity.[2]

The government which came to power in 1932 was composed of men who a few years before had been waging war on both Irish governments. In office they set themselves the task of reconciling the nationalist aspirations of the majority with the pro-British sentiments of the unionist minority. But their renunciation of force was on grounds of expediency rather than of principle; though they adopted constitutional methods themselves they were slow to take action against the extremists, and ready, as late as 1940, to make representations on behalf of I.R.A. men convicted of bombing attacks in England. Their problem was clearly stated by de Valera during the debate on the Executive Authority (External Relations) Bill in 1936. He had, he said, to balance two things—the sentiments of the unionists in the North and the sentiments of the majority in the rest of the country. The two were going in opposite directions. He was working towards a position when, he hoped, he would be able to satisfy the interests and aspirations of the majority to the point at any rate when they would say, 'We are prepared to sacrifice some of the rest in order to get a united Ireland'.[3] The constitution of 1937 marked the completion of his plan. When it was criticized on the ground that it placed further obstacles in the way of a united Ireland he replied that the majority had rights as well as the minority, that he could not have gone further than he had in the constitution to meet the view of those in the North without sacrificing to an extent that he was not prepared to sacrifice the legitimate views and opinions of the majority. In reply to a question about what there was by way of concession in the con-

[1] *Dáil Debates*, xvii. 658. [2] Ibid. xli. 584.
[3] Ibid. lxiv. 1470.

stitution that would not have been there if the Northern problem had not existed, he declared that but for it there would in all probability have been a flat downright proclamation of the republic.[1] On the other hand, after some years of working the new constitution he confessed that he would be quite satisfied with the existing arrangement if it functioned for the whole of Ireland.[2]

When the Northern unionists remained equally unmoved by blandishments and by threats Fianna Fáil politicians changed the emphasis in their attacks on partition. In reply to a parliamentary question in 1946 de Valera asserted that partition was created by the British parliament and could be ended by that parliament. He described it as a flagrant violation of the fundamental rights and sovereignty of the Irish people.[3] There was nothing new in this contention—it had been the basis of the claim put forward at practically every conference with British ministers since 1932—but in the post-war years it began to assume greater prominence. Concurrently with it a new inducement was offered to the Northern unionists in the form of a suggestion that they might retain their local parliament with its existing powers, but that the powers at present reserved to and exercised by the British parliament should be transferred to an all-Ireland parliament in which the unionists would be fully represented.[4] This proposal was endorsed by the coalition government which took office in 1948.

The conversion of Fine Gael to republicanism involved the abandonment of the party's former policy on partition. As leader of the coalition government in 1948 Costello bitterly denounced the intractability of the Northern government since 1922. The final break with the Commonwealth, he held, could make little difference to the unionist attitude and it would enable all political parties in Éire to unite in bringing pressure on the British government to end partition.[5] In 1936 Costello said that discreet work behind the scenes was the way to end partition;[6] in 1948 his government embarked on a widespread campaign designed to raise partition to the status of an international question.

The attempt of successive Irish governments to over-simplify the problem lends a certain air of unreality to much of the discussion on partition. No real cognizance has been taken of the differences in out-

[1] *Dáil Debates*, lxviii. 428–9.
[2] Ibid. xcix. 1–2.
[5] Ibid. cxiii. 385–91.
[3] Ibid. ci. 2194–5.
[4] Ibid. cvii. 786.
[6] Ibid. lxiv. 768.

look between the protestant majority in Northern Ireland and the catholic majority in the whole country. There has been little recognition of the fact that these differences have been confirmed and strengthened by the growth of vested interests on both sides of the border. The most hopeful sign in recent years has been the willingness of the two governments to co-operate on such practical matters as the Erne electricity scheme and the joint control of the Foyle fisheries and the Great Northern Railway.

APPENDIX

GEOGRAPHICAL DISTRIBUTION OF PARTIES

*Maps Showing First Preference Votes
Cast for the Three Principal Parties
in 1923, 1937, and 1948*

First preference votes
in thousands   Key

Under $2\frac{1}{2}$
$2\frac{1}{2}$ — 5
5 — $7\frac{1}{2}$
$7\frac{1}{2}$ — 10
10 — 15
15 — 20
20 or over

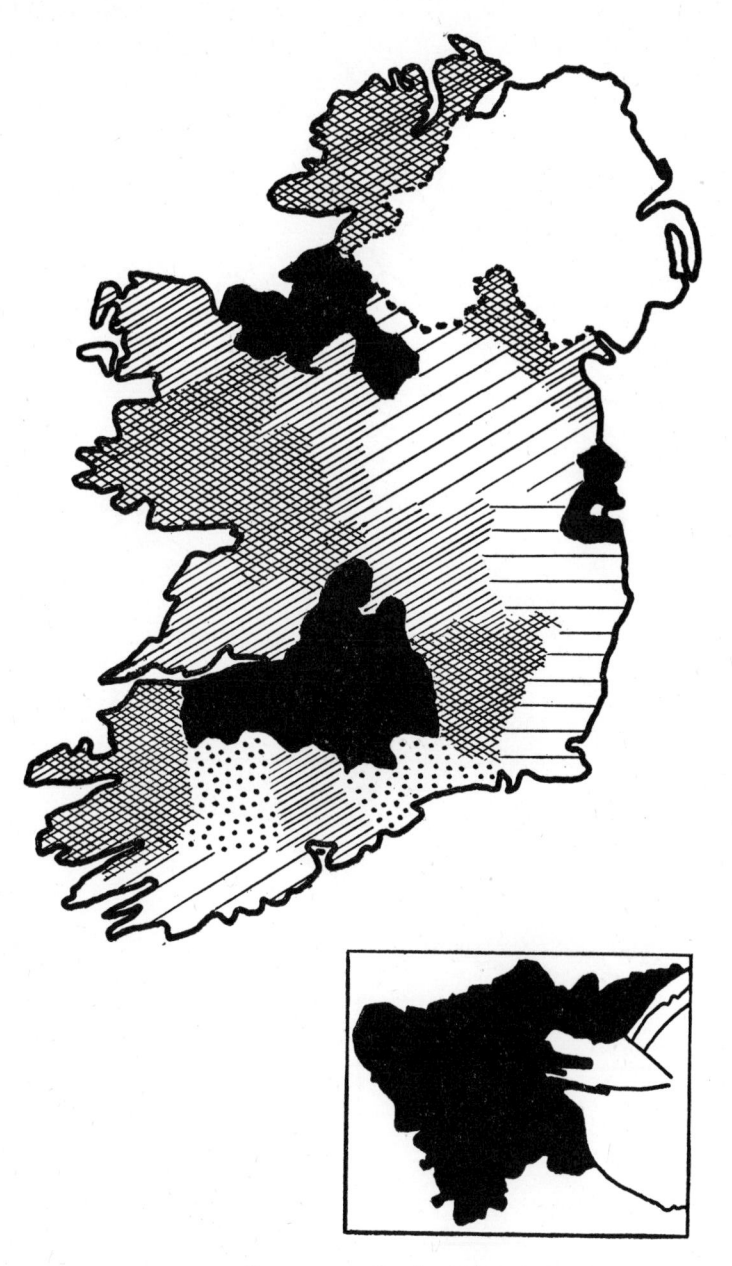

Cumann na nGaedheal 1923

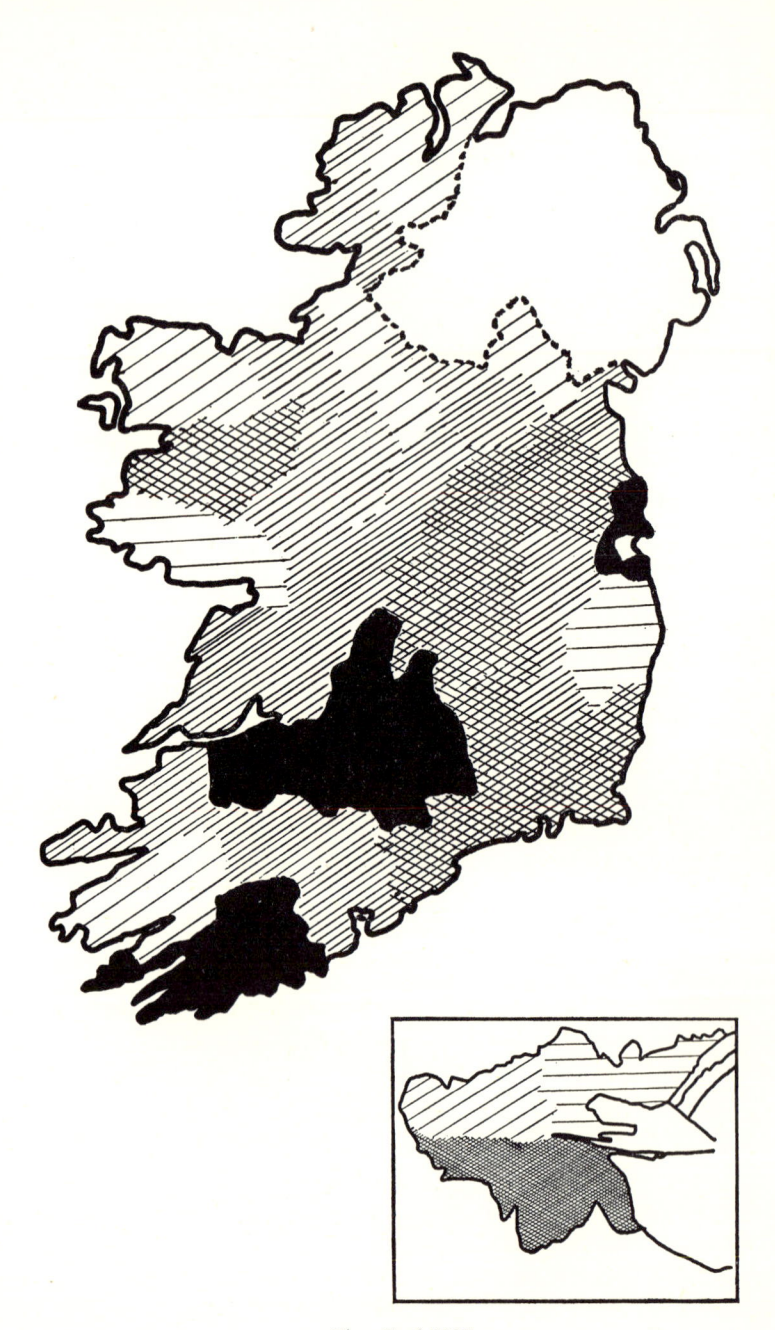

Fine Gael 1937

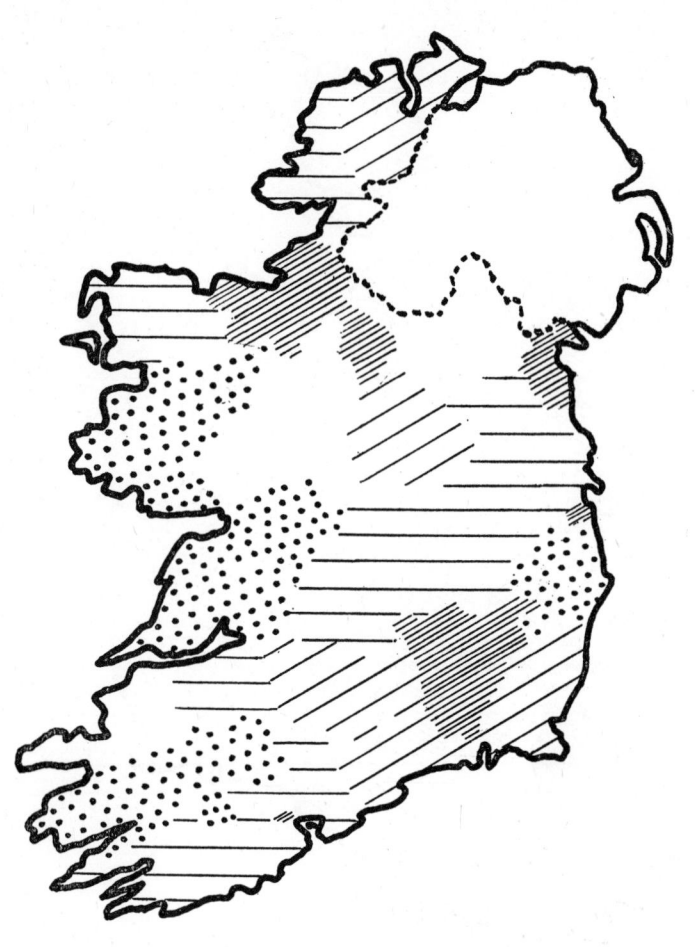

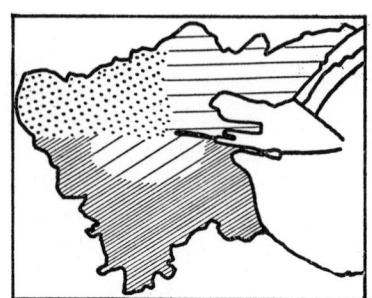

Fine Gael 1948

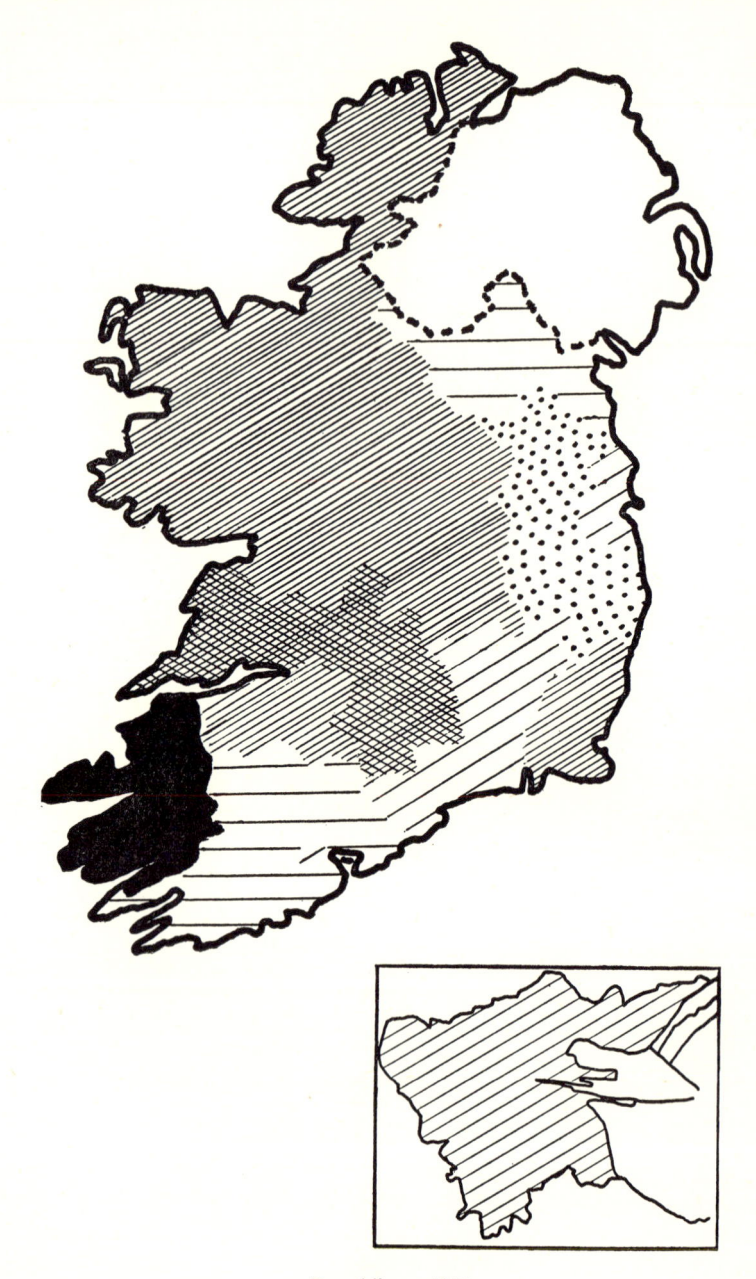

Republicans 1923

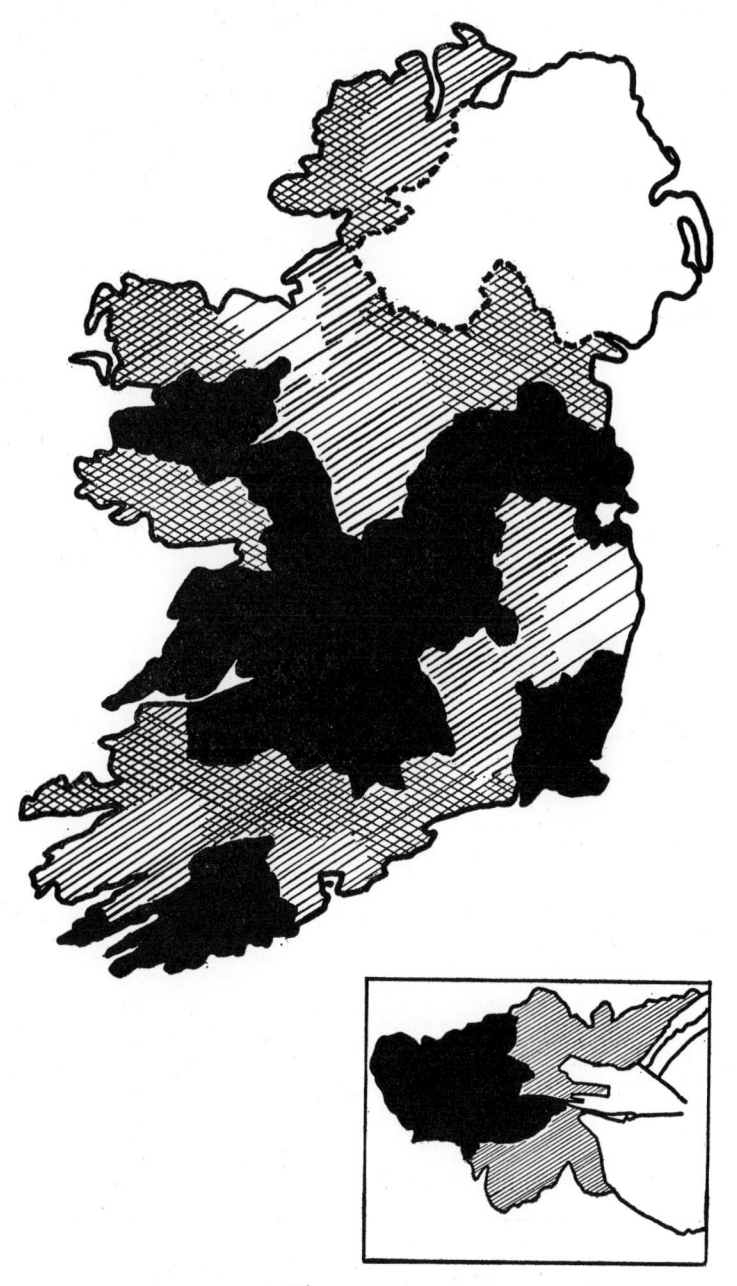

Fianna Fáil 1937

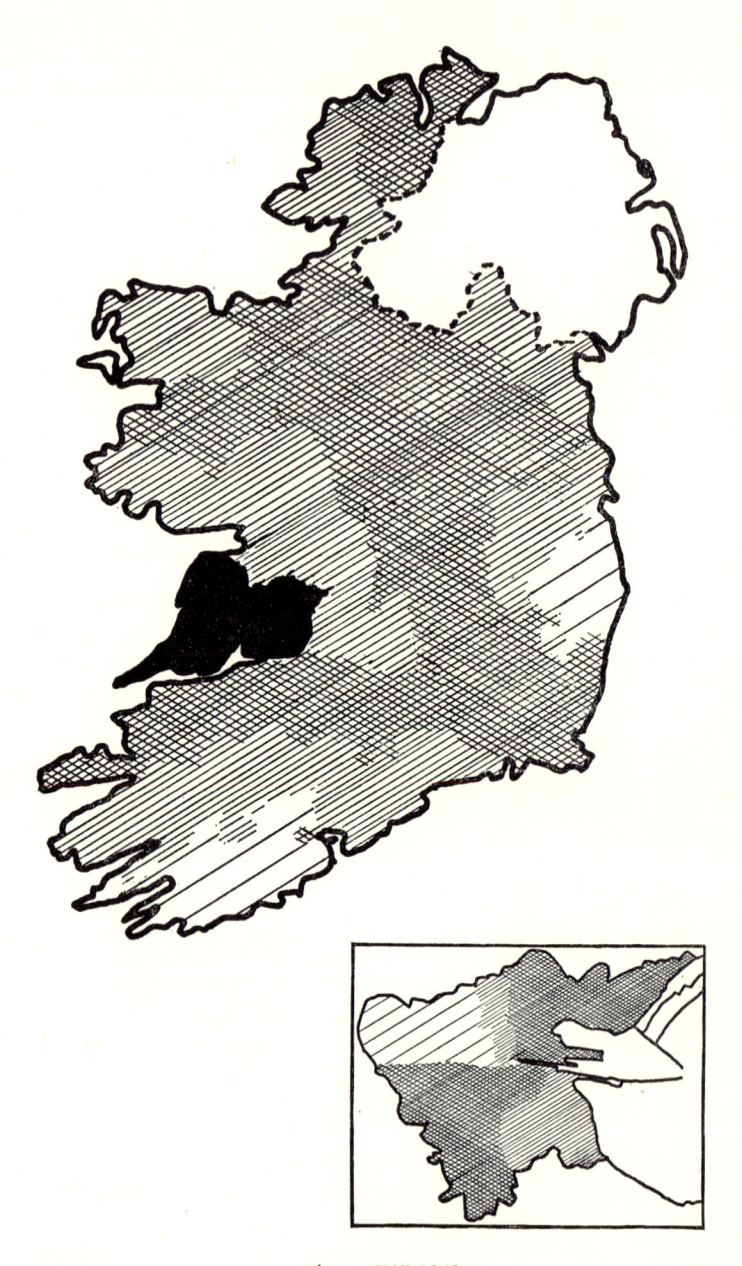

Fianna Fáil 1948

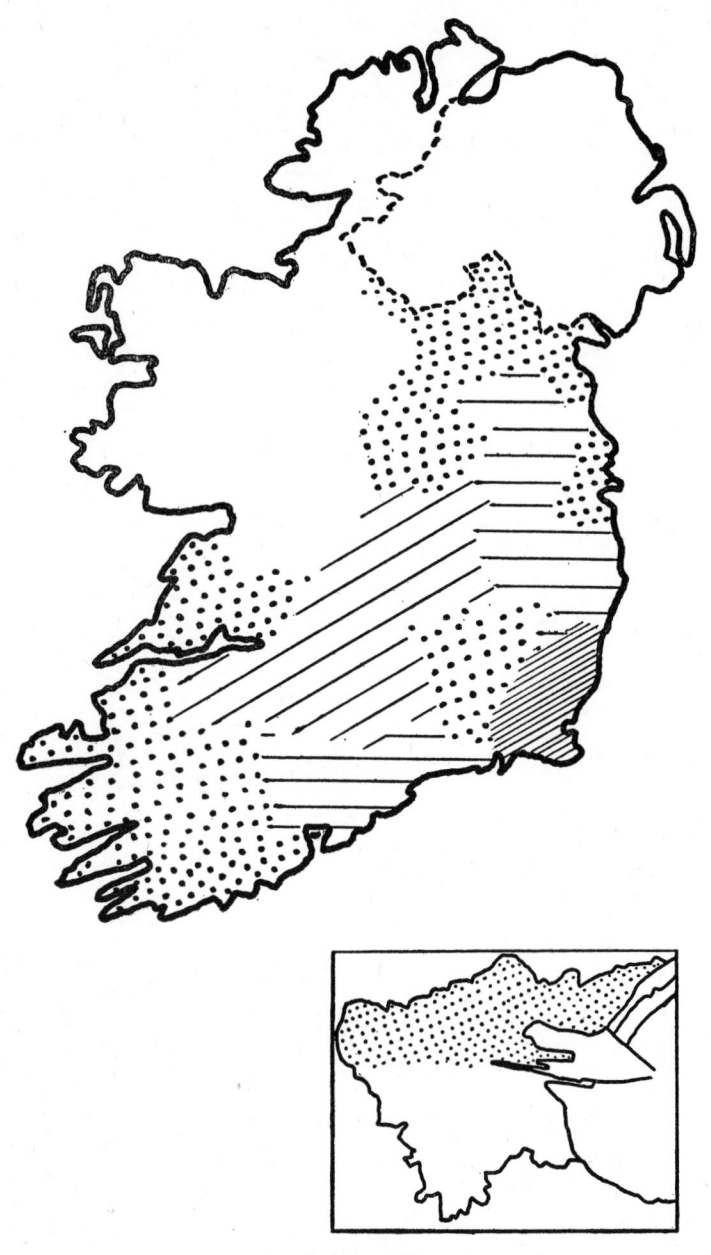

Labour 1923

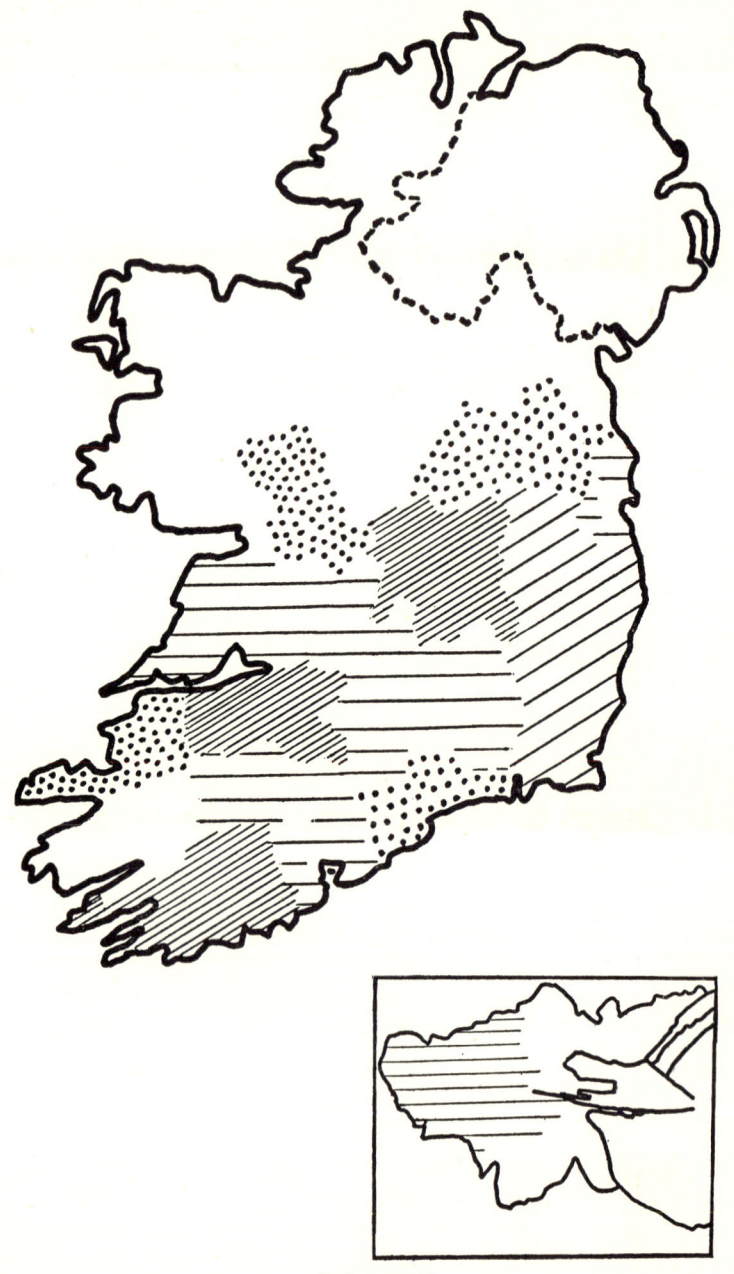

Labour 1937

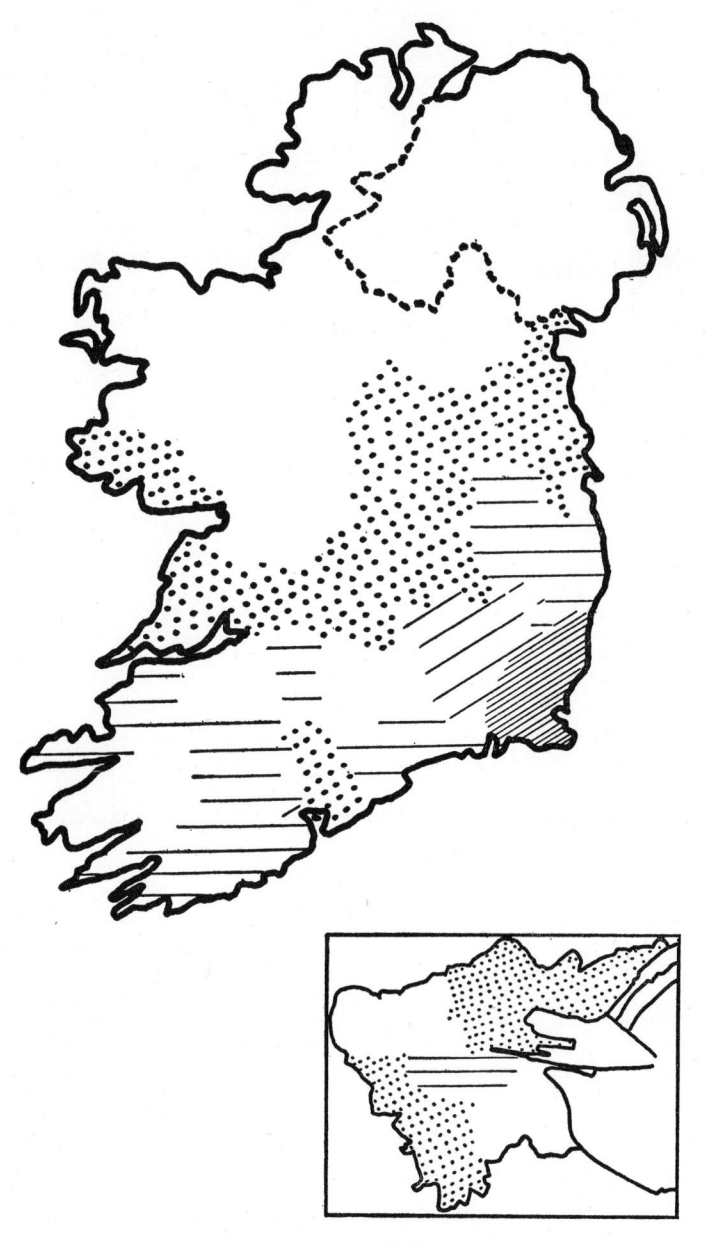

Labour 1948

BIBLIOGRAPHY

A. SOURCES

1. Parliamentary Debates and Other Official Publications

Constitution of Ireland. Dublin, 1937.
Constitution of the Irish Free State. Dublin, 1922.
Dáil Éireann. *Minutes of proceedings of the first parliament of the Republic of Ireland, 1919–21; official record.* Dublin, 1921.
Dáil Éireann. *Official report: debate on the treaty between Great Britain and Ireland signed in London on 6 December 1921.* Dublin, 1922.
Dáil Éireann. *Official report for periods 16–26 August 1921 and 28 February to 8 June 1922.* Dublin, 1922.
Dáil Éireann. *Parliamentary debates: official report.* Dublin, 1922–48.
Dáil Éireann. *Report of the committee on procedure and privileges re wearing of gown by ceann cómhairle.* Dublin, 1946.
Dáil Éireann. *Returns made annually for the years 1923–38 of private bills, questions in the dáil, sittings of Dáil Éireann, committees, closure of debate and public bills in the dáil.* Dublin, 1923–38.
Dáil Éireann. *Second report of the committee on procedure and privileges re office of leas-cheann cómhairle.* Dublin, 1928.
Dáil Éireann. *Standing orders relative to public business, 1950.* Dublin, 1950.
DUFFY, G. GAVAN, and O'CONNOR, A. (eds.), *A register of administrative law in Saorstát Éireann, including the statutory rules and orders from 6 December 1921 to 31 December 1933.* Dublin, 1935.
GROGAN, V. (ed.), *Index to the statutes, 1922–1948.* Dublin, n.d.
HANNA, H., and PRINGLE, A. D., *The statute law of the Irish Free State, 1922–8.* Dublin, 1929.
Index to statutory rules and orders, 1922–47, 3 vols. Dublin, 1944–55.
Irish reports: containing reports of cases determined in the High Court of Justice and in the Court of Criminal Appeal and by the Irish Land Commission and in appeal therefrom in the Supreme Court. Dublin, current.
MACCRÍOSTA, M., *Leinster House.* Dublin, 1955.
MALONE, S., *Notes on procedure in the houses of the oireachtas.* Dublin, 1947.
Parliamentary papers (British):
  Report of the royal commission on the rebellion in Ireland, [Cd. 8279], H.C. 1916, xi. 171; *Evidence and appendix*, [Cd. 8311], H.C. 1916, xi. 185.
  Summary of the proceedings of the imperial conference of 1930, [Cmd. 3717], H.C. 1930–1, xiv. 569; *Appendices*, [Cmd. 3718], H.C. 1930–1, xiv. 701.

Papers relating to the parliamentary oath of allegiance in the Irish Free State, and to the land purchase annuities, [Cmd. 4056], H.C. 1931-2, xiv. 273.
Financial agreements between the British government and the Irish Free State government, 17 February 1923, [Cmd. 4061], H.C. 1931-2, xiv. 239.
Correspondence relating to the land purchase annuities, [Cmd. 4116], H.C. 1931-2, xiv. 281.
Papers relating to a conference held in London, 14-15 October, 1932, [Cmd. 4184], H.C. 1931-2, xiv. 285.
Agreements between the United Kingdom and Éire signed at London on 25 April 1938, [Cmd. 5728], H.C. 1937-8, xxx. 1001.
Public general acts passed by the oireachtas. Dublin, 1922-48.
First report of department of local government and public health, 1922-5. Dublin, 1927.
Report of the second house of the oireachtas commission. Dublin, 1936.
Report of commission of inquiry into banking, currency and credit, 1938. Dublin, 1938.
Report of commission on vocational organisation, 1943. Dublin, 1943.
Seanad Éireann. Parliamentary debates: official report. Dublin, 1922-48.
Select constitutions of the world. Dublin, 1922.

2. Newspapers and Periodicals

Bamba, 1921-2.
Éire, 1914.
Freeman's Journal, to 1924.
Irish Bulletin: official organ of Dáil Éireann, 1919-21.
Irish Freedom, 1910-14.
Irish Independent, current.
Irish Jurist, 1935-48.
Irish Press, current.
Irish Statesman, 1923-30.
Irish Times, current.
Ireland Today, 1936-8.
Irish Worker: People's Advocate, 1911-14.
Journal of Comparative Legislation and International Law, 3rd series—to 1946.
Journal of the Parliaments of the Empire, 1920-48
Journal of the Society of Clerks-at-the-table in Empire Parliaments, 1932.
Nationality, 1915-16; new series, 1917-19.
New Ireland, 1915-19.
An t-Óglách: official organ of the Irish Volunteers, 1918-22.
Representation: the Journal of the Proportional Representation Society, to 1927.
Republic of Ireland: Poblacht na h-Éireann, 1922.

Round Table, 1910-48.
Scissors and Paste, 1914-15.
Sinn Féin, 1906-14.
Workers' Republic, 1915-16.

3. Pamphlets and Party Publications

The authority of Dáil Éireann. [Dublin, 1919].
The book of Clann na Talmhan. Drogheda, [1944].
The constructive work of Dáil Éireann. No. 1: the national police and courts of justice. Dublin, 1921.
The constructive work of Dáil Éireann. No. 2: i. *the department of agriculture and the land settlement commission;* ii. *the commission of inquiry into the resources and industries of Ireland;* iii. *the department of trade and commerce*. Dublin, 1921.
Clann na Talmhan (National farmers' organization): rules book. Dublin, n.d.
Clann na Poblachta constitution. Dublin, [1950].
COSTELLO, J. A., *The republic of Ireland*. Dublin, [1948].
—— *Ireland in international affairs*. Dublin, 1948.
DOUGLAS, J. G., *President de Valera and the senate, with an introduction by Professor D. A. Binchy*. Dublin, [1934].
Fianna Fáil: constitution and rules approved by eighteenth árd-fheis. Dublin, 1946.
Fighting points for Cumann na nGaedheal speakers and workers: general election 1932. Dublin, [1932].
Irish centre party: objects of the party. [Dublin, 1919].
Irish councils for Irish freedom. [1920?].
Irish dominion league: official report setting forth a summary of results achieved, together with the proceedings on dissolution. Dublin, 1921.
Irish republican army organization: the truth about the army crisis, with a foreword by Major-General Liam Tobin. Dublin, [1923].
The labour party. Annual report of the provisional administrative council and the report of the proceedings of the annual conference. Dublin, 1931.
The labour party. Official statement relating to the disaffiliation from the labour party of the Irish transport and general workers union, prepared by the administrative council for the information of party branches, divisional and constituency councils and the affiliated corporate bodies. Dublin, 1944.
The labour party constitution (revised September 1948). Dublin, [1948].
The labour party. Report of the administrative council for the year 1952-3. Dublin, 1953.
MACBRIDE, S., *Civil liberty*. Dublin, [1947].
—— *Our people—our money*. Dublin, [1949].
O'HIGGINS, K., *The new de Valera: a contrast and some disclosures, 24 March 1922*, [Dublin, 1922].

O'KELLY, J. J., *The republic of Ireland vindicated: presidential address at Sinn Féin árd-fheis, 4 October 1931*. Dublin, 1931.
Peace with Ireland council: objects. [London, 1920].
Peace with Ireland council: the situation in Ireland, a short history. [London, 1920–1].
Proportional Representation Society pamphlet, no. 72; The century of electoral reform. London, 1932.
Periodicals:
  Cumann na nGaedheal—Fine Gael papers:
    The Freeman (weekly), 1927–8.
    The Star (monthly), 1929–31.
    United Irishman (weekly), 1932–3.
    United Ireland (weekly), 1933–4.
    Forum (monthly), 1944–50.
    Fine Gael Digest (quarterly), 1950–6.
  Fianna Fáil papers:
    Fianna Fáil Bulletin (monthly), 1934–41.
    Gléas (monthly), 1952–7.
  Labour movement papers:
    Voice of Labour, 1917–27.
    Irishman, 1927–30.
    The Watchword, 1930–2.
    Labour News, 1936–8.
    Torch, 1939–44.
    Irish People, 1944–8.
    Citizen, 1949.
Sinn Féin tracts, no. 1: Sinn Féin in tabloid form. [Dublin, 1917].
Sinn Féin leaflets, 1917, no. 1: Colonial home rule: would it settle anything? Dublin, [1917].
Sinn Féin leaflets, Clare series, no. 2: The failure of parliamentarianism; lecture delivered at Ennis by Rev. J. Clany, 13 December 1917. Ennis, 1918.
The voice of Ireland. [Dublin, 1918].

4. Directories and Other Works of Reference

FLYN, W. J., *The oireachtas companion and Saorstát guide for 1928*. Dublin, 1928. Continued as: *Free State parliamentary companion*. Dublin and Cork, 1932, 1939, 1945.
Irish medical and hospital directory, current.
MACCABA, A. (ed.), *Leabhar na hÉireann: the Irish year book*. Dublin, 1922.
MacDonald's Irish directory, 1926. Dublin, 1928.
O'Neill's commercial who's who and industrial directory of Ireland, current.
Thom's directory of Ireland, current.
Who's who in the seanad election. Dublin, 1925.

5. Miscellaneous

Gavan Duffy Papers in the National Library of Ireland contain:
History and progress of department of publicity, August 1921.
Daily Bulletin, 1922 (Typewritten sheets).
Draft standing orders of first dáil.
Also in the National Library of Ireland:
Irish political miscellany, 1916–23: miscellaneous documents and illustrations.
Newspaper cuttings, 1919–23 (articles in *The Times* and the *Observer*).
Papers relating to the first dáil lent to the author by Mr. P. O'Keeffe.

B. SECONDARY WORKS

ALLEN, C. K., *Laws and orders: an inquiry into the nature and scope of delegated legislation and executive powers in England*. London, 1945.
ARMOUR, W. S., *Ulster, Ireland, Britain: a forgotten trust*. London, 1938.
BÉASLAÍ, P., *Michael Collins and the making of a new Ireland*, 2 vols. Dublin, 1926.
BENNETT, T. W. W., *Pro domo sua: being the speech of the chairman of the Seanad, Senator T. W. W. Bennett, in defence of his House of the Oireachtas against Mr de Valera and his government delivered in the Seanad on 30 May 1934*. Dublin, 1934.
BLAKE, R., *The unknown prime minister: the life and times of Andrew Bonar Law*. London, 1955.
BREEN, D., *My fight for Irish freedom*. Dublin, 1924.
BRETHERTON, C. H., *The real Ireland*. London, 1925.
BROMAGE, A. W., 'Constitutional development in Saorstát Éireann and the constitution of Éire', in *American Political Science Review*, vol. xxxi (1937), pp. 842–61, 1050–70.
BROMAGE, M. C., *De Valera and the march of a nation*. London, 1956.
BURCE, P. DE, *Free State or republic? Pen pictures of the historic treaty session of Dáil Éireann*. Dublin, 1922.
CALLWELL, C. E., *Field Marshal Sir Henry Wilson: his life and diaries*, 2 vols. London, 1927.
CAMPION, E., *An introduction to the procedure of the house of commons* 2nd ed. London, 1950.
CARTY, J., *Bibliography of Irish history, 1912–21*. Dublin, 1936.
CHUBB, F. B., 'Vocational representation and the Irish senate', in *Political Studies*, vol. ii (1954), pp. 97–111.
—— 'Cabinet government in Ireland', in *Political Studies*, vol. iii (1955), pp. 256–74.
CHURCHILL, W. S., *The world crisis: the aftermath*. London, 1929.
COOPER, B. R., 'Procedure of an Dáil', in *Freeman*, 31 March, 7 April, 14 April 1928.

COSTELLO, J. A., 'The long game', in *United Irishman*, 24 December 1932.
DANIELS, S. R., *The case for electoral reform, with an examination of the principal objections*. London, 1938.
FAUCON, G., *Le statut de l'État Libre d'Irlande*. Paris, 1929.
FIGGIS, D., *The Irish constitution explained*. Dublin, 1922.
—— *Recollections of the Irish war*. London, 1927.
FOX, R. M., *Labour in the national struggle*. Dublin, n.d. (1945).
GALLAGHER, F., 'Literature of the conflict', in *Irish Book Lover*, vol. xviii (1930), pp. 69–71.
—— *The indivisible island: the history of the partition of Ireland*. London, 1957.
[GRIFFITH, A.]. *The resurrection of Hungary, a parallel for Ireland*. Dublin, 1904.
GROGAN, V., 'Irish constitutional development', in *Studies*, vol. xl (1951), pp. 383–98.
GWYNN, D., *The life of John Redmond*. London, 1932.
—— *The Irish Free State, 1922–7*. London, 1928.
—— *The history of partition (1912–25)*. Dublin, 1950.
GWYNN, S., *John Redmond's last years*. London, 1919.
HANCOCK, W. K., *Survey of British Commonwealth affairs*, 2 vols. London, 1937.
HARRISON, H., *Ireland and the British Empire, 1937: conflict or collaboration?* London, 1937.
—— *Ulster and the British Empire, 1939: help or hindrance?* Dublin, 1939.
HEADLAM-MORLEY, A., *The new democratic constitutions of Europe*. London, 1928.
HENRY, R. M., *The evolution of Sinn Féin*. Dublin, 1920.
HERMENS, F. A., *Europe between democracy and anarchy*. Indiana, 1951.
—— 'Wartime elections in Ireland', in *The Review of Politics*, vol. v, (1943), pp. 509–16.
'History of the Dáil', in *Freeman's Journal*, 16 August 1921.
HOGAN, D., *The four glorious years*. Dublin, 1954.
HOGAN, J., *Election and representation*. Cork and Oxford, 1945.
—— 'Ireland and the British Commonwealth, 1931–7' in *Ireland Today*, vol. ii (1937), pp. 11–26.
HORGAN, J. J., *Parnell to Pearse*. Dublin, 1948.
HUMPHREYS, J. H., 'Éire's general election of 1944', in *Contemporary Review*, vol. clxvi (1944), pp. 16–20.
I.O. [C. J. C. STREET], *The administration of Ireland, 1920*. London, 1921.
JONES, F. P., *History of the Sinn Féin movement and the Irish rebellion of 1916*. New York, 1919.
KEITH, A. B., *Letters on imperial relations, Indian reform, constitutional and international law, 1916–35*. London, 1935.
—— *Letters and essays on current imperial and international problems, 1935–6*. London, 1936.

—— On certain legal and constitutional aspects of the Anglo-Irish dispute. With an introduction by Henry Harrison. London, 1934.
KENNEDY, H. 'Character and sources of the constitution of the Irish Free State', in *Journal of the American Bar Association*, vol. xiv (1928), pp. 437–45.
—— 'The association of Canada with the constitution of the Irish Free State', in *Canadian Bar Review*, vol. vi (1928).
KIELY, B., *Counties of contention: a study of the origins and implications of partition in Ireland*. Cork, 1945.
KING, F. C. ed., *Public administration in Ireland*, 3 vols. Dublin, 1944, 1949, 1954.
—— 'Drifting to absolutism?', in *Journal of the Statistical and Social Inquiry Society of Ireland*, vol. xvii (1952–3).
KOHN, L., *The constitution of the Irish Free State*. London, 1932.
LAW, H. A., 'The Irish elections and plebiscite', in *Contemporary Review*, vol. clii (1937), pp. 159–64.
LENNON, M. J., 'A retrospect', in *Bamba*, vol. ii (1922), pp. 209, 297, 395, 478.
MACARDLE, D., *The Irish republic*, 4th ed. Dublin, 1951.
MACDONAGH, M., *The home rule movement*. Dublin, 1920.
MCDUNPHY, M., *The president of Ireland: his powers, functions and duties*. Dublin, 1945.
MACNEILL, J. G. SWIFT., *Studies in the constitution of the Irish Free State*. Dublin, 1925.
MACNEILL, R., *Ulster's stand for the Union*. London, 1922.
MACREADY, C. F. N., *Annals of an active life*, 2 vols. London, 1924.
MALONE, A. E., 'The development of party government in the Irish Free State', in *Political Science Quarterly*, vol. xliv (1929), pp. 363–78.
—— 'Government: Irish Free State', in *Encyclopaedia of Social Sciences*, vol. vii, pp. 36–38.
MANSERGH, N., *The Commonwealth and the nations: studies in British Commonwealth relations*. London, 1948.
—— *The Irish Free State: its government and politics*. London, 1934.
MARJORIBANKS, E., and COLVIN, I., *The life of Lord Carson*, 2 vols. London, 1932, 1934.
'Meeting of the first dáil', in *Irish Press*, 21 January 1944.
MORRISON, H., *Government and parliament*. London, 1954.
MOSS, W. W., *Political parties in the Irish Free State*. New York, 1933.
NICHOLAS, H. G., *The British general election of 1950*. London, 1951.
O'BRIAIN, B., *The Irish constitution*. Dublin, 1929.
O'CONNELL, J. B., *The financial administration of Saorstát Éireann: with an epitome of the reports from the committee of public accounts 1922 to 1932*. Dublin, 1934.
O'DONOGHUE, F., *No other law: the story of Liam Lynch and the Irish Republican Army, 1916–23*. Dublin, 1954.

O'HEGARTY, P. S., *A history of Ireland under the Union, 1801–1922*. London, 1952.

—— *Victory of Sinn Fein: how it won it and how it used it*. Dublin, 1924.

O'KELLY, J. J. (Sceilg), *A trinity of martyrs*. Dublin, [1947].

O'KENNEDY, B. W., *Making history: the story of a remarkable campaign*. [Dublin, n.d.]

O'RAHILLY, A., *Thoughts on the constitution*. Dublin, 1937.

O'SHANNON, C., 'The 1919 democratic programme', in *Irish Times*, 31 January and 1 February 1944.

O'SULLIVAN, D., *The Irish Free State and its senate: a study in contemporary politics*. London, 1940.

PAKENHAM, F., *Peace by ordeal, an account from first-hand sources of the negotiation and signature of the Anglo-Irish treaty, 1921*. London, 1935.

PHILAN, E. J., 'The sovereignty of the Irish Free State' in *The Review of Nations*, March 1927, 35 et seq.

PHILLIPS, W. A., *The revolution in Ireland, 1906–23*. London, 1923.

ROSS, J. F. S., *Parliamentary representation*, 2nd ed. London, 1948.

SAUNDERS, A. E., 'The Irish constitution', in *American Political Science Review*, vol. xviii (1924).

SHAKESPEARE, E., *Let candles be brought in*. London, 1949.

SHEEHY, M., *Divided we stand: a study of partition*. London, 1955.

SKINNER, L. C., *Politicians by accident*. Dublin, 1946.

STRAUSS, E., *Irish nationalism and British democracy*. London, 1951.

WARD, N., *The Canadian house of commons*. Toronto, 1950.

WARREN, R. DE, *L'Irlande et ses institutions politiques, leur évolution—leur état actuel*. Paris, 1928.

WHEARE, K. C., *The Statute of Westminster and dominion status*. 4th ed. London, 1949.

WHITE, T. DE V., *Kevin O'Higgins*. London, 1948.

INDEX

Abdication crisis, 63, 158.
Abyssinian war, 108.
America, United States of, 23, 26–27, 36, 40, 44–45, 49, 54, 113, 184, 188–9.
Anglo-Boer war, 2, 4.
Anthony, R. S., 113.
Army Comrades Association, 78, 106–7.
Asquith, Rt. Hon. H. H., 6, 12–13, 46.
Atlantic Pact, 189.
Australia, 48, 51, 122, 129, 189, 198.
Auxiliary police, 37, 44.

Balfour, Lord, 191–2.
Barton, R., 31, 50–51, 53.
Béaslaí, P., 25, 35.
Belton, P., 112.
Bernard, Most Rev. Dr., 137.
Bills, classification of, and procedure on, 124–6.
Black and Tans, 44, 46.
Blue Shirt movement, 107–8, 143–4.
Blythe, E., 31, 75, 142, 155.
Boland, H., 21–22.
Botha, General L., 12.
Boundary Commission, 52, 104, 199–200, 201–2.
Breen, D., 156.
Brennan, R., 36.
Brugha, C., 18, 22, 26–27, 43–44, 53.
Burke, J. A., 142.

Cabinet system, 60, 65, 161–2, 165–6.
Canada, 51, 87, 122, 133, 154, 185, 189, 194, 198.
Carson, Sir E., 6, 49.
Casement, Sir R., 17.
Ceann cómhairle (Speaker), 26, 72, 77, 120–3, 130–2, 134, 136, 148, 160.
Childers, E., 31, 37, 51.
Citizen Army, 9, 11.
Civil war, 55, 62, 74–76, 85, 103, 137, 155, 173, 199.
Clann Éireann, 73, 104, 201.
Clann na Poblachta, 71, 73, 78–79, 110, 198.
Clann na Talmhan, 71, 73, 109–10, 116, 121.
Clarke, T., 2.
Clune, Most Rev. Dr., 48.
Coalition (inter-party) government, 72, 79, 109, 166, 198, 203.
Cockerill, Brigadier-General Sir George K., 48.
Cole, W. L., 24.
Collins, M., 18, 22, 26, 39, 43–44, 48, 50–51, 53–54, 74, 103, 166, 190.

Comerford, Maire, 62 n.
Commonwealth of Nations, 14, 50–51, 53–54, 57, 63–64, 116, 143, 153–5, 158, 172, 184–5, 190, 193–9, 202–3.
Comptroller and auditor general, 129, 169.
Connolly, J., 4, 10–11, 102, 108.
Conscription, 11, 14, 16–17, 21, 187.
Constituent assembly, 54–57, 61, 67, 74–75, 86, 119.
Constitution of Irish Free State, 54–62, 67, 70, 72, 74–75, 86–87, 106, 119, 130, 148, 154–8, 164–6, 171–3, 178–9, 183–4, 193–4, 197; of Ireland, 61, 63–65, 67, 70, 72, 74, 78, 86, 106, 120, 123, 133–4, 145, 147–8, 158–9, 164–5, 172, 179, 183, 197–8, 202.
Constitution committee, 54, 138, 162, 165.
Constitutional amendments, 59–61, 65, 72, 121, 139–41, 144, 148, 158, 160, 164, 172, 179, 184.
Cope, A. W., 48.
Cosgrave, W. T., 14, 53, 55, 58, 60–61, 71, 77, 84, 103, 105, 107–8, 121, 141–2, 166, 193, 200, 202.
Costello, J. A., 79, 142, 166, 198, 203.
Council of Europe, 189.
Council of Ireland, 14, 47, 49, 201.
Council of State, 64–65, 159–60, 179; Republican, 62.
Court: the High, 58, 64, 159, 178–80; the Supreme, 55, 64, 160–1, 178–80; of Appeal, 177, 179; Republican, 3, 15, 40–42, 170, 172.
Craig, Sir J., 49.
Cronin, Commandant, 108.
Cumann na mBan, 7, 10, 18.
Cumann na nGaedheal (cultural society), 2; (political party), 71, 73, 76–77, 82–84, 103–5, 107–8, 113–14, 116–17, 156, 168, 174, 190, 201–2, 207.
Curragh incident, 6.
Customs House, Dublin, 40.

Dáil Éireann: Revolutionary, establishment of, 1, 21–28; composition of, 29–34; work of, 35–44; and treaty, 48, 53, 55–56; Constitutional, competence of, 57–66; elections to, 67–85; composition of, 86–101; parties in, 102–10; meetings of, 119–20; officers of, 120–3; conduct of business, 123–9; committees, 122, 125, 127, 129–30 rules of debate,

131–3; Irish language in, 133–4; parliamentary privileges, 134–5; attendance, 123, 135; parliamentary papers, 136. *See also* Senate, Executive, Legislation and External affairs.
Davis, M., 142.
Derby, Lord, 48.
de Valera, E., 14–15, 21–22, 26–28, 38, 40, 43–44, 48–50, 53, 60, 62–63, 74, 76–77, 79, 83–84, 105–6, 108, 120, 143, 145–7, 150, 155, 158–9, 166, 186–9, 195–6, 198, 202–3.
Devlin, J., 28.
Dillon, J., 12–13, 19–20, 28.
Dillon, J. M., 107–8, 188.
Dolan, C. J., 3–4.
Donnellan, M. T., 110.
Douglas, J. G., 54.
Dowling, J., 17.
Dublin Castle, 11, 21, 38.
Dublin University, constituency of, 20, 29, 47, 53, 72, 92, 95, 149.
Duffy, G. Gavin, 21, 25, 35, 50–51.
Duggan, E., 50–51, 53.

Easter Rising, 1916, 2, 10–13, 32, 42, 166.
Economic war, 77, 107, 174, 187, 196–7.
Electoral college, 149–50.
Executive: the crown, 153–8; the presidency, 158–61; extern ministers, 60, 141, 161–4; nature of, and relations with dáil, 139, 141, 154, 164–9.
External affairs: constitutional powers of dáil and executive, 183–4; role of dáil in, 184; independent status emphasized internationally, 184–6; 'treaty ports', 186–7; neutrality, 188–9; attitude to Commonwealth, 190–9; partition, 199–204.

Fahy, F., 120–1.
Farmers' party, 73–74, 77, 84, 90, 94, 102, 104–5, 109, 116, 201.
Feetham, Hon. Mr. Justice, 200.
Fenians, 4.
Fianna Éireann, 7.
Fianna Fáil, 60, 63, 71–73, 76–84, 105–6, 110–18, 120–1, 140, 142, 149, 155–7, 168, 183, 185, 190, 194–5, 197, 202–3, 211–12.
Figgis, D., 54.
Financial control by dáil, 58–59, 64, 127–9, 138–9, 168–9.
Fine Gael, 71, 78, 81, 107–8, 110–18, 149, 188, 198, 203, 208–9.
Fisher, J. R., 200.
Fitzalan, Lord, 47.
Fitzgerald, D., 37, 191.

Fogarty, Most Rev. Dr. M., 40, 48.
Four Courts, Dublin, 74.
France, C. J., 54.
French chamber of deputies, 184.
French, Field Marshall Lord, 17.
Friends, Society of, 46.
Fundamental rights, 58, 64, 146, 180.

Gaelic Athletic Association, 31, 90.
Gaelic League, 1–2, 7, 18, 31
George V, King, 49, 53.
'German plot', 17.
Ginnell, L., 37, 61.
Gladstone, W. E., 1.
Gorey, D. J., 104–5, 201.
Governor-general of Irish Free State, 51, 63, 119–20, 139, 141, 146, 154, 157, 160.
Greenwood, Sir H., 44, 51.
Griffith, A., 2–3, 5, 10, 14–15, 17, 24, 27, 35, 48, 50–51, 53–54, 74, 103, 137, 144, 154, 166, 190.
Gunrunning: Larne, 6; Howth and Kilcoole, 8.

Hayes, M., 120–1, 135.
Healy, T. M., 154.
Heffernan, M. R., 84, 105.
Henderson, A., 46.
Hickey, J., 4, 109.
Hogan, J., 108.
Hogan, P., 121.
Hogan, P. J., 53.
House of Commons, 6, 8, 13–14, 17, 19–20, 31, 54, 87, 89, 93, 122–3, 125, 130–1, 193, 196, 198.
House of Lords, 1, 46, 193.
Hyde, Dr. D., 1, 160–1.

Imperial conference, 154, 157, 191–5, 199.
Independents, 65, 71, 73–74, 77, 87, 103, 149, 166.
Initiative, 59–61, 156.
Irish Bulletin, 24, 37–38, 41.
Irish convention (1917), 14, 16–17, 24.
Irish Republican Army (I.R.A.), 41, 43–44, 62, 77, 103, 105–6, 110, 144, 173, 188, 202.
Irish Republican Brotherhood (I.R.B.), 4–5, 7, 9, 11–12, 15–16, 103.
Irish republican congress, 21.
Irish socialist republican party, 4, 5.
Irish trades union congress, 4, 17, 102, 108.
Irish transport and general workers' union, 108–9.
Italy, 186.

Jameson, A., 137.

Index

Jewish member in dáil, 92, 116.
Johnson, T., 75, 103, 184.
Johnston, W., 5.
Judicial committee of privy council, 54–55, 63, 178, 191, 197, 200.

Kelly, T., 21.
Kennedy, H., 54–55.

Labour party (British), 46, 117.
Labour party, 4–5, 9, 11, 17, 20, 29, 61, 71, 73–78, 81–82, 89, 94, 102–4, 108, 110–18, 121, 130, 142, 149, 155, 157, 200–1, 213–15.
Larkin, J., 108–9.
League of Nations, 38, 50, 108, 184–6.
League of Youth, 107.
Legislation: dáil's ultimate control of, 170; analysis of, 171–5; relation of Irish to British, 175–7; influence of Roman Catholicism on, 177; inspired by judicial decisions, 177–8; limit to legislative competence of oireachtas, 179–80; delegated, 180–2.
Leinster House, Dublin, 119.
Lemass, S., 63, 145.
Liberal party, 1.
Lloyd George, Rt. Hon. D., 13–14, 16–17, 19, 45–51, 154.
Logue, Cardinal, 19, 48.

Macardle, Dorothy, 43.
McBride, S., 79.
McCabe, J. P., 28.
MacDermot, F., 107–8, 146.
MacEntee, S., 35.
McGilligan, P., 142, 192, 194.
McGrath, J., 53, 103.
McGuinness, J., 13.
MacNeill, E., 7, 11, 19, 22, 199–200.
MacNeill, J., 54, 63, 157.
Macready, General, Sir N., 44, 146.
MacSwiney, Mary, 106.
MacSwiney, T., 25.
Magennis, W., 104, 201–2.
Mansion House, Dublin, 15, 17, 21–22, 24, 30, 53.
Markievicz, Countess C., 7.
Martin, H., 45.
Maxwell, General Sir J., 12.
Midleton, earl of, 137.
Morrissey, D., 113.
Moylett, P., 48.
Mulcahy, R., 23, 166, 198.
Murnaghan, J., 54.

National centre party, 73, 107.
National corporate party, 108.
National council: (1903), 2; (1905), 3; (1917), 14.
National farmers' and ratepayers' league, 107.
National guard, 107.
National labour party, 71, 73, 109.
National league, 73, 76–77, 84, 104.
National party, 103–4.
National University of Ireland, 72, 75, 95, 104, 149.
Nationalist (or parliamentary) party, 1–2, 5, 7, 13–14, 16–20, 28, 31, 89, 100, 104, 201.
Neutrality, 78, 166, 186–7, 188–9.
New Zealand, 51, 122, 129 198.
Northern Ireland, 28–29, 49, 52–53, 176, 187, 189, 199–204.
Norwegian second chamber, 146.

Oath of allegiance: parliamentary, 47, 52, 54, 56, 58, 60, 63, 76–77, 79, 104, 106, 120, 143, 155–7, 162, 195–7; presidential, 159; republican, 27, 29, 43.
O'Brien, W., 109.
O Buachalla (Buckley), D., 157.
O'Byrne, J., 54.
O'Connor, A., 41.
O'Connor, J. (Lord Justice of Appeal), 48–49.
O'Duffy, E., 107–8.
O'Flanagan, Rev. M., 22, 48–49.
O'Hanlon, M. F., 104–5.
O'Hegarty, P. S., 12, 29–30.
O'Higgins, K., 53, 76, 106, 135, 142, 153–4, 156, 190.
O'Higgins, Dr. T. F., 106–8.
Oireachtas, 56–60, 62, 64–65, 76, 106–7, 112, 119–20, 126, 129–30, 133, 136, 141, 156–7, 159–60, 165, 167, 170–1, 176–7, 179–81, 183, 193, 199.
O'Keeffe, P., 24.
O'Kelly, J. J., 26, 62.
O'Kelly, S. T., 22, 25–26, 38, 161.
O'Mahony, S., 29.
O'Mara, J., 40.
O'Neill, J., 157.
O'Rahilly, A., 54.
O'Rahilly, The, 7.
O'Sullivan, Dr. D., 108.

Parliament of Southern Ireland, 28–29, 47, 52–54, 74.
Parliamentary allowance, 26, 94, 134–5.
Parliamentary constituencies, 19–20, 22, 25, 29–30, 40, 69–70, 72, 79–86, 90, 92, 95, 117, 135, 140, 145, 172.
Parliamentary elections: dáil, legal provision for, 67–72; elections and results, 73–79; size of poll, 79–80; selection of candidates, 79–81; campaign methods, 81–85; also 19–21, 75, 102–5, 138; senate, 140, 148–51.

Index

Parliamentary questions, 124, 141.
Parties, political: origin of, 102–10; organization, 110–13; funds, 113; newspapers, 113–14; social and geographical divisions, 114–18, 205–15. *See also* under names of parties.
Partition, 9, 14, 47, 51, 187–9, 196, 198–9, 203.
Peace conference, 11, 14, 19, 22, 36–38, 45.
'Peace with Ireland' council, 46.
Pearse, P., 2, 7, 11–12.
Petitions to dáil, 130–1.
Plebiscite, 61, 64, 78.
Plunkett, Count G. N., 13–15, 21, 23.
Plunkett, Sir H., 24.
Plunkett, J. M., 13.
President: of revolutionary republic, 26–27; of Ireland, 64–65, 78, 126, 129, 148, 159–61, 164–5, 179–80; of executive council, 59, 61, 105, 139–41, 154, 157, 160, 162–5, 168.
Presidential commission, 78, 159.
Press: separatist, 2–11, 21, 24, 42; attitude to dáil, 23–24, 29–30; attitude to Anglo-Irish war, 45–46.
Proportional representation, 27, 65, 67–72, 79, 91, 103, 107, 117, 140, 150, 159, 161, 166.
Protestant members of dáil, 31, 91–93, 116.
Provisional government, 52–54, 61, 138.

Radio, in elections, 85.
Redmond, J., 1, 4, 6–9, 12–14, 16.
Redmond, Major W., 14.
Redmond, Captain W. A., 16, 77, 84, 104, 201.
Referendum, 15, 59–61, 65, 139, 145–6, 148, 156–7, 160.
Roman catholic influence, 17, 31, 84, 91, 113, 138, 177.
Rossa, J. O'Donovan, 10.
Rotunda, Dublin, 7.
Royal Irish Constabulary, 42, 75, 195.

Senate: of Southern Ireland, 28, 47, 137; of Irish Free State, 54, 58–59, 60–61, 63, 119; composition, and dáil's distrust of, 137–8; powers of, 138–9; elections for, 139–40; strained relations with dáil, 140–4; abolition of, 144–6; commission on second chambers, 146–7; of Ireland, 64–65, 72, 124–5, 128–30, 134, 136, 160, 170; origin and nature of, 147–52.
Separatist groups, 1, 4–5, 8–11, 14–15, 102.
Sinn Féin, 1, 3–5, 7–11, 13–21, 24, 27– 31, 36–37, 39, 42–43, 46, 48, 62, 73– 74, 76–77, 94, 102–3, 105–6, 130, 155, 179.
Smuts, General J., 49.
Social policy, directive principles, 64.
South Africa, 12, 38, 51, 133, 194, 200.
Soviet Union, 189.
Spanish civil war, 186.
Stack, A., 53.
Statistics: relating to dáil, age analysis, 31; occupation analysis, 32–33; constituencies and members, 70; party representation, 71; general elections, 73; election results, 73; size of poll, 80; new members at elections, 86; members not re-elected, 87; parliamentary experience of members, 88; members of one dáil only, 86; pre-parliamentary experience of members, 89; birthplace and residence of members, 90; age distribution of members, 91; age distribution of new members, 92; protestants, 92; education of members, 93; occupations of members, 96–99; occupation analysis of members by parties, 114–16; questions, 124; closures, 133; use of Irish in debates, 134; numbers participating in debates, 135; relating to senate, ex-dáil members in, 151; bills amended by, 152; money bills on which recommendations made, 152; General, government and private members bills, 167; number of acts, 1922–48, 170; acts by subject, 171–2; delegated legislation, 181.
Statutory rules, orders and regulations, 167, 180–2.
Stephens, J., 12.
Sweetman, R., 44.
Swiss executive, 162.

Tánaiste, 159, 161, 164.
Taoiseach, 78, 120, 123, 126, 149, 151, 159–61, 164–5, 166–7, 198.
Teachtar dáil (T.D.), 132.
Thrift, W., 60, 166.
Treaty between Great Britain and Ireland, 1921, 50, 51–54, 57–58, 60–61, 63, 72, 74, 76–77, 88, 102–3, 116, 142, 153, 155–6, 161, 166, 179, 183–4, 186–7, 190, 194–6, 199–201.
Treaty debate, 53, 154, 190.

Unionists, 9, 13, 20, 29, 42, 75, 84, 89; Northern, 5–6, 14, 20, 39, 47, 190, 202–3; Southern, 50, 54–55, 67, 72, 137–8, 144.
United Ireland party, 107–8.

Index

United Nations Organization, 189.
University representation, 71–72, 92, 95, 145.

Vocational representation, 149–50.
Volunteers: Irish, 7, 9–11, 15–18, 27, 31, 42–44; National, 8; Ulster, 6–8.

Walsh, J. J., 35.
Westminster bills and acts: Home Rule Bill, 1912, 1, 4–8; Home Rule Act, 1914, 13, 47, 137; Amending Bill, 6; Suspensory Act, 6; Defence of the Realm Acts, 11; Man Power Bill, 1918, 17; Government of Ireland Act, 1920, 27–29, 47–49, 52, 67, 137, 199, 201; Irish Free State (Agreement) Bill, 53–54, 61, 74; Irish Free State Constitution Bill, 1922, 55; Irish Free State (Consequential Provisions) Bill, 1922, 55; Statute of Westminster, 1931, 56, 63, 193; Irish Free State (Special Duties) Act, 1932, 196.
Wilson, Sir H., 46, 49.
Wimborne, Lord, 17.
World War I, 6, 8–11; II, 78, 90, 166, 170, 173, 188.

Young Ireland Association, 107.

PRINTED IN
GREAT BRITAIN
AT THE
UNIVERSITY PRESS
OXFORD
BY
CHARLES BATEY
PRINTER
TO THE
UNIVERSITY

DARTMOUTH COLLEGE

3 3311 01042 0760